THE WITCHES OF SELWOOD

Millions of spiritual creatures walk the earth Unseen,
both when we wake and when we sleep.

John Milton, *Paradise Lost* (1667)

Frontispiece of Joseph Glanvill's Saducismus Triumphatus *(1681) depicting witchcraft episodes in Somerset and Wiltshire in the seven years between 1658 and 1665*

THE WITCHES OF SELWOOD

Witchcraft Belief and Accusation in Seventeenth-Century Somerset

ANDREW PICKERING

THE HOBNOB PRESS

First published in the United Kingdom in 2021
paperback edition with minor changes published 2023

by The Hobnob Press,
8 Lock Warehouse,
Severn Road, Gloucester GL1 2GA
www.hobnobpress.co.uk

© Andrew Pickering, 2021, 2023

All rights reserved. No part of this book may be reprinted or reproduced or utilised in any form or by any electronic, mechanical or other means, now known or hereafter invented, including photocopying, or in any information storage or retrieval system, without the permission in writing from the copyright holder or his heirs.

British Library Cataloguing in Publication Data
A catalogue record for this book is available from the British Library

ISBN 978-1-914407-49-9

Typeset in Adobe Garamond Pro 12/14 pt.
Typesetting and origination by John Chandler

Front Cover The Devil and witches in Selwood Forest; hand-tinted detail from the frontispiece by William Faithorne for the collection of 'relations' forming the second part of Joseph Glanvill's *Saducismus Triumphatus* (1681).
Back Cover: Witches and demons dancing in a circle. (Contemporary English woodcut.)

CONTENTS

	Foreword, *by John Chandler*	vi
	Acknowledgement	vii
	Preface	ix
	Notes on the Text	xix
	Illustrations, Maps and Tables	xx
1	The Devil's Cloister	1
2	The Demon Drummer	15
3	A Book of Examinations	50
4	A Hellish Knot of Witches	67
5	Pandaemonium	97
6	The Bewitching of William Spicer	123
7	The Bewitching of Mary Hill	144
8	Credible Ministers	190
9	Credulity and Incredulity	219
	Some Conclusions	240
	Chronology and Locations	245
	Bibliography	251
	Index	264

FOREWORD

Most of us, in the twenty-first century, regard witches as the stuff of children's fairy tales, hallowe'en hype, or a gullible counter-culture. And we tend to dismiss as unreliable superstition the graphic accounts of diabolical mischief that we come across in contemporary early-modern literature. But to the seventeenth-century psyche witchcraft, spirits and demons were tangible and ever-present hazards, a constant threat to health and happiness in a precarious world. And as Andrew Pickering demonstrates in this penetrating micro-history of the area where he lives and teaches, the names of the perpetrators, victims and witnesses which pepper these lurid descriptions attach to real individuals, whose lives and families can be pieced together through skilful analysis of a full range of historical sources.

Selwood Forest, along the Somerset-Wiltshire border, was a turbulent, poverty-stricken and lawless place in the later 17th century, and so a potent breeding-ground for witchcraft and associated practices. And because local churchmen and magistrates diligently chronicled their attempts to understand it and to contain its effects by punishment and persuasion, the region provides some of the fullest, most reliable evidence to be found of witchcraft anywhere. As Andrew so brilliantly explains, the subject should not be dismissed as a superstitious curiosity. Into his witches brew he pours philosophy, theology, psychology, folklore, politics, misogyny, law and subterfuge – all against the backcloth of a tumultuous civil war and its aftermath, and with a deep understanding of local circumstances and topography. It is a compelling account of ordinary people experiencing extraordinary events; but it is also a major contribution to the emerging study of this fascinating aspect of social history, by one thoroughly conversant with the debate over many years. Andrew wears his learning lightly, so that his respectable academic study will also be a compelling read for anyone who lives in and cares about this unique region of England's West Country.

John Chandler

ACKNOWLEDGMENTS

THIS BOOK IS a major revision of a previous publication, *The Witches of Selwood Forest: Witchcraft and Demonism in Somerset, 1625-1700* (Cambridge Scholars, 2017). The chapters at the heart of the work—3, 4, 6 and 7—have been rewritten following my further research and the subsequent publication of articles in the academic press including, 'Great News from the West of England: witchcraft and strange vomiting in a Somerset village', in *Magic, Witchcraft and Ritual* (University of Pennsylvania), 13:1, 2018, 70-97; 'Witchcraft and evidence in a seventeenth-century Somerset parish', in *The Local Historian: Journal of the British Association for Local History*, 48:1, 2018, 30-40; 'The Devil's Cloyster: putting Selwood Forest on England's seventeenth-century witchcraft map' in Klüsener, B., and Nate, R., (eds.), *Remembering Places* (Katholische Universität Eichstätt-Ingolstadt: Königshausen & Neumann, 2019), 35-54. I am indebted to the generous advice of at least a dozen editors, reviewers and academic referees, in particular Professor Claire Fanger of Rice University, Texas, Dr Heather Falvey of the University of Cambridge and the University of Oxford, and Professor Richard Nate of the University of Eichstätt-Ingolstadt, Bavaria. I have welcomed the interest in my continuing studies shown by Professor Peter Marshall (University of Warwick), Professor David Amigoni (Keele University), and Professor Ian Atherton (Keele University) and Dr Rachel Adcock (Keele Uinversity), and I am immensely grateful to Marion Gibson, Professor of Renaissance and Magical Literatures at Exeter University, for her encouraging review of the original version of this book in *The Seventeenth Century*, 34:1, 2019, 138-140, and also to Mark Stoyle, Professor of Early Modern History, University of Southampton, for his kind review in *Southern History: a Review of the History of Southern England* 40 (2018). My thanks are also extended to others working in the field who have scrutinized my research in undertaking their own, notably Dr Davide Ermacora, Honorary Fellow at Ca' Foscari University of Venice, for his extensive commentary on my thoughts regarding episodes of 'strange vomiting' in his 'Embedded Pins and Migratory Needles: A Historical Folklore Perspective', *Contemporary Legend*, 3: 9 (2019), 1-53. I am honoured too to have been invited to publish this revision by Dr John Chandler, former county editor, Gloucestershire, for the *Victoria County History*, chair of the Publishing Committee of the British Association for Local History, and owner of Hobnob Press.

Most of all my gratitude is extended to my wife, Lisa, who has shared my witch-finding adventures with me with great interest and enthusiasm since our first perusal of the Beckington registers at the Somerset Heritage Centre in Taunton on All Hallows Eve 2014. It is to her that this book is dedicated.

Andrew Pickering
Bruton in Selwood

PREFACE

Historians of witchcraft in early modern England spend much of their time grappling with narratives published three or four hundred years ago. While all literature from the period sheds light on past mentalities, this kind of material is notoriously unreliable when used in attempts to reconstruct past events and past lives: 'Those who work with stories about witches should regard them as a fascinating and important resource, but must avoid the pitfalls of regarding them as if they were objective and unproblematic, of taking them as read' warns one eminent expert in the field.[1]

The writers of many of the tracts, seeking to prove the reality of spirits, demons and their witch-acolytes, were no fools – often they were highly educated, erudite and even in some cases, given the intellectual context in which they operated, progressive. Nevertheless, the thought at the back of the researcher's mind is that it might all be hogwash. Some tracts from the period are recognised as fraudulent;[2] others contain clear evidence of hoax by one or more of the protagonists in the tales,[3] if not the authors who told them.

A good place to begin the study of any witchcraft case is to ascertain whether the people said to have been involved existed in the first place. What Malcolm Gaskill has described as the 'supporting cast' in witch-trial dramas is not entirely invisible, and plenty of leads, not least in the names of its chief protagonists, provide ample opportunities for further inquiry.[4] Searches of registers for baptisms, marriages and burials, lists of affidavits confirming burial in wool, hearth tax records, and wills demonstrate the veracity of much of what is contained in seemingly *incredible* accounts. This in turn validates attempts to make sense of the more remarkable aspects of the stories without relying entirely on such interpretative tools as metaphor and imagination. The task of the student of witchcraft narratives, as Peter Marshall has put it, is that 'of making connections, assessing plausibility, and scratching for meaning out of the hard soil of the historical record'.[5]

The witchcraft narratives explored in this study concern the ancient royal forest of Selwood,[6] which straddled the Somerset–Wiltshire border and extended south of Frome almost into Dorset.[7] The poverty and disorder in parts of Selwood Forest[8] in the seventeenth century were notorious.[9] On its southern edge at Stoke Trister, a place that would become notorious for witchcraft, a great crowd attended a bull-baiting, defying orders to disperse.[10] Disafforestation schemes in particular provoked riots in the region. Several Selwood communities, including the parishes of Beckington, Batcombe and Mells, were puritan strongholds in the bitter political and religious struggles of the Civil War period.[11] Woodlands, close to Frome, was remembered in about 1800 as having been 'within the memory of man, the notorious asylum of a desperate clan of banditti, whose depredations were a terror to the surrounding parishes'.[12]

This forest, roughly 20 miles north to south and 15 east to west, has an exceptionally rich, though largely unrecognised, witchcraft history. Here two of the most important books on the subject ('demonologies') were written: Richard Bernard's *Guide to Grand-Jury Men* (1628) and Joseph Glanvill's great work, posthumously published as *Saducismus Triumphatus or, Full and Plain Evidence Concerning Witches and Apparitions* (1681). The most detailed accounts of 'black Sabbath' meetings in early modern England come from the area—allegedly the activities of two substantial covens, one centred upon Bayford and Stoke Trister at the southern end of the forest and the other close by at Brewham near Bruton. The formal accusation for maleficent witchcraft[13] of almost thirty women and men can be identified for the Selwood Forest region between 1658 and 1690. Of these at least nine were examined by a local magistrate and some had their cases heard at the assizes. Between 1694 and 1730 at least four so-called witches, who did not receive a formal hearing, were subjected to the trauma of an extra-judicial public 'swimming'—a lynching, in effect—that left one of them dead. Involving at least twenty-four named participants, the alleged witchcraft conspiracy in villages around Bruton and Wincanton at the start of the 1660s bears comparison with the supposed gathering of witches at Pendle, Lancashire, who were tried in 1612. Until its suppression by higher authorities, the Selwood Forest panic looked set to become one of the more severe witch-hunts in English history. The better-known Selwood Forest cases were considered by Walter Scott in his *Letters on Demonology and Witchcraft* (1830), and by Margaret Murray in her highly influential *The Witch-Cult in Western Europe: A*

PREFACE xi

Study in Anthropology (1921), but of the equally significant Beckington case in 1689, the main focus of the second half of this book, they made no mention.

The timing of the major episodes considered below and their prosecution, the time of the Restoration and the era of Monmouth's Rebellion and the Glorious Revolution, has invited consideration of these in the light of Peter Elmer's observations that 'those in authority, steeped in demonological thought, were more likely to act upon them, only at such times when their own sense of religious or political order was threatened or challenged'[14] and that the outcome of trials was largely determined by the local and national political contexts. This in turn, he argues, helps explain the uneven distribution of witchcraft trials both geographically and over time.[15]

Only by exploring the multiple links that existed between the perpetrators of witch-hunts, the record keepers, and others who wrote about them can we begin to understand the extraordinary concentration of seventeenth-century witchcraft-related records in the vicinity. Biographies and papers have been produced about those who recorded Selwood Forest's witchcraft beliefs and history at the time, most recently, Julie Davies' *Science in an Enchanted World: Philosophy and Witchcraft in the Work of Joseph Glanvill* (2018), but usually without much regard for the immediate geographical and social contexts in which they wrote. Jonathan Barry's recent investigation (2012) of one of the less well-known of these, Robert Hunt, the Justice of the Peace who was Glanvill's principal informer, ventured into the largely uncharted waters that this book further explores.[16]

Little is known of the scale and nature of witchcraft trials in Somerset in the period before the Civil War (1642–1651). Barry has summed up the paucity of the available evidence for the South-West in the sixteenth and seventeenth centuries: 'Before 1670', he has written, 'we have only some bail books (1654–1677) and the orders of the courts (largely administrative though occasionally mentioning witchcraft cases), and even after 1670, when we have the gaol books, we do not have indictments or depositions, so we have only a minimal amount of information about each case'. Legal records detailing assize court trial proceedings have not survived.[17] However, there are numerous unexplored indictments for Somerset for the period after 1670. The Q/SI catalogue reference leads the researcher to sixty-eight files of this material covering the period 1571–1971. The file for 1689–1690 is a box containing a dozen or so rolls of documents, each comprising a considerable number of parchments tightly bound in ancient ribbons and string. They are filthy to handle, covered in the accumulated dust of ages. Among many other points of interest they include, in addition to indictments, bastardy cases, recognizances and the like, lists of JPs and jurors, the signed oaths of constables, and details of the crimes of named individuals from all over Somerset recently released from local houses of correction such as Shepton Mallet gaol.

Malcolm Gaskill,[18] citing C. L'Estrange Ewen, the early-twentieth century compiler of two still much-used compendia of witchcraft cases,[19] has reasserted how unusual such cases were—1000 trials in 9000 parishes across the course of 200 years—but witchcraft *accusation* at a local and extra-judicial level, though unquantifiable, must have been much more frequent. Bewitchment, at all social levels, still played a central part in mainstream thinking.[20] Building on Ewen's work, James Sharpe was able to produce a valuable summary of patterns of witchcraft accusation in the region using the evidence of the gaol deliveries after 1670 recorded for the Western Circuit (Somerset, Wiltshire, Dorset, Southampton, Devon, Cornwall). In this period of decline he found these records 'especially tantalizing as they show that levels of prosecution [...] were higher in the South-West than in the South-East, possibly pointing to a peak of indictments, now lost to the historical record, in the middle of the seventeenth century'.[21] From the seventy indictments for the period after 1670, Sharpe was able to conclude that thirty-five occurred before 1679, twenty more in the next ten years up to 1689, eleven between 1690 and 1699, with a final four culminating in 1704. The most common crime for which they were charged appears to have been harming people, more commonly females than males, and sometimes (but less frequently) killing them. The vast majority of those accused (94 per cent) were female.

A great deal has been written about the witch-hunting phenomenon in early modern Europe over the last forty years. For students of the period the subject provides an ideal vehicle for exploring different historical approaches and modes of interpretation. For the academic historian, it is a battlefield of conflicting ideas. For the lay reader, it is a fascinating mystery and a shocking illustration of the capacity of individuals and communities to persecute. Although witchcraft accusation accounts for a tiny fraction of the punishments meted out by courts in the period, this crime has received a disproportionate amount of attention. Barry has identified in recent work on witchcraft 'three themes or approaches [...] of particular importance in our understanding'; these are the nature and extent of the decline of belief, the need for the close analysis of case studies, and the language of witchcraft narratives that involves 'an interest in the intertextuality of witchcraft cases, that is their shaping by reference to previous stories, authorities or cultural models'.[22] These three elements are at the core of this enquiry into the subject.

The evidence of the contemporary accounts in this book corroborates modern historians' characterisations of, and explanations for, witchcraft accusation in the close-knit communities of early modern England. The further investigation into the lives of the chief protagonists and their families has helped explain the social and economic contexts in which accusations were made. It sheds further light on motivational factors including tarnished reputations, social conditioning and popular beliefs. It has prompted consideration of patterns of witchcraft-related phenomena such as swimming tests and strange-vomiting. The Selwood cases affirm many of the conclusions drawn by Barry and other historians of the subject. As Sharpe concluded in a consideration of witchcraft in Pendle Forest, one can suppose the inhabitants of Selwood Forest in the seventeenth century were also living 'in an intellectual and social milieu where gossip about witchcraft, knowledge of witchcraft and worry about witchcraft were commonplace'.[23] Accusations began as petty squabbles among neighbours. The accused and the accusers knew each other well, even to the point of being related. Those identified as witches were elderly, female and impoverished. Their supposed victims were also vulnerable— typically young and emotionally troubled or economically deprived, or both. Witches acquired their reputations over a period of time counted in years, possibly decades.[24] Some may have been practising 'witches' insofar as they encouraged a reputation for having the wise woman's knowledge of mysterious matters pertaining to life and death. Keith Thomas and many after him have confirmed the reality of practitioners of magic in early modern England.[25] Their prosecution was entirely in the hands of the local elite. Magistrates, in particular, were the gatekeepers who determined whether or not the complainants from the parishes had a case that should be heard. Legal business cost money and, when those in litigation had not a penny to spare, the attitudes of those who held the parish purse strings were of paramount importance.

Most of the Selwood witchcraft narratives entered the historical record because of the philosophical wars that were waged through the printed works of members of the Royal Society, churchmen and other intellectuals. The first blast of the trumpet in Selwood Forest in the campaign against Restoration era witchcraft scepticism was sounded by Glanvill in the 1660s. For a short while, through its inclusion in Richard Baxter's *Certainty of the Worlds of Spirits* (1691), the Beckington case, which has since shrunk into relative obscurity, took centre stage, when, as Jacqueline Pearson has observed, ghost stories and other supernatural phenomena gained a new lease of life because of their 'didactic usefulness' in confuting 'an alleged epidemic of atheism'.[26]

* * *

THE OPENING CHAPTER of this book considers the nature and influence of the work of one of the most influential English demonologists, Richard Bernard, who lived in Selwood at Batcombe, close to Bruton and Frome. His *Guide to Grand Jury Men,* first published in 1627, is widely regarded as a comprehensive exposition of the witchcraft paradigm in seventeenth-century England, at least until the Restoration era. It is an obvious starting place for the telling of the unfolding Selwood witchcraft story, and its considerable influence upon its development is beyond doubt. His professional relationship with other worthies who played a part in the Selwood witchcraft story, notably the clerics Richard Alleine and his son, are also explored.

Chapter 2 introduces an even more famous seventeenth-century Selwood demonologist: Joseph Glanvill, the vicar of Frome Selwood for most of the 1660s. Glanvill's scientific and spiritual beliefs are a focus as are his connections with other protagonists in Selwood's witchcraft history; this chapter develops the hypothesis that the demonological texts produced in the region during the period, their authors, and the tales they told, were more closely connected than has previously been recognised.

The third chapter analyses the evidence for two witchcraft cases in the vicinity of Selwood Forest recorded in Joseph Glanvill's writings and the source for these, the magistrate Robert Hunt's 'book of examinations'.

PREFACE

Parish registers, wills and other contemporary documents are used in an attempt to place these remarkable accounts in their historical contexts.

Chapter 4 consolidates existing understanding of, and attempts to develop, the history of the supposed covens active in and around Stoke Trister and Brewham at the time of the Restoration. The principal protagonists are revealed as ordinary people leading ordinary lives which are disturbed by some extraordinary allegations regarding episodes of witchcraft and night-time meetings with a demonic man in black.

The next chapter, Chapter 5, considers the turbulent years between the Hunt-Glanvill cases of the early 1660s and the next significant episode of witch-hunting in Selwood Forest, at Beckington, in 1689. Political and religious discord in this post-Restoration period, as discussed in this chapter, are part of the story, and fear of a return of the Great Plague in the mid-1680s, twenty years after it last struck London in 1665, another.

The shocking news from Selwood, concerning the bewitchment of two teenagers in the Somerset parish of Beckington in 1689, is introduced in Chapter 6. This focuses on the bewitchment of William Spicer by an octogenarian named Elizabeth Carrier whose fascinating history regarding her contribution to her community during a dreadful epidemic in 1686 is revealed through the close analysis of a register recording burials in woollen cloth.

Chapter 7 concerns a case study furnished in considerable detail by two contemporary accounts. Psychoanalytical and medical explanations are considered in an attempt to unravel fiction from fact. The outcome of the subsequent trial is explored with particular attention paid to the judges who heard the evidence at Bruton's Quarter Sessions and the Taunton Assizes.

The 'Credible Ministers' considered in Chapter 8 include Richard Baxter, who was keenly interested in the Selwood witchcraft cases, and others endeavouring to keep the banner of belief in the spirit world alive in the decades following Glanvill's death in 1680. This chapter also explores the vigorous and sometimes violent attempts to crush emergent Quakerism, and it further develops the discussion regarding the connections made in the period between witchcraft and other forms of religious dissent.

The closing chapter covers some late cases of witchcraft accusation in the region. These are discussed in the context of the continuing witchcraft debate in intellectual quarters in which sceptical opinion gained the upper hand in the second half of the century and helped end the judicial witch-hunt in England well before the repeal, in 1736, of the 1603 Jacobean witchcraft act.

In writing this book I have frequently made reference to James Sharpe's *Instruments of Darkness* (1996)—an excellent single-volume account of the rise and decline of witch-hunting in early modern England, the evocative title of which, incidentally, is derived from Glanvill. The wide variety of approaches found in the most admired publications of the last twenty years, notably Robin Briggs's *Witches and Neighbours* (1996, 2002), Wolfgang Behringer's *Witches and Witch-hunts* (2004), Stuart Clark's *Thinking with Demons* (1997), and Malcolm Gaskill's *Crime and Mentalities in Early Modern England* (2000) have influenced my own approaches to, and interpretations of, the Selwood Forest cases. The historiographical context has been further explored through such volumes as *Witchcraft Historiography* (2007), compiled by Jonathan Barry and Owen Davies, and by Brian Levack's important compendium, *The Oxford Handbook of Witchcraft in Early Modern Europe and Colonial America* (2013). Barry's essay on Robert Hunt in his *Witchcraft and Demonology in South-West England, 1640–1789* (2012) has been invaluable as a stimulus for my own research. Several more micro-histories also have proved very helpful. These include Sharpe's fascinating account of a case in Oxfordshire in 1604, *The Bewitching of Anne Gunter: A Horrible and True Story of Football, Witchcraft, Murder and the King of England* (1999, 2000), Philip C. Almond's analysis of the famous late-Elizabethan Throckmorton case, *The Witches of Warboys* (2008), Gilbert Geiss and Ivan Bunn's study of accusations at Lowestoft in 1662, *A Trial of Witches* (1997), Tracy Borman's study of the Belvoir Castle case of 1613, *Witches: James I and the English Witch-hunts* (2013), and David L. Jones's *The Ipswich Witch: Mary Lackland and the Suffolk Witch Hunts* (2015). Emmanuel Le Roy Ladurie's hunt for the origins of a witchcraft case in south-west France, commemorated by a poem penned over 200 years later in 1842, provided further inspiration in revealing how much could be made of so little; he published his findings as *La Sorcière de Jasmin* (1983), subsequently translated into English as *Jasmin's Witch* (1987). This much revised reworking of the original 2017 version of this book is further informed by the new information and fresh perspectives contained in a range of recent publications, notably Peter

PREFACE   xvii

Elmer's *Witchcraft, Witch-Hunting, and Politics in Early Modern England* (2016).

The Witches of Selwood complements the handful of other regional and micro-histories that focus on witchcraft in the west of England, the most recent being John Callow's *The Last Witches of England* (2021). In a field of study where the micro-historical approach has played such an important part in testing and developing the broad conclusions historians have claimed, these publications and my own work demonstrate the merit of close analyses of the south-west. Here witchcraft belief remained strong well-beyond the Restoration, and the enduring fascination with it is of particular interest for those attempting to unravel the complexities of the demise of witch-hunting.[27]

1. Marion Gibson, *Reading Witchcraft* (Routledge, 1999), 10.
2. For example, *The Tryals, Examination and Condemnation of Four Notorious Witches at the Assizes held at Worcester* (1690): purporting to be a reliable account of a trial at Worcester in 1647 it contains the unlikely claims that 'Witchfinder-General' Matthew Hopkins (who seems to have operated exclusively in eastern England) was involved in these interrogations, and that all four were burned at the stake (an exceptionally rare event in the English record, since English law stipulated hanging for witch-felons). It seems to be based in part upon a 1645 pamphlet concerning the trial of four 'witches' in Essex, not Worcester.
3. For example, the cases of Anne Gunter of North Moreton in Oxfordshire (1605) and William Perry, 'The Boy of Bilson', in Staffordshire (1621).
4. 'Witch-trials were not simple social reflexes; they were intricately plotted human dramas with a large, but often historically invisible, supporting cast': Malcolm Gaskill, 'Witchcraft, politics and memory in seventeenth-century England', *Historical Journal*, vol. 50, no. 2 (2007), 289-308.
5. Peter Marshall, *Mother Leakey and the Bishop: A Ghost Story* (Oxford: Oxford University Press, 2007), 189.
6. 'Selwood' is thought to derive from the Saxon word 'sealhwudu' meaning woodland where willow ('sallow') trees grow.
7. See Michael McGarvie, *The Bounds of Selwood* (Frome: Frome Society for Local Study, 1978) for a full examination.
8. The term *forest* derives from the Latin word *foras* meaning outside - originally it had no particular association with woodland. Royal forests, where special rules applied, were not absolutely subject to (were 'outside') the common law. The king's foresters were much resented for the special privileges that came with their appointment.

9 David Underdown, *Revel, Riot, and Rebellion: Popular Politics and Culture in England, 1603–1660* (Oxford: Oxford University Press, 1985), 34.
10 *Ibid.*, 264.
11 *Ibid.*, 78.
12 George Alexander Cooke, *Topographical and Statistical Description of the County of Somerset* (*c.*1800), 167.
13 Harm caused by supernatural means.
14 Peter Elmer, *Witchcraft, Witch-Hunting, and Politics in Early Modern England* (Oxford: Oxford University Press, 2016), 7.
15 Elmer, *Witchcraft*, 293.
16 Jonathan Barry, 'Robert Hunt and the Somerset Witches' in *Witchcraft and Demonology in South-West England, 1640–1789* (London: Palgrave Macmillan, 2012).
17 Barry, *Witchcraft and Demonology*, 9.
18 Malcolm Gaskill, 'Witchcraft and neighbourliness in early modern England', in S. Hindle, A. Shepard and J. Walter (eds), *Remaking English Society: Societal Relations and Social Change in Early Modern England* (Boydell, 2013), 211.
19 C. L'Estrange Ewen, *Witch Hunting and Witch Trials* (Kegan Paul, 1929); *Witchcraft and Demonianism* (Frederick Muller, 1933).
20 Ryan J. Stark, *Rhetoric, Science and Magic in Seventeenth-Century England* (Catholic University of America Press, 2009), 115.
21 James Sharpe, *Instruments of Darkness: Witchcraft in Early Modern England* (Philadelphia: University of Pennsylvania Press, 2007), 120.
22 Jonathan Barry, 'Public infidelity and private belief? The discourse of spirits in Enlightenment Bristol' in Owen Davies and Willem de Blécourt (eds), *Beyond the Witch Trials: Witchcraft and Magic in Enlightenment Europe* (Manchester: Manchester University Press, 2004), 117.
23 Sharpe, *Instruments*, 202.
24 For example, when Elizabeth Johnson was accused of killing a child in Kent in 1582 she found herself facing further charges for *maleficia* against other women in 1566, 1569 and 1576: deeds she was believed to have committed over a period of sixteen years. Sharpe, *Instruments*, 118.
25 Keith Thomas, *Religion and the Decline of Magic* (Penguin, 1971); Owen Davies, *Popular Magic: Cunning-folk in English History* (Hambledon, 2003).
26 Jacqueline Pearson, '"Then she asked it, what were its Sisters names?': Reading between the lines in seventeenth-century pamphlets of the supernatural', *The Seventeenth Century*, 28:1 (2013), 64.
27 This has been most recently and comprehensively addressed by Michael Hunter in *The Decline of Magic: Britain in the Enlightenment* (New Haven and London: Yale University Press, 2020).

NOTES ON THE TEXT

Abbreviations

DNB: *Dictionary of National Biography*, First Series (London: Smith, Elder and Co., 1885–1900).

ODNB: *Oxford Dictionary of National Biography*, Second Series (Oxford: Oxford University Press, 2004).

PRO: Public Record Office (now The National Archives).

SRO: Somerset Record Office (now Somerset Archives and Local Studies).

VCH: *Victoria County History.*

Dates

Except where indicated, January, February and March dates have been adjusted to match the modern convention (New Year's Day: 1 January), in place of the pre-1752 custom (New Year's Day: 25 March).

ILLUSTRATIONS, MAPS AND TABLES

Illustrations

Cover The Devil and witches in Selwood Forest hand-tinted detail from the frontispiece by William Faithorne for the collection of 'relations' forming the second part of Joseph Glanvill's *Saducismus Triumphatus* (1681).

Back Witches and demons dancing in a circle. (Contemporary English woodcut.)

Frontispiece Frontispiece of Joseph Glanvill's *Saducismus Triumphatus* (1681) depicting witchcraft episodes in Somerset and Wiltshire in the seven years between 1658 and 1665.

Fig. 1-1 Detail from the frontispiece of *Saducismus Triumphatus* (1681) depicting the Devil and witches in Selwood Forest.

Fig. 1-2 Richard Bernard (1568-1641), Pastor of Batcombe in Somerset.

Fig. 1-3 Richard Bernard, *A Guide to Grand-Jury Men Divided Into Two Bookes: In The First, Is The Authors Best Advice To Them what to doe, before they bring in a billa vera in cases of witchcraft, etc.*, first published in 1627.

Fig. 1-4 A 1614 account of the Devil's manifestation in Ditcheat in 1584.

Fig. 2-1 Detail from the frontispiece of *Saducismus Triumphatus* (1681) depicting the demon 'Drummer of Tedworth'.

Fig. 2-2 Joseph Glanvill (1636-80), Vicar of Frome Selwood (1662-72), member of the Royal Society and collector of Selwood witchcraft cases

Fig. 2-3 Glanvill's posthumous *Saducismus Triumphatus, or, full and plain Evidence concerning Witches and Apparitions* (1681).

Fig. 2-4 Adam Hill, *The Defence of the Article* (1592).

Fig. 2-5 Henry More, 1614-87, member of the Royal Society and editor of *Saducismus Triumphatus*.

Fig. 2-6 Robert Boyle, 1627-91, Glanvill's Royal Society ally in the search for scientific proof of God and the existence of spirits.

Fig. 3-1 Detail from the frontispiece of *Saducismus Triumphatus* (1681) depicting the levitation of Richard Jones.

Fig. 3-2 Woodcut showing pipe-smoking Cox, her toad-familiar and her astonished neighbour, from W.P., *The History of Witches and Wizards* (1720).

Fig. 3-3 Detail from the frontispiece of *Saducismus Triumphatus* (1681) depicting Julian Cox in magical flight.

Fig. 3-4 Woodcut depicting Robert Hunt and attendees.

Fig. 4-1 The witches of Selwood engaged in image magic with the Devil,

ILLUSTRATIONS, MAPS AND TABLES   xxi

from W.P., *The History of Witches and Wizards* (1720).

Fig. 4-2 The witchcraft of Elizabeth Style(s) of Bayford, from W.P., *The History of Witches and Wizards* (1720).

Fig. 4-3 Elizabeth Styles makes her pact with the Devil who pricks her finger, from W.P., *The History of Witches and Wizards* (1720).

Fig. 4-4 A black-faced man in black (note the clerical band around his neck) presents a witch with a demon-familiar, from W.P., *The History of Witches and Wizards* (1720).

Fig. 4-5 The witches of Selwood; detail from the frontispiece of *Saducismus Triumphatus* (1681) depicting the baptizing of poppets by the man in black and the forging through the Devil's touch of a diabolical pact.

Fig. 4-6 Witches and demons dancing, from W.P., *The History of Witches and Wizards* (1720).

Fig. 4-7 Witches and demons feasting, from W.P., *The History of Witches and Wizards* (1720).

Fig. 5-1 Devils bewitching Monmouth's army in Somerset in the summer of 1685.

Fig. 5-2 Pamphlet illuminating the constant and universal fear of plague in seventeenth-century England.

Fig. 5-3 Illustration showing various forms of sorcery in Richard Bovet's *Pandaemonium* (1684).

Fig. 5-4 Contemporary playing cards illustrating the impact of the Monmouth rebellion upon Frome Selwood.

Fig. 6-1 Seventeenth-century woodcut depicting stereotypical witches and their familiars, from *The wonderful discoverie of the witchcrafts of Margaret and Phillip Flower*, 1619.

Fig. 7-1 Contemporary woodcut depicting a bewitched girl vomiting nails, from W.P., *The History of Witches and Wizards* (1720).

Fig. 7-2 A search for the Devil's mark in a mid-nineteenth-century depiction of the Salem witchcraft examinations a couple of years after similar events in Beckington. (*Examination of a Witch* by T.H. Matteson)

Fig. 7-3 Late seventeenth-century bellarmine stoneware 'witch bottles' in Andover Museum found buried in the foundations of what was once a house in Abbotts Ann in Hampshire.

Fig. 7-5 *Great News from the West of England* tract (1689).

Fig. 8-1 The Devil seemingly conjured by gentlemen-wizards who appear to be standing within a magic circle, from W.P., *The History of Witches and Wizards* (1720).

Fig. 8-2 Lord Chief Justice Sir John Holt, 1642-1710.

Fig. 8-3 Richard Baxter (1615-91), theologian and demonologist.

Fig. 8-4 Statue of Richard Baxter at Kidderminster erected in 1875 in recognition of 'his Christian learning and his pastoral fidelity'.

Fig. 8-5 Richard Baxter, *The Certainty of the Worlds of Spirits* (1691).

Fig. 8-6 The Quaker and prophetess Anna Trapnel who was imprisoned after being accused of witchcraft in Cornwall in 1654.

Fig. 8-7 The Quaker's Dream (1655) depicting Satanic interventions and a range of supposed Quaker offences.

Fig. 8-8 Anti-Quaker propaganda, dated 1659, concerning such matters as the recent problem with Quaker-witches in Sherborne.

Fig. 8-9 Contemporary illustration of the punishment received by Quaker leader, James Nailor, in London in 1656.

Fig. 8-10 Image from Henry Hunt, *A Peep into a Prison; or, the Inside of Ilchester Bastile* (1821).

Fig. 9-1 A group of (Quaker?) witches dance in a circle around a central figure.

Fig. 9-2 Graphic contemporary account of the swimming for witchcraft of Ruth Osborne (1680-1751) and her husband at Tring in Hertfordshire in 1751.

Fig. 9-3 The swimming in a millpond of Mary Sutton at Bedford in 1613.

Fig. 9-4 By the time Royal Academian Henry Fuseli painted *The Weird Sisters or the Three Witches* (1783) the English witchcraze was long passed.

Fig. 9-5 Thomas Hobbes, *Leviathan*, 1651.

Fig. 9-6 'Credulity, Superstition and Fanaticism' by William Hogarth (1762).

Except where noted or where the provenance is unknown all images are deemed to be licensed under the Creative Commons Attribution-Share Alike 3.0 Unported license. https://creativecommons.org/licenses/by-sa/3.0/deed.en

Maps

Map 1 The West of England.
Map 2 The Selwood Forest region of Somerset and Wiltshire.

Tables

Table 1 The accused and their alleged victims in the Brewham witchcraft cases of 1664-5.
Table 2 Ejected ministers with Selwood Forest associations.
Table 3 Number of Beckington burials 1660-1709 recorded in the extant parish registers.
Table 4 Burials in wool, Beckington Register, 1681–7.
Table 5 Witchcraft cases featuring voiding of strange objects and other related phenomena.
Table 6 Ordeal by water ('swimming') episodes.
Table 7 Selwood connections.

1

THE DEVIL'S CLOISTER

Fig. 1-1 *Detail from the frontispiece of Saducismus Triumphatus (1681) depicting the Devil and witches in Selwood Forest.*

I have observed that there were neither witches nor bewitched in a village
until they were talked about and written about.
– Alonso de Salazar Frias, c. 1612.[1]

ONE OF THE most influential English demonologies published in the first half of the seventeenth century was written by Richard Bernard (*c.*1568–1642), a prolific writer of theological and other texts and the rector of Batcombe, a parish on the western edge of Selwood Forest. It was first printed in 1627 under the title *A Guide to Grand-Jury Men Divided Into Two Bookes: In The First, Is The Authors Best Advice To*

Fig. 1-2 *Richard Bernard (1568-1641), Pastor of Batcombe in Somerset.*

Them what to doe, before they bring in a billa vera in cases of witchcraft, etc. Bernard's *Guide* endeavoured to define witches and witchcraft, and to detail the activities of witches, none of which were precise concepts in popular culture.[2]

Raised in Nottinghamshire and educated at Cambridge, Bernard had resided for many years in the north of England before being presented with his Batcombe living in 1613. In doctrine he was a puritan and in practice a nonconformist. He objected to what he regarded as unnecessary religious ceremonies, refusing, for example, to make the sign of the cross in baptisms. His writings leaned towards the apocalyptic. He was assisted in his work at Batcombe by his fellow puritan and his successor, Richard Alleine, the son of the rector of nearby Ditcheat, also named Richard. Together Bernard and Richard Alleine senior wrote an exposition of Psalms 1–3.[3] Alleine junior would eventually be licensed to preach as a Presbyterian at Beckington.[4] At much the same time it is recorded that he, 'Master Bernard of Batcombe', played a prominent part in the exorcism of John Fox of Nottingham as one of the 'godly ministers' assisting Richard Rothwell.[5] According to his own testimony Bernard had exorcised another demon while he was vicar of Worksop in the years before he came to Somerset.[6]

Dedicated to the judges of the Western Circuit, Bernard's *Guide to Grand Jury Men* defined the legal and metaphysical position of witch-finders in England in the seventeenth century. The book was republished in 1629 and its many readers included the notorious mid-1640s witch-hunters in the Home Counties, Matthew Hopkins and John Stearne. It was cited by Increase Mather in an address delivered in 1692 at the height of the Salem witchcraft scare of 1692.[7]

Bernard's *Guide* 'serves as an exemplar of a distinctively English demonological style'[8] in Sharpe's reckoning. His commentary was informed by accounts of well-known witchcraft cases, including the Pendle episode of 1612, and by the writings of famous continental and English demonologists, including Bodin, Del Rio, Gifford, Roberts, and Scot. These, together with the pamphlet literature he also used, formed the 'rich and well-documented foundation for contemporary witchcraft beliefs'[9] that was in place by the end of James I's reign in 1627. Typical of the literature of this type, his was full of what Stuart Clarke has described as the 'dismal misogynisms' of the age.[10] Bernard's views were further dispersed through their incorporation in the third edition (1630) of Michael Dalton's highly influential *Country Justice*, first published in 1618.

In the 1620s he was involved in a Somerset witchcraft case – probably the trial of Edmund Ball and Joan Greedie at Taunton assizes in 1626[11] – and this seems to have prompted his writing of the *Guide*. Another demonologist with Somerset connections, Meric Casaubon,[12] recounted what appears to be the same case in *Of Credulity and Incredulity in Things natural, civil and divine*, published in 1668. At the time of the Taunton trial he was the rector in the parish of Bleadon, Somerset. After the accused (Edmund Ball?), a gardener by profession and a 'desperate atheist', was captured following a remarkable escape from Bridgwater Gaol 'he was speedily executed. Thus the Devil deals with his vassals'.[13] Bernard's *Guide* begins with the premise that human afflictions are ordained by God and, while witches might be the 'instruments of evil' that punish humanity for its sins, it is far more important for the afflicted to mend their ways than seek out and punish witches. Furthermore, citing the work of an expert 'physician', he insisted that many traumatic medical diseases, commonly attributed to witchcraft, have natural causes. The physician in question was John Cotta, author of *The Tryall of Witch-Craft* (1616). Quite logically Bernard concluded that grand jurymen should always consult medical experts before attributing an affliction to unnatural causes. This is no simple task since the Devil and his acolytes will sometimes attempt to disguise satanic diseases as natural ones. Citing the well-known case of 'The Boy of Bilson' and his own observation of a pretended bewitchment in Wells, Bernard warned against pretenders mimicking the behaviour of the possessed.

The first of the two books into which the *Guide* is divided concludes with a tackling of the disconcerting absence of explicit references to witches and witchcraft in the Holy Scriptures. His earlier point that the Devil initiates acts of evil and the witch is merely his instrument is reasserted. Consequently, it is argued, there are few references to witches because the Bible directly attributes evil in the world to the activities of the Devil: 'witches are Satan's slaves who cannot do that evil which men accuse them of – the Devil does it for them. Therefore, the Scriptures ascribe the acts to the Devil as his own and not to witches (though they consent) because they do not do them themselves'. The second book begins by outlining the evidence for, in Bernard's view, the incontrovertible reality of witches and witchcraft. Using the evidence of numerous confessions of witches, he was able to construct an up-to-date mythology of witchcraft and diabolism.

Keith Thomas's research, resulting in his *Religion and the Decline of Magic* (1971), confirmed the reality of practitioners of magic in early modern England. These 'cunning folk', who were vilified by Bernard, were found throughout the land peddling herbal remedies, prophecies and love potions. The herbalist Nicholas Culpeper noted in 1649 how 'All the nation are already physicians. If you ail anything, everyone you meet, whether a man or woman, will prescribe you a medicine for it'. They relied on their own knowledge and that of their neighbours, including the local wise woman or cunning man. In the opinion of the contemporary philosopher Francis Bacon, this was not such a bad thing since 'empirics and old women [were] more happy many times in their cures than learned physicians'. Even the controversial and frequently sceptical philosopher Thomas Hobbes (1588–1679) was of the same opinion, preferring to 'take the advice or take physic from an experienced old woman that had been at many sick people's bedsides, than from the learnedest but unexperienced physician'.[14] Macfarlane concluded that in Elizabethan times 'nowhere in Essex was there a village more than ten miles from a known cunning man/wise woman. The county was covered by a network of magical practitioners'.[15] They had a range of occupations and included among their number schoolmasters, medical practitioners and yeomen farmers. In his list of sixty-three, forty-four are men – an interesting contrast to the preponderance of women (c.90 per cent) charged with witchcraft in seventeenth-century Essex.

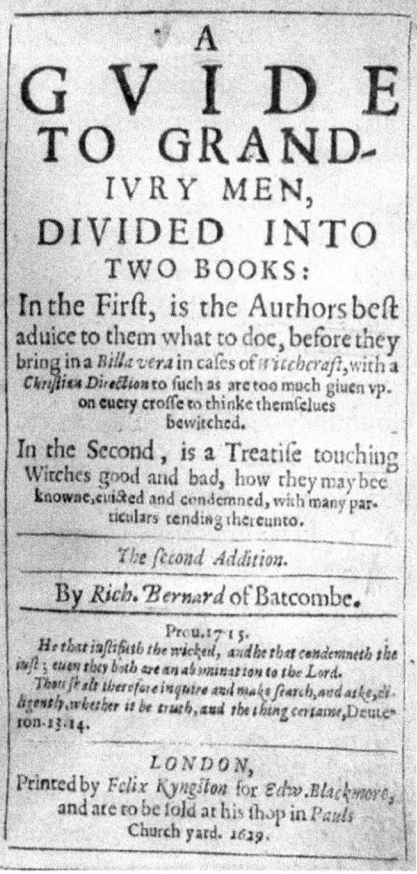

Fig. 1-3 *Richard Bernard,* A Guide to Grand-Jury Men Divided Into Two Bookes: In The First, Is The Authors Best Advice To Them what to doe, before they bring in a billa vera in cases of witchcraft, etc., *first published in 1627.*

In Bernard's (and Cotta's) opinion these 'white' witches and wizards, 'commonly called blessers, healers, cunning wise men or women', who offered cures for maleficent witchcraft were as despicable as those who caused it. This was an age in which the traditional healers and dealers of helpful magic were demonised; in the new construction these were open to condemnation as much as their imagined Devil-worshipping counterparts. Although the 'bad' witch, typically, was female, Bernard remarked that these so-called 'good' witches were often male – an observation substantiated by modern historians. These cunning folk he depicted as central players in the common culture of rural England, rich in 'fantasy' and plagued by 'fear', its inhabitants 'superstitiously addicted' and prone to 'heathenish practice'. That their spells sometimes worked was not contested by Bernard – he maintained that they did not have any magical powers but, in laying claim to supernatural abilities, they opened themselves up to a subtle pact with the Devil and through him alone their charms took effect. Like the black witch, the white witch was in league with Satan and reliant on a demon-familiar: 'Through their spirit they learn who are bad witches and where they dwell, who are stricken, forespoken, and bewitched, and through them they find out about those whom they undertake to cure for the spirit is sent to their patients by them'. For the most part, in Bernard's reckoning, white witches served different purposes from black witches in the divine scheme of things, but 'though these witches be almost all healing witches, and cannot do to man or beast any harm, except when they procure some other to do it, yet we may find that some of these sometimes have the double faculty both to bless and to curse, to hurt, and to heal'. Of this phenomenon Bernard provided a well-known example: 'one Hartley[16] in Lancashire and a woman witch, both of which, Master Cooper in his *Mystery of Witchcraft* makes mention'.[17]

In his summary of the characteristics of a white witch Bernard provides fascinating insights into the ways in which these cunning folk operated in seventeenth-century England. For some the provision of magical cures was a profession, but others, it appears, offered their services free despite their poverty. Bernard explained this surprising behaviour as a whim of the Devil who had mastered them:

> Their reward is for their curing, what people commonly will give them; some take more, some take but a little, often nothing, and some may not take anything at all, as some have professed, that if they should take anything they could do no good; of such a one Bodin[18] makes mention, who went about in patched and ragged

clothes. Here also the Devil will imitate Christ, who said 'Freely ye receive, freely give'.[19]

White witches, according to Bernard, were 'commonly very ignorant of religion' and very superstitious. They avoided both clergymen and physicians, unwilling to discuss with them their activities 'lest their works of darkness should come to light, and they be discovered to be witches'. They gave themselves away by their 'private and secret whisperings, mumblings and muttering with a low voice' and by claiming they could 'help those that are bewitched and forespoken'. They would endeavour to cure sufferers of such conditions as the 'ague' and toothache with a touch and the recitation of prayers, 'many of which are Popish prayers', and 'by charms and spells, absurd, barbarous and ridiculous forms of words and such like which have no power from natural working'. They prescribed remedies, hung amulets and passages from the scriptures around the necks of the afflicted, advised their patients to scratch the suspected witch until he or she bled, to burn some of his or her hair, 'to prick a needle or bodkin under the stool where the witch sits', or 'to make a witch-cake of baker's meal' to undo black magic. If the patient was cured it was the Devil's work, these spurious remedies having no effect at all. Likewise, when they displayed powers of prophecy they were instructed by the Devil: 'This foreknowledge, physicians have not by their Art, neither have these ignorant persons this by divine inspiration, and therefore by it must be acquired through their pact with the Devil'. With the Devil's assistance they could reveal the image of a maleficent witch in a glass – the art of 'scrying' as it was called in the West of England. Those who resorted to the cunning folk were themselves 'usually wicked and evil people, haunted themselves by an evil spirit, who suggests this course of action to them'.[20]

In making such remarks Bernard was upholding a tradition that can be traced in England back at least as far as William Perkins[21] at the turn of the century. Perkins abhorred 'all diviners, charmers, jugglers, all wizards commonly called wise men and wise women' because 'they deny God, and are confederates with Satan'. However, while people 'do commonly hate and spit at the damnifying sorcerer, as unworthy to live among them', the cunning man was 'so dear to them, that they hold themselves and the country blessed that have him among them, they fly unto him in necessity, they depend upon him as their god'. In Perkins's opinion death 'is the just and deserved portion of the good witch'.[22] Bernard echoed this declaration in stating: 'There ought be no such distinction of witches as good and bad, blessing and cursing, white and black witches [...] They may differ in name, but all are abomination to the Lord, and ought to die'. He considered the practices of faith healers and other cunning folk a throw-back to Catholic times, the legacy of which was to be found in 'their superstitious ceremonies, lip-prayers, *Ave-Marias*, creeds, and *pater-nosters* by set numbers'. He claimed that 'when Popery held sway here, then devils and spirits often appeared, and at that time there were many more witches than now'.[23]

Although some were more likely to succumb to the Devil's wiles than others, all of humanity, in Bernard's opinion, was at risk. After all, in Bernard's puritanical view, 'man has lost the image of God, in which he was created, and is wholly polluted with sin and corruption'.[24] Despite his recognition in the first part of the *Guide* that natural ailments could be misconstrued as having supernatural causes, the evidence of bewitchment provided by Bernard in the second part persuades the modern reader that little-understood conditions such as strokes and epilepsy might nevertheless have deceived the author. The popular folk cures for witchcraft, familiar from the pamphlet literature of the period, are catalogued, but Bernard had no faith in their efficacy; he concluded, 'God only can free us from devils and witches'.[25]

According to Bernard's definition, a witch is someone who is in league with the Devil. Until this could be proven the jury should not condemn the accused. At the top of his list of sufficient proofs is the 'witch's mark' – the place where she has been touched by the Devil or her blood is sucked by her familiar. This preoccupation with familiars is a defining characteristic of the English witchcraft tradition, unheard of in German confessions,[26] and uncommon elsewhere in Europe except in the Basque Country.[27]

Bernard identified such marks as those that would be found on the body of the Beckington witch Elizabeth Carrier in 1689 as certain proof of the witch's pact with the Devil and explained to the judges what it was they should look for. 'The witch's mark', he wrote, 'is insensible, and being pricked will not bleed'. Sometimes it might resemble a teat but sometimes it might be 'a bluish spot' like a bruise or 'red spots like a fleabite'. Sometimes it might be a dimple where 'the flesh is sunk-in and hollow'. Since, he maintained, witches had the power to hide their marks, it was good practice to search the witch more than once in order to discover the tell-tale mark.[28] It is quite evident from all this that the women engaged in the search would be able to find the Devil's mark on the body of anyone presented before them. He further clarified the phenomenon with reference to a number of well-known English cases.

He explained how 'they meet together to 'christen' the spirits (as they describe it) when they give the spirit a name' and listed some of these: 'Mephastophilus, Lucifer, Little Lord, Fimodes, David, Inde, Little Robin, Smack, Lightfoot, Non-such, Lunch, Makeshift, Swart, Pluck, Blue, Catch, White, Callico, Hardname, Tibb, Hiff, Ball, Puss, Rutterkin, Dick, Pretty, Griffet and Jace'. In the English tradition, as Bernard reiterated, it was firmly believed that 'By these familiar spirits they do what they do; of these they ask advice, they send abroad to fulfil their desires, if God allows'. In so doing the witches are deceived into thinking they control the demon themselves.

The great majority of the people accused of being witches in Selwood in the second half of the century were women. Bernard's misogynistic *Guide*, reiterating ideas voiced by previous commentators such as Alexander Roberts,[29] both explained and encouraged this pattern of persecution.

The book ends with the argument that Satan mimics God, sometimes copying God, sometimes inverting God's work. In his conclusion he challenged those sceptics who, like Scot and Weyer, would attribute witchcraft to 'brainsick conceits, and mad melancholy'.[30]

Jonathan Barry has explored connections between Bernard and the two men responsible for the most complete record of the Selwood Forest witch trials of the late 1650s and early 1660s – Joseph Glanvill and his fellow political and religious moderate,[31] Robert Hunt Justice of the Peace. Noting that Bernard lived halfway between two of the places where these witchcraft accusations were made – Shepton Mallet and Brewham – Barry has written, 'It seems very likely that he [Bernard] was personally known to Hunt; intriguingly Hunt's appeal as sheriff in 1654 to the county bench to subscribe to a fund for preaching to the prisoners is very close in sentiment and wording to Bernard's pleas for funds to help poor prisoners, addressed to the same bench in 1627'.[32] Furthermore,

Bernard's *The Isle of Man: or the legal proceeding in Manshire against sinne* (1627) was dedicated to the Thynne family of Longleat, who later installed Joseph Glanvill, first as the Vicar of Frome Selwood and then as Vicar of Street and Walton. Barry concluded: 'It is hard to believe that Hunt and Glanvill did not both know and discuss Bernard's writings on witchcraft, and Hunt might well have used it as a guide to his own work in examining witches'.[33] Thirty years on, many of the witchcraft traditions and assumptions written down by Bernard were evident in the Selwood cases recorded by Hunt. Another thirty years thereafter, notably in the extraordinary symptoms of the bewitched – fits, displays of supernatural strength, strange vomiting – they would appear once more in the 1689 case recounted by the rector of Beckington.

Richard Alleine succeeded Bernard as rector of Batcombe in 1642. In 1654 he and his father, both committed Calvinists, were appointed as assistants to a parliamentary commission established for the purpose of 'ejecting scandalous ministers'. Alleine was a charismatic preacher who, despite his hellfire and brimstone sermonizing was 'idolised by his parishioners'.[34] He was ejected from his Batcombe living following the imposition of the Act of Uniformity in 1662, as was his father from Ditcheat. After the passing, in 1665, of the Five Mile Act, which obliged ejected ministers to abandon their parishes, he moved to Frome Selwood whose vicar, Glanvill, and, one must suppose, his acquaintance, was beginning to make a name for himself as a member of the Royal Society who happened to have a deep interest in local witchcraft cases. Eventually, Alleine was licensed to preach as a Presbyterian in neighbouring Beckington from 1672.[35] It is most probable that he and Beckington's rector, who would be instrumental in bringing the 1689 case to light, became closely acquainted. All these men of the cloth, to some degree at least, can be assumed to have shared what Elmer has described, referring to Robert Hunt, as a 'providentialist world-view', finding evidence in all kinds of preternatural episodes for a post-Restoration world 'out of kilter'.[36]

Alleine was a prolific writer and, although he did not write on the subject of witchcraft, his sermons and published texts are rich in references to the Devil and the terrible danger of leading a sinful, irreligious life. During his Frome retirement he published *Godly-Fear* (1674) – a weighty tome concerned with 'the nature and necessity of fear and its usefulness both to the driving sinners to Christ and to the provoking Christians on in a Godly life, through the several parts and duties of it, till they come to blessedness'. In the rhetorical style of the period, and alert to the new threat of emerging atheism, Alleine alluded to the subtle activities of the Devil in the world, including the Tidworth haunting of Mr. Mompesson's home near Salisbury, recently witnessed and reported by Glanvill. These Alleine contrasted with the horrors of eternal damnation:

> What is it to dwell in an earthly house that's haunted with the Devil? What terror do they live in, whose dwelling is in haunted houses? How are they feared, and frightened, to see the face of that dragon, though shaped into the most beautiful form? Those that tremble so to see the Devil in their own houses, what will it be to them, to be carried with him into his house where he will be unclothed of all his vizors and no longer appear in the shape of a man, no, nor of a lion or bear, but will show himself a devil. All the legions of those unclean and damned spirits together with all those damned souls their fellow-sinners. All the filth and garbage of the Earth must lie rotting and stinking together in this dismal hole. All the atheists and blasphemers, all the adulterers and their whores, all the rioters and drunkards, that have spent so many days, and sat up so many nights at the wine and the strong drink, shall now be filled with the company they loved, and shall have an everlasting night to lie drinking up the wine of the wrath of the Almighty, and of the Lamb, and suck up the dregs and bottom of that deadly cup, which the fury of the Most High hath mingled and appointed for them. This is their sentence.[37]

As a child growing up in Ditcheat, Alleine no doubt was familiar with the tale, derided by the great Elizabethan sceptic Reginald Scot, of the occasion when, in 1584, the Devil was at large in the village. His reference to the Devil taking the shape of a bear in the passage above was probably inspired by it. The tale was told in a pamphlet, *A true and most Dreadfull discourse of a woman possessed with the Devill*, published in London that year. It concerned the manifestation of a hideous creature in the form of a headless bear that appeared in the bedroom of one Stephen Cooper's sick wife, Margaret.

In his sermons Alleine urged constant vigilance against the subtle intrusions of the Devil: 'Brethren, who is there with you at this house? Here you are before the Lord, but who is there with you? Search every room, look into every corner; is there none within that should not be there? Is there no messenger of Satan, hath the world no agitator at work within you?'[38] 'The Devil', he once warned another congregation, 'is with you wherever you are, he watches you wherever you go'.[39] Elsewhere he conjured up images of demonic armies – Hell's 'black regiments' – and, invoking the terminology of his mentor, Bernard (and after him, Glanvill), the Devil's 'instruments',[40] hunting the souls of worldly sinners. Witchcraft he listed with adultery, drunkenness, sodomy, buggery, blasphemy, idolatry and atheism, as abominations encouraged by Satan.[41]

A 1614 account of the Devil's manifestation in Ditcheat in 1584.

1. In Gustave Henningsen, 'The Greatest Witch-Trial of All: Navarre, 1609–14' in *History Today*, 30:11 (1980).
2. Malcolm Gaskill, 'The Pursuit of Reality: Recent Research into the History of Witchcraft', *The Historical Journal*, 51: 4 (2008), 1086.
3. DNB 'Bernard, Richard'; ODNB 'Bernard, Richard'; Richard Bernard and Richard Alleine, *David's Musick, or, Psalms of that royall prophet, once the sweete singer of that Israel* (1616).
4. ODNB, 'Alleine, Richard'.
5. DNB, 'Bernard, Richard'; Stanley Gower (?), *A General Martyrologie* (1651), a biography of Richard Rothwell, in Darren Oldridge, *The Devil in Tudor and Stuart England* (Stroud: The History Press, 2011), 209.
6. ODNB, 'Bernard, Richard'.
7. Bernard Rosenthal, *Salem Story: Reading the Witch Trials of 1692* (Cambridge: Cambridge University Press, 1993), 135-6; the 'gold standard' for Massachussetts magistrates according to Stacy Schiff, *The Witches: Salem, 1692, a History* (London: Weidenfeld and Nicolson, 2015), 211.
8. Sharpe, *Instruments*, 82.
9. *Ibid.*,102.
10. Clark, Stuart, *Thinking with Demons: The Idea of Witchcraft in Early Modern Europe* (Oxford: Oxford University Press, 1997), 114.
11. Brit. Mus., Add. MSS., 36,674, fol. 189.
12. Meric Casaubon was born in Geneva, the son of an influential French intellectual, Isaac Casaubon. In common with Bernard and Glanvill, he challenged the perceived threat of atheism by forming arguments for the reality of the existence of spirits based on biblical and classical precedent together with modern accounts of supernatural phenomena.
13. Meric Casaubon, *Of Credulity and Incredulity in Things natural, civil and divine* (London: 1688), 170–72.
14. Thomas, *Decline of Magic*, 15–17.
15. Alan Macfarlane, *Witchcraft in Tudor and Stuart England* (London: Routledge, 1970, 1999), 120.
16. Itinerant conjuror, herbalist and faith healer, Edmund Hartley was executed in 1597 following charges of demonic possession.
17. Richard Bernard, *A Guide to Grand-Jury Men Divided Into Two Bookes: In The First, Is The Authors Best Advice To Them what to doe, before they bring in a billa vera in cases of witchcraft, etc.*, (1627), 131; Cooper's influential demonology was published in 1617.
18. French author of the most influential demonology produced in the late sixteenth century: *On the Demon-mania of Sorcerers* (1580).
19. Bernard, *Guide*, 131–32.
20. *Ibid.*, 132–43.
21. Cambridge theologian and puritan.

22 William Perkins, *A Discourse of the Damned Art of Witchcraft* (1608), 255–57, in Sharpe, *Instruments*, 101–02.
23 Bernard, *Guide*, 99–100.
24 *Ibid.*, 118.
25 *Ibid.*, 196.
26 Lyndal Roper, *Witch Craze* (New Haven and London: Yale University Press, 2004), 92.
27 Sharpe, *Instruments*, 70.
28 Bernard, *Guide*, 218–20.
29 Alexander Roberts, *A Treatise of Witchcraft: wherein sundry Propositions are laid downe, plainely discovering the Wickednesse of that damnable Art* (1616), 42–3, in Sharpe, *Instruments*, 109.
30 Bernard, *Guide*, 267.
31 See Barry, *Witchcraft and Demonology*, 29; Elmer, *Witchcraft*, 217.
32 Barry, *Witchcraft and Demonology*, 47.
33 *Ibid.*, 48; see also Julie Davies *Science in an Enchanted World: Philosophy and Witchcraft in the Work of Joseph Glanvill* (London: Routledge, 2018), Chapter 2.
34 Stephen Wright, 'Alleine, Richard' (*Oxford Dictionary of National Biography*, 2004).
35 *Ibid.*
36 Elmer, *Witchcraft*, 218.
37 Richard Alleine, *Godly-Fear* (1674), 176.
38 Richard Alleine, *The World Conquered or A Believers Victory over the World* (1668), 238.
39 Richard Alleine, *A Rebuke for Backsliders and a Spur for Loyterers* (1684), 110.
40 Richard Alleine, *The Godly Mans Portion and Sanctuary Opened in Two Sermons Preached August 17 1662* (1662), 33–4; this fascinating book includes a succinct point-by-point guide to achieving the mid-seventeenth-century puritan lifestyle (125–36). He mostly avoided the derogatory term 'puritan', substituting for it the word 'precision' to define those who were precise in their reading of the scriptures: 'Whosoever is not truly a person of a precise life, is certainly in the state of damnation' (*A vindication of Godlinesse*, 1664, 91).
41 Alleine, *The Godly Man's Portion*, 49.

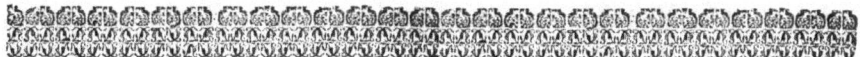

2

THE DEMON DRUMMER

Fig. 2-1 *Detail from the frontispiece of Saducismus Triumphatus (1681) depicting the demon 'Drummer of Tedworth'.*

If the notion of a spirit be so absurd as is pretended, that of a God, and a soul distinct from matter, and immortal, is likewise an absurdity.
– Joseph Glanvill, 1668.[1]

IF WHAT SURVIVES of the Selwood Forest witchcraft story can be deemed to start in Batcombe, the Restoration-era phase is centred upon Frome. A short time before he arrived in Frome, where he would stay until his death in 1681, Richard Alleine became engaged in a public debate with a man he named a friend, Frome's vicar and Joseph Glanvill's predecessor, John Humfrey,[2] another prolific and well-connected writer who played a vital part in the unveiling of witchcraft in the region.

Born at St Albans in 1621, and graduating from Pembroke College, Oxford, in 1641, he had been the incumbent of St John's, Frome, since 27 June 1654. He received a Presbyterian ordination in 1649, and was aged forty-one at the time of the Uniformity Act and the 'Great Ejectment' which led to the removal of around 2,000 nonconformist ministers.

Humfrey was no puritan and most certainly not a republican – Calamy noted, 'As he never took the covenant, so did he never join in the association with the Presbytery'. He was 'counted a man of the old stamp, and no favourite of those times' and 'all along for bringing in the King', and he was even issued with a warrant shortly before the Restoration as a 'seditious person'. This danger 'blew over when the King returned'.[3] Nevertheless his position remained in jeopardy until he agreed to an orthodox episcopalian re-ordination, conducted by the Bishop of Bath and Wells, William Piers. Although at first he attempted to justify his action in print, clearly it caused him a crisis of conscience. This was the focus of a correspondence he had at the time with the celebrated Richard Baxter, who had been ejected (from Kidderminster) in 1661 and, three decades later, would publish the best-known account of the Beckington witch trial.[4] When, subsequently, he reneged on his decision and renounced his re-ordination, he was ejected from his Frome Selwood office in August 1662 and replaced by Joseph Glanvill. Calamy recorded the declaration Humfrey made regarding this difficult decision:

> I [...] who was ordained by a class of Presbyters in 1649, and again ordained by a Bishop in 1660, do profess before the world, in order to the glory of God and the peace of my conscience, that though I hold re-ordination to be in some cases lawful, and agreeable to the word of God, and have publicly appeared in defence of it; yet having been convinced I did not do right, in yielding to what there was really no occasion for, having tried all other ways to ease my mind, but without relief, and having no other method left, (to say nothing of the absurdity of the form used, which runs back again to Deaconship, where there was already an higher order, which is so reproachful that it deserves indignation) I do of my own accord, and proper motion, influenced to it by none, but by the hand of God, profess before him my penitent grief and sorrow for that whole action and all that belonged to it, in will, word, and deed, when

I, without due consideration, yielded to be re-ordained; I retract, revoke, renounce, and reject it, and by these present lines do, as far as in me lies, render what was done undone again: and being fully persuaded that my former ordination was sufficiently valid, I restore myself to my former state, and to that I will adhere.[5]

Having read his statement to the bishop's registrar he then took out and tore up his Holy Orders in front of him. The furious registrar promptly went into another room to denounce Humfrey before others assembled there. Humfrey confirmed to them what he had done, and, gathering up all the pieces of the torn document, he threw them into the fire.

Humfrey was already a well-known theologian and had now become a well-known controversialist as a moderate nonconformist and a pioneer of the Congregationalist movement. His publications on the re-ordination issue had prompted Richard Alleine, the ejected rector of Batcombe who retired to Frome and Beckington, to respond, also in print. In a fifteen-page appendix item at the end of a tract published in 1661 he conceded that 'Mr Humfrey being a scholar and having sought God upon his knees for direction, it would be somewhat unchristian to adhere to my former determination [Alleine was firmly opposed to re-ordination] without so much as considering what he had written and printed against it'.[6] Quite possibly Alleine's powerful counter-argument that re-ordination is a 'moral evil' was instrumental in Humfrey's brave decision to renege on his initial compliance when he accepted re-ordination in 1660. It is highly likely that the two men knew each other personally, both having held Selwood Forest livings during the era of the Commonwealth. That they both had associations with writers of some of the most famous demonologies in English history, as well as close connections with the village of Beckington, is especially interesting.

Humfrey's correspondence with Baxter can be traced back at least as far back as 1654. The two men maintained a lively correspondence which would continue over several decades, during which time they also exchanged manuscripts of their work,[7] and became close neighbours in London. Glanvill was also an admirer of Baxter and he heard him preach on a number of occasions.[8] He too corresponded with him on a range of theological matters over the course of several years. In time all three would reveal a deep interest in demonology and publish material in the field, and they all played a vital in preserving for posterity reports of witchcraft in Selwood Forest. Together they were part of, in the words of Michael Hunter, 'an alliance of Anglicans and nonconformists in confronting the irreligious threat'.[9]

The Restoration in 1660, Peter Elmer has concluded, 'marked a major turning point in English history, for the fate of demonology and witchcraft as well as the religious and political direction of the country'.[10] In Beckington the old Laudian, Alexander Huish, was reinstated as rector, and Glanvill became vicar of neighbouring Frome Selwood in November 1662. As a convinced 'latitudinarian'[11] Glanvill doubtless was sympathetic towards Humfrey and others in his situation. In appointing Glanvill, Thynne placed one of the most promising young thinkers of his age in the heart of an area which, it seems, was in the midst of something amounting to a witchcraft panic. Glanvill would contribute much to the revival of interest in witchcraft and other supernatural phenomena in this era of uncertainty.[12] He had already secured admiration for his publications *The Vanity of Dogmatizing or Confidence in Opinions manifested in a Discourse of the Shortness and Uncertainty of our Knowledge, and it's causes with some Reflexions on Peripateticism, and an apology for Philosophy* (London: 1661) and *Lux Orientalis; or an enquiry into the Opinion of the Eastern Sages concerning the Pre-Existence of Souls*. In the latter in particular he placed himself firmly in the camp of the Cambridge Platonists,[13] exploring the possibility that the soul endures to be recast in an ethereal or terrestrial form. Inspired by Henry More's pioneering *Antidote against Atheisme* (1653), he would undertake his own investigations into preternatural phenomena in the scientific 'garb of the naturalist' as More had put it,[14] using empirical evidence to proves its reality. The mid-century revival of interest in Reginald Scot's sceptical *Discoverie of Supposed Witchcraft*, reissued in 1651, had helped reopen the debate as to the reality of wicked spirits and witchcraft. Glanvill would reject Scot's arguments as 'trifling and childish', his 'ventures at philosophy' as 'little better than absurd'. None but 'boys and buffoons', he concluded, could be impressed by such impotent arguments.[15]

Montague Summers once wrote, 'There is no more important figure in the history of English psychical research than Joseph Glanvill'.[16] The controversial twentieth-century ghost-hunter Harry Price remembered him as 'the Father' of the science.[17] The famous collection of Glanvill's writings on witchcraft, *Saducismus Triumphatus*, has long been regarded among historians of English demonism as one of the most important of all of the seventeenth-century texts on the subject. Furthermore, as Ryan

Fig. 2-2 *Joseph Glanvill (1636-80), Vicar of Frome Selwood (1662-72), member of the Royal Society and collector of Selwood witchcraft cases*

Stark has commented, he was writing at a time, more than any other in the history of the western world, when the study of bewitchment played 'such a central role in mainstream thought'.[18]

Born in Plymouth in 1636 and raised in a puritan household, Glanvill had graduated with an MA degree from Lincoln College, Oxford, in 1658. Ordained in 1660, he held the Frome living until 1672 when he exchanged it for the combined livings of Street and Walton near Glastonbury. From 1666 he also held office as a rector of Bath Abbey, and Bath became his principal place of residence until his death in 1680.

In the winter of 1662–3, at the time of his arrival in Frome, Glanvill, in the company of a 'gentleman', visited the home, thirty-four miles away, of John Mompesson at Tidworth (then known as Tedworth) on the edge of Salisbury Plain, a few miles north-east of Amesbury. Here he spent a night during which he witnessed various forms of what would now be called poltergeist activity associated with the so-called 'Drummer of Tedworth', the most famous episode of its kind in early-modern England.

The events at the home of the Tidworth magistrate gave rise to much speculation that he was being victimised by devils. The affair began when Mompesson confiscated a drum belonging to a vagrant named William Drury, a former regimental drummer turned trick-dancer at country fairs. Subsequently the sound of drumming was heard throughout the Mompesson home, though the source of the thumping and tapping could not be located. When the vagrant's drum was destroyed these noises grew louder still. Drury was arrested again early in 1663 on a charge of stealing pigs and was sentenced to transportation. However, he managed to escape from the convict ship and acquired a new drum. Mompesson had the vagrant seized once more and the drummer found himself charged with both witchcraft and pig-stealing. Drury was alleged to have admitted to a visitor while he was in prison that he was responsible for the disturbance, but the witchcraft charge could not be proved. For the pig-stealing he was transported to Virginia. Those who claimed to have heard the noise explained that the unseen drummer seemed to tap out responses to their questions. Contemporary demonologists found various other phenomena reported at the house significant and clearly indicative of the demonic origins of the trouble – they drew obvious conclusions, for instance, from the smell of brimstone that was said to pervade the house. Other reports spoke of strange lights, children lifted into the air, furniture moved by unseen hands, Bibles covered in ashes, chamber-pots emptied onto beds, drops of blood found and bedclothes disturbed. On occasion the cacophony was loud enough to wake up the whole village. The extraordinary phenomena attributed to the phantom drummer continued for two years. The king, Charles II, became interested in the case and sent a committee to investigate but they failed to witness anything unusual, unlike Glanvill and his companion:[19]

> About this time I went to the house to investigate the truth of the matter of which there was so loud a report. It [the poltergeist] had ceased from its drumming and ruder noises before I came thither, but most of the more remarkable circumstances [...] were confirmed to me there by several of the neighbours together who had been present at them. At this time it used to haunt the children as soon as they lay down. They went to bed the night I was there at about eight o'clock,

when a maid-servant, coming down from them, told us it was come. The neighbours that were there, and two ministers who had seen and heard it many times, went away, but Mr Mompesson and I, and a gentleman that came with me, went up. I heard a strange scratching as I went up the stairs, and when we came into the room, I perceived it was just behind the bolster of the children's bed, and seemed to be against the tick.[20] There was as loud a scratching as one with long nails could make upon a bolster. There were two little girls in the bed, between seven and eleven years old as I guessed. I saw their hands out of the bedclothes and they could not have contributed to the noise that was behind their heads. They had become used to it, and, since they still had someone or other in the chamber with them, seemed not to be much affrighted. Standing at the bedhead, I thrust my hand behind the bolster, directing it to the place from whence the noise seemed to come. Thereupon the noise ceased there and was heard in another part of the bed. But when I took my hand out it returned and was heard in the same place as before. I had been told that it would imitate noises and I tested this by scratching several times – five, seven and nine – upon the sheet, and each time it followed and stopped at the same number. I searched under and behind the bed, turned up the clothes to the bed-cords, grasped the bolster, sounded the wall behind, and searched as much as I possibly could to find out if there was any trick, connivance, or common cause of it; so did my friend, but we could discover nothing. Thus I was entirely convinced, and am so still, that the noise was made by some demon or spirit. After it had scratched away for half an hour or so it went into the middle of the bed, under the children, and there seemed to pant, very loudly, like a dog out of breath. I put my hand upon the place and felt the bed bearing up against it, as if something within had thrust it up. I grasped the feathers to feel if any living thing were in it. I looked under everywhere about to see if there were any dog or cat, or any such creature in the room, and so we all did, but found nothing. The motion it caused by this panting was so strong that, quite perceptively, it shook the room and windows. It continued thus for more than half an hour while my friend and I were in the room and, we were told, for as long after. During the panting [episode] I chanced to see something (which I thought was a rat or mouse) moving in a linen bag that was hung up against another bed that was in the room. I stepped over and caught it by the upper end with one hand, with which I held it, and drew it through the other, but found nothing at all in it. There was nobody near who could have shaken the bag, and even if there was, no-one could have made such a motion as if a living creature was moving within it.[21]

Such experiences are rare but have been recorded for many hundreds of years and continue to crop up from time to time, mostly read as minor items in tabloid and online newspapers. Glanvill and his companion might have been deceived or imagined these extraordinary happenings. Some level-headed commentators on historic poltergeist cases do not entirely rule out the possibility that those involved witnessed actual phenomena, phenomena that are 'supernatural' only because no known natural law explains them. In his 2011 review of the famous poltergeist episode in Enfield in the late 1970s, its investigator, Guy Playfair, noted that what 'appears to us today as strange, unbelievable and impossible as, say, the idea of an internet would have appeared to Newton [Glanvill's Royal Society contemporary] or even Einstein' might become a recognised scientific fact.[22] Where seventeenth-century 'believers' in poltergeist activity found explanations in the reality of a world of spirits, modern-day researchers are more likely to resort to psychokinetic theory. Richard Sugg, Lecturer in Renaissance Literature at the University of Durham,[23] finds the evidence for poltergeist activity in the past and present hard to ignore,[24] 'Poltergeists', he has written, 'are clearly real. Or, rather: the set of bizarre effects [...] clustered under that name are clearly real'.[25] Whatever their cause the

Fig. 2-3 *Glanvill's posthumous Saducismus Triumphatus, or, full and plain Evidence concerning Witches and Apparitions (1681).*

experience for observers is a real one and and one which might reaffirm or even realign their existing world-view. Shortly before his death in 2006 the controversial parapsychologist and Professor of Psychology at the University of Edinburgh, John Beloff (1920–2006), announced:

> I have never seen an apparition or been present at a poltergeist disturbance [....] However, that is no reason to doubt the testimony of those who have. After all, most of our topographical and all our historical knowledge is, perforce, knowledge at second hand. If there are compelling cases of poltergeist activity then it is futile to dismiss, in principle, all reports of such phenomena, although we have an intellectual duty to be as cautious and critical as we can.[26]

With the tale of the Drummer of Tedworth in mind, he further observed, '[In] cases from the past where the investigator was a prominent academic with a reputation to uphold [...] I find it easier to believe than disbelieve, however much believing may complicate my world view'.[27]

Of all the supernatural cases Glanvill cited in his 'Relations' in his subsequent *Saducismus Triumphatus*, this was the only one of which he had personal experience. Thereafter he readily accepted the validity of the accounts of respectable people, notably Robert Hunt, as further affirmation of the reality of spirits – malign and benevolent. 'It will be said by some', he acknowledged, 'that my friend and I were under some affright, and so fancied noises and sights that were not'. However, he contested, 'This is the eternal evasion. [...] I know what I heard and saw'.[28] Then again, as Darren Oldridge has put it, 'what today might be dismissed as 'tricks of the mind' could be readily explained within a belief system that acknowledged demonic visitations as unproblematically real'.[29] Regardless, Glanvill had the evidence attested by 'thousands of eye and ear witnesses, and those not of the easily deceivable vulgar only, but of wise and grave discerners; and that, when no interest could oblige them to agree together in a common lie'.[30]

Glanvill's Royal Society associate, the antiquarian and author of *Brief Lives* John Aubrey, despite his sensitivity towards preternatural providential phenomena,[31] considered the whole business a hoax.[32] He found Glanvill, though 'an ingenius person', one who was 'a little too credulous'. He added that when one Mr Ettrick investigated the activity he found requests to make a knocking noise were only responded to when spoken aloud – the 'ghost' would not respond when the request was whispered. When Sir Christopher Wren stayed at Tidworth for a night 'he observed that this drumming was only when a certain maid-servant was in the next room'. Furthermore, Aubrey observed, 'the Devil kept no very unseasonable hours: it seldom knocked after twelve at night, or before six in the morning'.[33] In 1716 Glanvill's famous account was the inspiration for Joseph Addison's comic play *The Drummer*.

'The gentleman', Glanvill wrote, 'who was with me at the house' is referred to elsewhere as 'Mr Hill'.[34] Jonathan Barry has declared, 'It is impossible to identify Hill given the commonness of the name', and he is probably correct. However, there is a tantalising possibility, as Barry has noted, that this 'very sober, intelligent and credible person'[35] could have some connection with other people by the name of Hill linked to the Selwood Forest cases. Richard Hill of Stoke Trister, as described below, launched an attack on Elizabeth Style for the alleged bewitchment of his thirteen-year-old daughter, and May Hill was the rector who recorded the bewitchment of his parishioner, Mary Hill (no relation), at Beckington in 1689. It is reasonable to rule out Richard Hill since he is defined as a yeoman in the Style case of 1665 and there is no hint whatsoever that he had established any direct connection with Glanvill. In any case, their homes were more than sixteen miles apart – this certainly could not have been a neighbourly relationship that somehow transcended class boundaries. May Hill (1644-1700), at first sight, is the much more promising candidate for the gentleman Glanvill called 'my friend'.[36]

Hill's origins are illuminated through the records of his matriculation and family wills. His was very much a Selwood Forest family, and one of considerable local importance as landowners and clerics. May and his brother, Stephen (1655-1737), graduates of Magdalen Hall,[37] came from a place once called Brookway Gate,[38] very close to Frome, on the western edge of the parish of Westbury, Wiltshire. Their mother, Frances Seaman, was the daughter of the rector[39] of their local church of St. Mary's in Upton Scudamore. When the older brother matriculated in March 1661, aged about seventeen, his college had a reputation for its puritan zeal; its inspirational Principal from 1648, Henry Wilkinson, was in post from 1648, until he was ejected following the passing of the Act of Uniformity in 1662. Among the famous Magdalen Hall *alumni* was the great puritan lawyer Mathew Hale (1609–1676).[40]

Hill graduated as a Bachelor of Arts in 1664. He was ordained deacon at Salisbury Cathedral by the bishop, John Earle. Stephen became rector of nearby Hemington in Somerset, six miles west of Beckington.

* * *

IT IS LIKELY Hill was a related to the famous late-Elizabethan theologian, Adam Hill, and vicar of Westbury from 1577, who was probably born there in the mid-sixteenth century, perhaps hailing, like so many Hills in the period, from Dilton.[41] He was also rector of Gussage St Michael on the south side of Cranborne Chase in Dorset at the same time and, in 1586, he was installed as prebendary and succentor of Salisbury Cathedral where, according to Foster's *Alumni Oxonienses*,[42] and, subsequently, the nineteenth- and twenty-first-century editions of the *Dictionary of National Biography*, he was buried in 1595. However, a search of the parish registers reveals that Adam Hill, 'Professor of Theology', was in fact laid to rest, on 19 January 1595, at Westbury.[43] Adam Hill was twice married; his first wife, Margaret, died in 1584 and was buried at Westbury on 20 May, just a couple of weeks after the burial of a daughter, Elizabeth. His second wife, Margery, died in 1596.[44] A graduate of Balliol College, Oxford (1568–73), with a reputation as a 'practical preacher',[45] his major work, 140 pages long, was *The Defence of the Article: Christ descended into Hell* (1592) – a response to the ardent Scottish Calvinist Alexander Hume (1560–1609), who had published a critique of one of Hill's published sermons. Hill railed against those who denied the reality of Christ's sojourn in Hell before his resurrection.[46] He was insistent upon the existence of both Hell and the Devil, vehemently rejecting the claim of those who argued 'Christ by his death destroyed the Devil, therefore his descending into Hell was needless'.[47] Instead, he insisted, '[the Devil] snares, binds and devours the wicked: he accuses, slanders and tempts the godly'.[48] Hell must be regarded, in Hill's opinion, as a very real place: 'For if Hell [...] should be taken metaphorically as some will have it, so may you allegorise the whole creed as do the heretics, and so overthrow the whole substance of our faith'.[49] In so doing, this cleric who lived on the edge of Selwood Forest, anticipated the arguments of later writers connected with the area who were concerned with the Devil, his acolytes and the reality of spirits: Bernard, Glanvill, Baxter and his supposed descendant, May Hill. Like these and others after him, he firmly believed that in casting a shadow of doubt over diabolical truths 'the atheist is hardened'.[50]

It might be no coincidence that Adam Hill had a contemporary with the same surname, William Hill, who was the rector of Mells, and who also had studied at Balliol and become a Doctor of Divinity. Mells is in Somerset, just a couple of miles west of Frome Selwood and a short distance from Adam Hill's Westbury living. He graduated at the start of 1581, shortly after Adam Hill, and received his MA in 1583, a year after Adam became vicar of Westbury. Having received his BD and licence to preach in 1591, he served as rector of Mells from the November of that year until his death in September 1619. Foster's *Alumni Oxonienses* records that he was 'perhaps prebendary of Bristol 1607–15' and his will reveals he had property in Bristol. Certainly he was a Wells Cathedral prebend between 1596 and 1606. This highly qualified and successful theologian may have been closely related to Adam Hill – a cousin perhaps, or a younger brother.

Like Adam, William Hill is recorded as having had two wives. The Mells parish register records the children he had with Sarah from the birth of her namesake in 1593. Baby Sarah did not survive infancy but at least four of her nine children, for whom the records survive (up to the birth of William in 1605), apparently did since they are named as beneficiaries in the will their father wrote on his deathbed in September 1619.[51] The will reveals that, after the death and burial of Sarah in 1613, William Hill married again, by which time he must have been in his early fifties.

William Hill of Mells almost certainly[52] was the same William Hill, 'Doctor of Divinity', who wrote a widely read pamphlet of around fifty pages entitled *The First Principles of a Christian: or Questions and Answers upon the Creed, the Ten Commandments, and the Lord's Prayer* (1605). It was already in its third edition by the time Hill had it reprinted in London in 1616, and it was still in print, and into its fourteenth edition, in 1636. He wrote it 'chiefly for the benefit of the people of his own charge', and it was aimed specifically at children. He was dismayed by the abundance of young men who 'to the disgrace of the Gospel, are riotous swaggerers, horrible blasphemers, filthy drunkards, and a great deal more'. In his preamble he warned 'all Christian children, especially to them of mine own charge' that Satan could 'seize upon your souls in childhood'. In answer to the question 'What mean you by the Devil?' he responded, 'I mean all those spirits of aposty, ever at hand to suggest evil motions into mine heart'.

* * *

MAY HILL was the curate to, and son-in-law and successor of, the illustrious Alexander Huish, recently reinstated as rector of Beckington. Glanvill had doubtless studied the writings of Adam Hill and he would have worked in close conjunction with his diocesan neighbour, Huish. The notion of Glanvill *not* having some kind of connection with May Hill or other members of his influential family at this time is difficult to countenance.

Although Hill had yet to graduate and would not take up his curacy at Beckington until 1665, it is possible that he knew Glanvill even before he took up the position: Hill was only about twenty years old at the time of the Tidworth trip, but Glanvill himself was only twenty-seven or so, and their homes were a mere three miles apart. These two young men, mounted on stout horses, could have made the journey together to Tidworth in a single day. At first sight, not least because of their shared interest in witchcraft cases and their mutual association with Richard Baxter, the famous author of *Certainty of the Worlds of Spirits* in which Hill's account of the Beckington case of 1689 would be published, it seems a plausible solution to the 'Mr Hill' riddle.[53] However, the Mr Hill who rode out with Glanvill had a wife[54] and May Hill would not marry for another ten years. The elusive Mr Hill could well have been May Hill's father, also called May.[55] May Hill senior's will, drawn up in 1694,[56] reveals him as a wealthy man with estates on the eastern side of Selwood Forest.[57] The son of Stephen Hill, he was baptised in Dilton with the name 'Mahew' on 12 May. When he married his second wife, Elizabeth Daniel, a widow of Upton Scudamore, in 1664, he was given the staus of 'yeoman'.

Glanvill heard Baxter preach several times and corresponded with him on a range of theological matters over the course of several years. Glanvill's visit to the haunted house in Tidworth in 1663 can be fairly precisely dated by the evidence of a letter Glanvill wrote to Baxter on 21 January: 'I came yesterday from Mr Mompesson's house at Tedworth'.[58] It is conceivable that Glanvill's travelling companion was another Magdalen College man, Thomas Hill, rector of Wylye from 1660 to 1664.[59] Even closer than Wylye to Glanvill's home in Frome, or for that matter, young May Hill's home near Chapmanslade, was the prebendary Thomas Hill held at Heytesbury from 1661 until his death in 1671. This was a mere six miles from Brookway Gate and it is possible Thomas and May were closely related.

An account of the haunting, thought to date from January 1663, survives among the State Papers. Of this Michael Hunter has written, 'This paper was evidently based on oral testimony rather than on the written accounts dealt with here, since events were presented in a

THE DEFENCE OF

the Article:

Chri∫t de∫cended into Hell.

With Arguments obiected again∫t
the truth of the ∫ame doctrine: of one
Alexander Humes,
All which reasons are confuted, and the same doctrine
cleerely defended.

By *Adam Hyll*, D. of Diuinity.

Magna e∫t veritas & praualet.

AT LONDON
Printed for *William Ponsonbie.* 1592.

Fig. 2-4 Adam Hill, *The Defence of the Article* (1592).

different order and certain of them were conflated together'. However, Hunter notes that this account 'also included details of a visit to Tedworth by the author of the piece, who had witnessed the poltergeist in the children's bed'. Although it has much in common with Mompesson's letters, 'The tone of the piece is rather different: it is written in an impressionistic, almost journalistic way, describing the events, though 'strange', as 'tricks', and giving an impression of a 'boisterous' yet intriguing atmosphere'. That it ended up in the State Papers, Hunter has concluded, 'implies that it was sent to court, perhaps with a view to arousing interest in the affair there'.[60] Hunter continues, 'Although the author of the paper is not identified, and although the extant copy is not in his handwriting, a strong candidate for its authorship is none other than Joseph Glanvill, since various aspects of the author's experiences in the children's bedroom as reported in this paper recur in almost identical autobiographical terms in Glanvill's published account of the case'. However, Glanvill was not alone when he visited the house in January 1663. An obvious explanation for why the summary of their shared experiences is not in Glanvill's hand is that his colleague, Mr Hill, wrote it on his behalf. The account in the State Papers is very similar to Glanvill's published version, as one would expect if indeed it was written by Mr Hill; this was a shared experience – '*we* went up into the chamber', 'it tore up the clothes and shook the room under *us*' – and yet it is different in the detail. The strange movement of the linen bag hanging from another bed in the room, as though an animal were inside it, is found only in Glanvill's later account of their visit.

That this Mr Hill took more than a passing interest in the case is evident in Glanvill's comments on his friend's further investigation into the matter: 'The gentleman, who was with me at the house, Mr Hill, being in company with one Compton of Somersetshire, who practiced physic, and pretends to strange matters, related to him this story of Mr Mompesson's disturbance'. This 'physician' and cunning man, Compton, is another of the fascinating characters in the story of witchcraft in and around Selwood Forest. He appears in Glanvill's account of the contemporary witchcraft case in Stoke Trister, the details of which Glanvill also received from the investigating JP, Robert Hunt. In this he is identified as coming from Ditcheat, a village three and a half miles west of Bruton, on the western edge of Selwood Forest. Compton told Mr Hill the house at Tidworth was nothing less than 'a rendezvous of witches, and that for a hundred pounds, he would undertake to rid the house of all disturbance'.⁶¹ Mr Hill, though at first sceptical, was then treated to another remarkable experience:

> In pursuit of this discourse he talked of many high things, and having drawn my friend into another room apart from the rest of the company, said he would make him sensible he could do something more than ordinary, and asked him who he desired to see. Mr Hill had no great confidence in his talk, but yet, earnestly pressed to name someone, he said he desired to see no one so much as his wife, who was then many miles distant from them at her home. Upon this Compton took up a looking glass that was in the room and, setting it down again, bid my friend look in it, which he did, and there, as he most solemnly and seriously professes, he saw the exact image of his wife in that habit which she then wore, and working at her needle in such a part of the room (there presented also) in which and about which time she really was, as he found upon enquiry when he came home. The gentleman himself averred this to me, and he is a very sober, intelligent, and credible person. Compton had no knowledge of him before, and was an utter stranger to the person of his wife.⁶²

According to Glanvill, Compton 'was by all accounted a very odd person' and regarded with suspicion by his neighbours and by others who came into contact with him. Barry has found several men by the name of Compton in the period – a Francis Compton, gentleman, of East Pennard, near Ditcheat, recorded in 1680, and Bernard Compton, Henry Compton and Joseph Compton, who all signed the Protestation Oath in 1641 at East Pennard. This was also signed by one Ferdinand Compton, who lived in nearby Pilton. Barry has concluded that 'he was probably from this family, who may have been related to various minor gentry families of Compton in Somerset at Sutton Bingham [south of Yeovil] or near South Petherton'.⁶³ Such a man, Barry suggests, could have made a significant contribution to the local witchcraft panic in the early 1660s by 'spreading news and fears about witchcraft' among other members of the local elite, not least Hunt, Glanvill and Hill. In turn, Barry concludes, clergymen like Glanvill and gentlemen like Hill further fanned the flames of witchcraft suspicion.

It is impossible to determine where Hill had his encounter with Compton but, given the fact that Hill 'related to him this story of Mr

Mompesson's disturbance' when they met, it does not appear to have been at the haunted house itself.[64] It is much more likely that they met in the vicinity of their homes in the Selwood area, perhaps at Hunt's manor house in Compton Pauncefoot. If so, and if Mr Hill was May Hill's father, his wife was indeed many miles away, at home on the other side of Frome, when he saw her in the looking glass. Certainly Compton was known by this time to the folk of nearby Stoke Trister – at some point not long after the Christmas of 1662, a local butcher, Richard Vining, consulted Compton who told him that his wife's disease had been provoked by a neighbouring witch, who proved to be Elizabeth Style. In the Style case ('Relation III') Glanvill was not entirely clear as to where Vining met Compton; he wrote: 'the Examinant [Vining] went to one Mr Compton, who lived in the parish of Ditcheat (the same person that showed my friend his wife in a glass, as I have related in the story of Mr Mompesson) for physic for his wife'. He did not say, categorically, that they met at Ditcheat, eleven miles away; Compton could well have been in the vicinity of Hunt's home at the time of Glanvill's and Mr Hill's return from Tidworth. Quite possibly Hunt had invited Compton, an acknowledged expert in such matters, to his home in January 1663 to receive his advice on both the Style case and the Tidworth affair. The small community of Ditcheat on the edge of Selwood Forest, as mentioned above, was home to the Alleine family and Richard Alleine senior was its rector until his death in around 1660. Compton, it is reasonable to suppose was well known to the family, Richard Alleine junior was Glanvill's neighbour in Frome who, in turn, was Hunt's friend. It is tempting to think Hunt could have employed Compton's services in his Stoke Trister investigations and that Alleine brought his attention to him in the first place.

Even if Beckington's future rector, May Hill, did not have a close connection with Glanvill, there can be no doubt that he would have been very much aware of the extraordinary events at Tidworth, the most celebrated supernatural narrative of the early Restoration era, and he would most probably have attended closely to the emerging tales of witchcraft even nearer his home on the edge of Selwood Forest. These too would be told by Glanvill, for whom proof of witchcraft amounted to proof for the existence of the soul. In his writings he invoked the contemporary language of his day in defining those that doubted the existence of spirits and the reality of the afterlife as 'sadducees' and 'atheists'.

Glanvill's position in relation to spirits, demons and witches was summarised in twelve points spread over sixty-five pages of the *Saducismus*. He opened with the assertion that the denial of the notion of spirits, and hence of witches, makes belief in God and humans' souls equally absurd. On the premise that the soul and body are separable he argued that extraordinary tales of witches flying on broomsticks and transforming themselves into cats were not necessarily fictions. He speculated upon the possibility that the power of witches was limited to frail and tender bodies, particularly those of children and weak-minded adults. The presence of pins found in the bodies of the bewitched in many cases was sufficient proof for Glanvill that supposed bewitchment could not be brushed aside as simply the consequence of melancholy and imagination. That some of those who claimed to be bewitched in past cases were exposed as cheats was not, in his opinion, sufficient reason to reject the truth of others. He explained his understanding of the term 'the Devil' as a 'body politic' – multiple demonic entities comprising the whole, 'aspects of the same malignant force', as Darren Oldridge has put it.[65] Most people, he maintained, are protected by good spirits, 'angels', hence the bad spirits, 'genii', are prevented from preying on humanity at large.

Glanvill's late nineteenth-century biographer, rather uncharitably in an otherwise balanced appreciation of Glanvill's output, observed, 'It is strange fortune of some men to be immortalised by their follies rather than by their virtues',[66] and Glanvill's 'follies' were his writings about witches – 'his ardent advocacy of a dying superstition'. When Ferris Greenslet wrote these words he also remarked on the revival of interest in, and admiration for, Glanvill in the wake of the new fad for psychical research, one that would inspire a number of fresh appraisals of the author.[67] In fact Glanvill was a most progressive thinker and, as a member of the Royal Society, one fully committed to the principle of knowledge by observation and experiment over dogma. For Glanvill, as historians recognised by the early twentieth century, his writing about witchcraft was no aberration – 'this work fitted in quite harmoniously with his others'.[68] While on the one hand Glanvill was keenly interested in the Royal Society's revelations of mechanical 'laws', his faith and conviction that some phenomena defied the mechanical explanation of atomic principles prompted his determination to find proof of immaterial forces in nature. As Moody E. Prior once pointed out, for Glanvill the suspension of disbelief when presented with evidence that defied simple explanation was 'a necessary part of the scientific attitude'. 'Hence', Prior continued, 'the paradox that Glanvill believed in witches because he was a skeptic'.[69]

In 1664, along with his Longleat patron's nephew and successor Thomas Thynne, who would become the first viscount of Weymouth, Glanvill joined the recently formed society and in the same year he began in earnest his study of poltergeists and witches. The Royal Society had its origins in the mid-1640s but became a formal, organised society in the early 1660s shortly before being incorporated by Royal Charter on 15 July 1662. Glanvill was elected a fellow of the society on 14 December 1664, and in 1670 he became secretary of its short-lived Somerset branch. It seems likely that a founding member, Robert Boyle (1627-91), author of *The Sceptical Chymist* (1661) and one of Glanvill's principal intellectual allies, had something to do with his nomination since his brother, Lord Broghill, earl of Orrery, owned Marston House, three miles to the south-west of Frome, a place Boyle is known to have visited.[70] Notable among Glanvill's early works was *Plus Ultra* (1668), celebrating the great scientific discoveries of the age and Boyle's personal contribution to these discoveries. Boyle encouraged him in his investigations of witchcraft and provided him with details of a French case – the account of the devil of Maçon – in order to convince sceptical readers. Elmer has further noted 'Robert Boyle and his brother the earl of Orrery were almost certainly responsible for securing the inclusion of those cases of Irish witchcraft and other preternatural occurrences that were published by Glanvill and More in 1681'.[71]

The reconciliation of his theological beliefs with a scientific outlook in relation to witchcraft was well summed up by Stanley Redgrove: 'It was because Glanvill was a whole-hearted believer in the new experimental philosophy, because he was so thoroughly imbued with the scientific spirit, that he saw that the question of witchcraft was one to be settled, not by argument, but by the evidence of fact'. Furthermore, 'a far more important question was involved: a demonstration of the reality of witchcraft meant a proof of the reality of spirit, and, hence, would provide weighty evidence in favour of the Christian doctrine of immortality'.[72]

In February 1665 Glanvill was far from Frome and attending a meeting held at Ragley Hall, the home of Lady Conway, close to the old Roman town of Alcester on the western edge of Warwickshire. Here he exchanged his thoughts with Conway's teacher and friend Dr Henry

Fig. 2-5 *Henry More, 1614-87, member of the Royal Society and editor of* Saducismus Triumphatus.

More, and other luminaries among the Cambridge Platonists, regarding supernatural phenomena. No doubt he brought to the table his own knowledge of the dramatic witchcraft episodes that were causing such consternation back in Selwood Forest. In return he collected other stories that would eventually join his own 'relations' in print. A year later he published his findings and theories on the matter for the

Fig. 2-6 *Robert Boyle, 1627-91, Glanvill's Royal Society ally in the search for scientific proof of God and the existence of spirits.*

first time in *Some Philosophical Considerations Touching Witches and Witchcraft*. The first run of copies was largely destroyed in the Fire of London; it was reprinted in two further editions in 1667 and in 1668.[73] One of the first to read it, Samuel Pepys, was unimpressed, commenting in his diary in November 1666 that he considered it 'well writ, in good style' but 'not very convincing'.[74] A 1668 edition, with the addition of the accounts of the ghostly Drummer of Tedworth and the witchcraft of Jane Brooks of Shepton Mallet, appeared as *A Blow at Modern Sadducism in some philosophical Considerations about Witchcraft*. The completed version, much augmented by Henry More, appeared for the first time in 1681 in the year after his death. Its full title is *Saducismus Triumphatus, or Full and Plain Evidence, concerning Witches and Apparitions, in two Parts, the First treating of their Possibility, and the Second of their real Existence*. The third and final edition of the *Saducismus* appeared with additional Glanvill texts in 1689, the year of the Beckington witchcraft case.[75]

An earlier version of the material that eventually evolved into the *Saducismus Triumphatus* was a philosophical debate without recourse to 'the evidence of the Divine Oracles' or 'Relations of Fact'. It took the form of a letter addressed to 'the much honoured Robert Hunt, Esq.' and was inspired by Hunt's 'ingenious industry for the detecting of those vile practicers'.[76] He wrote it as a contribution 'to the defence of the truth, and certainty of matters' which Hunt had determined 'by experiments that could not deceive'.[77] The accounts of Hunt's examinations he withheld until the extended second edition of his essay.

A Blow at Modern Sadducism[78] (1668) was accredited on its frontispiece, not to Joseph Glanvill, but 'a Member of the Royal Society'. Throughout Glanvill adopted a modern 'scientific' approach in advancing empirical evidence and historical precedent as proof for the existence of spirits and witchcraft rather than relying exclusively on theology and biblical texts. 'All histories', he declared, 'are full of the exploits of those instruments of darkness, and the testimony of all ages, not only of the rude and barbarous, but of the most civilised and polished world, brings tidings of their strange performances'.[79] These provided 'thousands of eye and ear-witnesses' drawn from all social groups including many 'wise and grave discerners'. To deny them amounted to the absurd possibility that they were all engaged, and continued to be so, in a monstrous lie. Indeed, to reject this mountain of evidence required, in Glanvill's opinion, a vastly bigger leap of faith than to accept it as fact. If such phenomena were mere 'fancies', he declared, 'tis somewhat strange that imagination which is the most various thing in the world, should infinitely repeat the same conceit in all times and places'.[80] After all, some things, he wrote, 'we cannot conceive how they can be performed', such as how the foetus is formed in the womb and how a plant springs from the earth.[81] For the same reason the mysterious appearance of pins and nails under the skin of the supposedly bewitched cannot be satisfactorily explained 'by the power of imagination'.[82]

Science, Glanvill maintained, was not the enemy of religion but the antidote to atheism. Science might yet prove certain key religious doctrines, notably that of belief in the supernatural. His was, as Stuart Clark has put it, a scientific demonology that was absolutely relevant in Restoration science[83] – he was concerned with witchcraft because of, not in spite of, the 'mechanical philosophy' of the era. Clark has concluded that 'At one level, [Glanvill and his allies] were simply compiling a natural history of the demonic'[84] – just one among the several natural histories members of the Royal Society were busy describing. He toyed with various possibilities concerning the identity of witches' familiars. They might, he supposed, be the spirits of 'sorcerers and witches in this life',[85] those 'forsaken of God and goodness'.[86] Alternatively they might be 'devils' quite separate from the humanity with which they consort. He considered it likely 'there may be as great a variety of intellectual creatures in the invisible world as there is of animals in the visible'.[87] The term 'Devil', Glanvill proposed, should be interpreted as a collective noun – 'a name for a body politic in which there are very different orders and degrees of spirits'. This 'body politic' he further defined as 'the Kingdom of Darkness'.[88] The wicked spirit, like his counterpart in human society, 'desires vassals to pay him homage, and to be employed like slaves in the services of his lusts and appetites';[89] the soul he seizes in making his pact with a witch becomes his property – his own 'instrument of darkness'. The witch herself falls prey to the wicked spirit because of her own 'vile disposition', her 'malice, envy, and desire of revenge', qualities contrary to life and nature.[90]

That children and 'timorous persons' were most often identified as the victims of maleficent witchcraft must be, Glanvill concluded, 'because their spirits and imaginations being weak and passive, are not able to resist the fatal invasion; whereas men of bold minds [...] are secure from the contagion, as in pestilential airs clean bodies are not so liable to infection as are other tempers'.[91] However, he warned, 'tis very likely that many of the strange accidents that befall us may be the infliction of evil spirits, prompted to hurt us by the delight they take in their mischief'. It is possible, he thought, that we might feel the 'effects of their malice [...] in more instances than we are aware of'.[92]

Clark has argued that this seemingly contradictory defence of witchcraft belief among the advocates of the new science of 'mechanical philosophy' was in fact quite compatible with contemporary scientific as well as religious beliefs: 'This situation continued as long as natural philosophy was tied [...] to a theology of nominalism and voluntarism that while it justified the law-like regularity of natural occurrences, also required the energy of providentially inspired activity in the natural world'.[93] As deism replaced theism and rational philosophy replaced natural theology 'it became unnecessary to impose causal activity on passive matter or find spirit testimony to illustrate this'.[94] Clark, in the opinion of other experts in the field,[95] revealed the great seventeenth-century demonologists as cutting-edge philosophers of their day, engaged in 'an inquisitive and empirical discourse that would talk itself out of existence precisely because of its appetite for truth and proof'.[96]

For the time being, and until well into the next century, the search for 'spirit testimony' was a valid scientific endeavour. Why this mattered so much was plain: although those who denied the existence of spirits were not necessarily atheists, they were 'anti-scripturists' in the sense that they so plainly attested the contrary. Although opinions were forming in educated circles that posed a serious challenge to belief in witchcraft, Glanvill was not a lone voice in his insistence on its reality, and he was not defending it from an antiquated philosophical position. Henry More had written *An Antidote to Atheism* (1653), which had been conceived along similar lines to Glanvill's *Saducismus*:

> It is not to be imputed to any vain credulity of mine, or that I take a pleasure in telling strange stories, but that I thought fit to fortify and strengthen the faith of others as much as I could; being well assured that a contemptuous misbelief of such like narrations concerning spirits, and an endeavour of making them all ridiculous and incredible, is a dangerous prelude to atheism itself, or else a more close and crafty profession or insinuation of it. For assuredly that saying was nothing so true in politics, *no bishop, no king*; as this is in metaphysics, *no spirit, no God*.[97]

Glanvill's search for proof took him beyond the scriptures to some remarkable cases, some already well known, and others that were not – a spate of recent witchcraft episodes that he knew plenty about from his study of Robert Hunt's records of recent cases in east Somerset. Hunt, Glanvill stated, 'was pleased to send me his book of examinations of witches', which, he continued, 'contains the discovery of such an hellish knot of them, and that discovery so clear and plain, that perhaps there is nothing I have seen with stronger evidence to confirm the belief in witches'. Of these accounts, in his preface to *A Blow against Modern Sadducism* (1668), Glanvill had declared:

> I have no humour nor delight in telling stories, and do not publish these for the gratification of those that have; but I record them as arguments for the confirmation of a truth which hath indeed been attested by multitudes of the like evidences in all places and times. But things remote, or long past, are either not believed or forgotten: whereas these being fresh and near, and attended with all the circumstances of credibility, it may be expected they should have the more success upon the obstinacy of unbelievers.[98]

Originally a Dorset man, born in 1609, Hunt trained as a lawyer and relocated to Somerset in 1618 when he purchased the estate of Speckington, near Ilchester. It was probably during the Civil War that he acquired the manor of Compton Pauncefoot, a village close to the Wincanton and Bruton locations of the witchcraft cases he heard at the Quarter Sessions. The area of his jurisdiction included a substantial part of Selwood Forest. A committed Parliamentarian, he sat in the Long Parliament, representing Ilchester, which, in 1640, opened proceedings against Alexander Huish, rector of Beckington. Having performed his duties well in trying Royalists after Penruddock's Rising and supervising elections to the second Protectorate Parliament, he was called to represent the county in Richard Cromwell's Parliament. In the general election of 1660 he was returned as the Member for Ilchester, subsequently losing his seat to Edward Phileps. By the time of his death, aged seventy, in 1680, the same year in which Joseph Glanvill died, he had become the 'most reputed justice in Somerset'.[99] His interest in the Selwood Forest witchcraft cases has, however, blackened his reputation. In his *Letters on Demonology and Witchcraft* in 1885, Walter Scott portrayed Hunt as a man with the potential to become a Somerset version of Matthew Hopkins, the notorious 'Witchfinder General' active in Essex and East Anglia in 1645.[100] In his own lifetime however, Hunt – JP, MP and, in the mid-1650s, Sheriff of Somerset – was a vastly more reputable figure than the young unestablished upstart of Manningtree, Essex, who indulged in his short-lived and quasi-legal witch-hunting activities in the chaos of the English Civil War. In Barry's reckoning 'Hunt may well be regarded

[…] as a perplexed man trying to make sense of strange events, rather than as a zealot imposing his own vision'[101] but certainly not a fanatic like Hopkins.[102] His rigorous investigation of witchcraft accusations at the time of the Restoration chimes with Elmer's conviction that 'godly magistrates were far more likely to invoke the threat of witchcraft at moments of acute political crisis such as regime change'.[103]

In 1666, when he first published on the subject of witchcraft, Glanvill had discussed with Hunt 'the late and frequent dealings you have had in the examination of witches' and presented his book to Hunt as 'a way of accounting for some of those strange things you have been a witness of' and as a contribution 'to the defence of the truth of matters which you know by experiments that could not deceive against the little exceptions of those that are resolved to believe nothing in affairs of this nature'.[104] Although the cases Hunt had been involved in are not found in *Some Philosophical Considerations*, Barry has made a case for the likelihood of Glanvill's familiarity with these, arguing that in Glanvill's general discussion 'one can relate some of his assumptions about the nature of witchcraft cases to the details of the cases as published later'.[105] If Hunt, as Barry has suggested was acquainted with Richard Bernard before the latter's death in 1642,[106] Glanvill's friendship with Hunt also connected him with the long-deceased demonologist. It is inconceivable that he did not become closely acquainted with Bernard's curate and successor, Richard Alleine, who lived in Frome for most of the time Glanvill was vicar there.[107]

Hunt's 'book of examinations' has not survived although a copy of a manuscript derived from it is held in the Somerset Record Office (SRO).[108] Glanvill suggested in his preface to the *Saducismus* that it contained details of more, now unknown, local cases, writing, 'Out of that book I have collected some of the major cases, the clarity of which I think will be enough to overcome and silence any indifferent prejudice'. The SRO manuscript contains some information concerning the Selwood cases that does not appear in any of the Glanvill texts, but no additional cases.[109]

Glanvill deeply regretted the suppressing of Robert Hunt's pursuit of witches in Selwood Forest. For, 'had not his discoveries and endeavours met with great opposition and discouragement from some then in authority', he wrote, 'the whole clan of those hellish confederates in these parts might have been justly exposed and punished'. In Glanvill's opinion the evidence was overwhelming and 'Matters of fact well proved ought not to be denied because we cannot conceive how they can be performed'. 'On the contrary', he argued empirically, 'we should judge the action by the evidence, and not by the measures of our fancies about the action'.[110] The same logic underpins all scientific endeavours in the modern world.

In 1669 John Wagstaffe published *The Question of Witchcraft debated, Or a Discourse against their opinion that affirm Witches*, the first critique of Glanvill's arguments. This was to little effect beyond prompting Meric Casaubon to write a much weightier riposte, this time in defence of Glanvill, entitled *Of Credulity and Incredulity*, published in 1670. Glanvill acknowledged the doubts some had regarding his claims in later editions of his witchcraft text. This, in turn, helped provoke a physician, John Webster, into mounting a much more effective assault in *Displaying of Supposed Witchcraft* (1676), albeit one in which the author did not question the reality of fairies. Glanvill and More rallied their defence with the developed work that would be published as *Saducismus Triumphatus* in 1681.

Glanvill did not live to see the *Saducismus* printed, dying on 4 November 1680 at the age of forty-five. He was buried in Bath Abbey where his commemorative stone in the floor, partly obscured by pews, can still be seen.

The story of the Drummer of Tedworth remained a keystone upon which further arguments for belief in the reality of spirits would be based. The *Saducismus* provided a model for John Beaumont's *An Historical Physiological and Theological Treatise of Spirits, Apparitions, Witchcrafts, and Other Magical Practises* (1705), a 400-page exploration of the principle that a mostly invisible 'spirit' world coexists with the visible 'natural' world, written 'to caution men not to be over hasty in rejecting things that may seem strange, and do not presently fall within their comprehension'.[111] Among many other relations, the book included a telling of the drummer's tale.

Beaumont (c.1640–1731) was a Somerset man from a Roman Catholic family based in Ston Easton, a few miles north-east of Wells and just a dozen or so miles away from the Forest of Selwood. His growing reputation, founded on his work in natural philosophy and geology, led to his election to the Royal Society in 1685 where he would count among his colleagues such eminent individuals as Sir Hans Sloane, Robert Hooke and John Aubrey. His 1705 treatise contains a few other cases of supernatural phenomena, the records of Matthew Hopkins's and

John Stearne's witch-finding activities in 1645, Cotton Mather's studies in New England, and the remarkable episodes of witchcraft at Salem in 1691. He also recounted his own disturbing experience of encounters with spirits, which we can presume he probably had at his Ston Easton home, and a couple of local episodes he knew of, one at Bristol, the other in the village of Butleigh near Glastonbury. In 1705 Beaumont echoed Glanvill's by now unfashionable argument that the reality of witches and demons proved the presence of God as the ultimate authority above all things:

> Now, if there are any witches, enchanters, etc., it necessarily follows that there are demons, by whose help and power, they cause these prodigious effects to come to pass, which men wonder at, and look upon with horror and amazement, it being impossible that those things should be done by any human power. The histories therefore and writings of all nations, and even of the heathens themselves, are full of examples of the Devil's apparitions and of their strange effects. Now, […] if there were any demons (as it cannot be denied) it follows that there is a deity above them, which so restrains them, that they shall not overthrow all things by their might, for they have strength and malice enough to do it.[112]

Beaumont's was just one of at least thirteen books on the subject of witchcraft published between 1680 and 1718. Glanvill was widely regarded by their authors as the great authority on the subject. The coincidence of Glanvill being appointed to a living in Frome in the early 1660s must surely explain why he wrote so extensively on the subject. Without his immediate contact with the Selwood Forest cases it seems unlikely that he would have engaged so fully in this debate and thus, without the Selwood witches, the history of the decline of learned witchcraft belief might well have been very different.

The early eighteenth-century historian of witchcraft, the Anglican bishop Francis Hutchinson, helped establish the simple myth that the emergence of the Royal Society was the decisive factor in determining the decline of belief in witchcraft among the elite.[113] In fact, through the advocacy of More, Glanvill and Beaumont, it played a vital role in maintaining, possibly even reviving, belief in England and America in the closing decades of the seventeenth century. A recent historian of the Salem witch trials has observed that, together with the writings of William Perkins, 'These [witchcraft] ideas the New England settlers imported wholesale, derived primarily from the work of Glanvill'.[114] In Wallace Notestein's opinion it was Hutchinson himself who levelled the 'final deadly blow at the dying superstition'.[115] Notestein's own pioneering narrative of the history of witchcraft in England, for this reason, culminated in the year Hutchinson published.

1. Joseph Glanvill, *A Blow at Modern Sadducism* (1668), 8.
2. 'Humfrey' was the more common spelling of his surname in his lifetime, although the name appears in a range of forms in different documents – Baxter spelled it 'Humphreys'; 'Humphry' and 'Humfrye' were the names recorded in the register at the time of the baptism of two of his and his wife Hannah's children, Hannah (St John's, Frome, 02/01/1657/8), William (St John's, Frome, 08/01/1658/9); in Edmund Calamy, *The Nonconformists' Memorial*, ed. Samuel Palmer (London: 1725), his name is 'Humphrey' in the index and 'Humfrey' in the main text; the parish register for St John's for 29 May 1657 identifies 'John Humfris', 'Minister of Froome', as a witness to the marriage of Joan Avery and Thomas Napper.
3. Calamy, *Memorial*, 362.
4. Humfrey wrote to Richard Baxter on this matter in May 1662.
5. Calamy, *Memorial*, 362.
6. Richard Alleine, *Cheirothesia tou presbyteriou, or, A Letter to a friend* (1661), 64.
7. In 1684, for example, Humfrey sent Baxter a presentation copy of his latest work, 'The Axe Laid at the Root of Separation'; Geoffrey K. Nuttall, and N. H. Keeble (eds), *Calendar of Correspondence of Richard Baxter*, Vol. 2, (Oxford: Clarendon Press, 1991), letter 1147.
8. Elmer notes, 'Glanvill admired Baxter's commitment to the rational investigation of providences, which mirrored his own', Elmer, *Witchcraft*, 216.
9. Michael Hunter, 'The Decline of Magic: Challenge and Response in early Enlightenment England', *The Historical Journal*, 55:2 (2012), 408.
10. Elmer, *Witchcraft*, 11.
11. Defined by Elmer as 'a small but influential group within the re-established church, labelled by their opponents as latitudinarians, who sought to construct a more inclusive religious settlement built upon consensus and dialogue', Elmer, *Witchcraft*, 177; he notes it is a 'slippery term, its origins complex and with no fixed 'membership' or set of beliefs'; Elmer, *Witchcraft*, 212.
12. 'The years after 1660 also witnessed a revival of interest in witchcraft and related phenomena, much of which [...] was related to the religious and political turmoil and uncertainty of that period.' Elmer, *Witchcraft*, 11.

13 A term coined in the nineteenth century to define a group of theologians and philosophers associated with Henry More. While advocating reason and rationalism as the way towards resolving contemporary religious disputes, and having a keen interest in the new 'mechanical philosophy', they were convinced by the reality of immaterial substance including the soul and spirits.
14 Thomas Harmon Jobe, 'The Devil in Restoration Science: Glanville-Webster Witchcraft Debate', *Isis*, 72: 3 (1981), 347.
15 Glanvill, *Blow*, 72.
16 Montague Summers (ed.), *Pandaemonium by Richard Bovet, 1684* (Aldington: Hand and Flower Press, 1951), xi.
17 Harry Price, *Poltergeist Over England: Three Centuries of Mischievous Ghosts*, (London: Country Life Ltd., 1945), Chapters 6 and 7.
18 Ryan J. Stark, *Rhetoric, Science, and Magic in Seventeenth Century England* (Washington DC: The Catholic University of America Press, 2009), 115.
19 This summary of the case of the 'Drummer of Tedworth' is derived from my brother's entry in David Pickering, *Dictionary of Witchcraft* (London: Cassell, 1997), 77.
20 Ticking: fabric covering a pillow/bolster.
21 Joseph Glanvill, *Saducismus Triumphatus: or full and plain Evidence concerning Witches and Apparitions* (1681), 328–29.
22 Guy Playfair, *This House is Haunted* (Guildford: White Crow Books, 2011), 274.
23 Author of *The Smoke of the Soul: Medicine, Physiology and Religion in Early Modern England* (Basingstoke: Palgrave Macmillan, 2013) and *Mummies, Cannibals and Vampires: The History of Corpse Medicine from the Renaissance to the Victorians* (London: Routledge, 2011).
24 Richard Sugg, 'Ghosts and poltergeists: more common than you think?', article posted on the *History Today* website, 29/10/2015, http://www.historytoday.com/richard-sugg/ghosts-and-poltergeists-more-common-than-you-think.
25 Richard Sugg, *A Century of Supernatural Stories* (Createspace, 2015).
26 John Beloff, 'Foreword' in Houran and Lange, *Hauntings and Poltergeists: Multidisciplinary Perspectives* (Jefferson: McFarland, 2001), 2.
27 The opening chapter of the book for which Beloff wrote this foreword began with a discussion of Glanvill and the Tidworth case.
28 Glanvill, *Saducismus*, 330.
29 Darren Oldridge, *The Devil in Tudor and Stuart England* (Stroud: The History Press, 2010), 62.
30 Glanvill, *Saducismus*, 3.
31 In Elmer's opinion 'he fits the profile of the latitudinarian demonologist'; Elmer, *Witchcraft*, 151.
32 Jo Bath and John Newton, 'Sensible Proof of Spirits: Ghost Belief during

33 John Aubrey, *The Natural History of Wiltshire* (1691), Part II, Chapter 18.
34 Glanvill, *Saducismus*, 333.
35 *Ibid.*, 334.
36 *Ibid.*, 330, 334.
37 Later renamed Hertford College.
38 Between Chapmanslade and Old Dilton. Andrew's and Dury's *Map of Wiltshire* (1773), inditifies 'Brokeway Gate' as a small cluster of buildings on the southern edge of Gibbet ('Gibbitt') Wood, halfway along the road between Beckington and Warminster.
39 William Seaman (1603-1680), rector 1628-1680. In May Hill junior's will an aunt is mentioned as a beneficiary – Sarah Whittaker. He left her an annuity of £30 for the remainder of her life. In 1634 Sarah, the sister of William Seaman, rector of Upton Scudamore, had married William Whittaker at Upton Scudamore. PROB 11/459/353 May Hill.
40 Hale was the presiding judge in the 1662 witchcraft case heard at Bury St Edmunds. The death sentence he imposed on two elderly women, Amy Denny and Rose Cullender, became an important post-Restoration precedent for the continuation of witchcraft trials in the decades that followed, including those at Salem, Massachusetts (1692–1693).
41 According to his entry in the original *Dictionary of National Biography*; however, Henry Summerson in the more recent ODNB (2004) has him as a 'native of Salisbury' where he certainly spent part of his life.
42 Foster, *Alumni Oxonienses*, 623.
43 Furthermore, I found no record of him at Salisbury Cathedral in the ledger for burials available for consultation in the nave (seen in October 2015).
44 On 15 October 1584 Adam Hill married Margery Greenhill in the church at Westbury. The Hills baptised at least five children there: Katherine (1587), John (1588), Edward (1589), Mary (1592) and Alice (1594). The register for the last two of these records the name of the father as Doctor Hill. That this Adam Hill was indeed the highly learned vicar is further confirmed by the will of another Margery Greenhill of Westbury, who remembered the four children of 'Doctor Adam Hill' in her will dated 9 October 1613, in which she bequeathed to them items of furniture, bedding (bolsters and coverlets), and two brass pots and gowns that had belonged to their mother. She named them as Edward, Katherine, Mary and Alice. John Hill is not mentioned and, although I have not traced a burial record for him, it seems likely that he had already died, perhaps in infancy. Incidentally, a Margery Greenhill in the parish was married to one Robert Hill in 1599. The Margery Greenhill who wrote the will had a sister (or sister-in-law) named Elizabeth Marchant – almost certainly she was married into the same local family as Sarah Marchant (several decades later), daughter of May Hill senior and sister of May Hill junior. Adam's descendants have

not been clearly identified. His son Edward, might well have spent his life in the vicinity of Frome – an Edward Hill witnessed the will of Thomas Smith, a fuller of Frome, in 1657, and Thomas Hill, the son of Edward Hill, 'gentleman' of Frome, matriculated at Lincoln College, Oxford, in 1671 at the age of sixteen. This Edward was too young to be Adam Hill's son, of course, but he could well have been a great-grandson bearing a family name. Although the surviving records do not prove the matter, there is a good chance that the clerical Hill brothers, students at Magdalen Hall half a century after Adam Hill's death, were his close relations.

45 'a most noted and eloquent preacher of his time [...] had he not been untimely snatched away by death, he would have been advanced to an high degree in the Church'; Foster, *Alumni Oxonienses*, 238.

46 'a war of sermons and books on the subject between Alexander Hume and Adam Hill in 1589–94'; . Beatrice Groves, 'Hal as Self-styled Redeemer: the harrowing of hell and *Henry IV Part I*' in Peter Holland (ed.), *Shakespeare Survey*, 57 (2004), 236–48 (237–8).

47 Adam Hill, *The Defence of the Article: Christ descended into Hell* (London: 1592), 18.

48 *Ibid.*, 19.

49 *Ibid.*, 25.

50 *Ibid.*, dedication to John, Archbishop of Canterbury.

51 PROB 11/135/286 William Hill. Doctor Hill was buried on 15 September 1619.

52 He is the only William Hill in the *Alumni Oxonienses* who fits the bill.

53 A further candidate is one Edward Hill, a gentleman of Frome, whose son, Thomas, matriculated at Lincoln College, Oxford, in 1671.

54 Glanvill, *Saducismus*, 334.

55 The editor of the *Alumni Oxonienses 1500–1714* (1891), John Foster, or whoever it was who first transcribed the original hand-written ledger, with some uncertainty, recorded the name of Stephen Hill's father, in parentheses, as *Mau*. The equivalent note for his brother, May, identifies the father with the curious name simply as *M*. These can be read as abbreviations for May or, in its Latinised form, *Maius*. Foster, *Alumni Oxonienses*, 711.

56 PROB 11/501/2 May Hill. The will of May and Stephen Hill's father, also called May, is dated 10 January 1693 (i.e. 1694). His home is identified as Short Street – the settlement half a mile to the east of Brookway Gate. Clearly May Hill was a wealthy man – he left his Short Street 'living' to his son Francis, £400 to his daughter Elizabeth Hill, £200 to his son Stephen, £50 to his married daughter Sarah Marchant, and everything else (not stipulated) to his eldest son and executor, May. To his three servants he bequeathed 5 shillings each and he pledged £5 in bread to the poor of Dilton.

57 In 1664 he married again, this time to Elizabeth Daniell of the neighbouring

parish of Upton Scudamore. They were married at the church of St Mary's in the hamlet of Dilton, a mile from Hill's Short Street home. In its register May Hill is identified as 'Mr' – a title usually reserved for gentlemen and clerics. When Elizabeth died in 1685, and he died in 1694, the Upton Scudamore register for each of them identifies their Short Street residence.

58 Michael Hunter has noted: 'Although it lacks a year, the letter is addressed to a house where Baxter resided only in January 1663', Michael Hunter, 'New light on the 'Drummer of Tedworth': conflicting narratives of witchcraft in Restoration England', *Historical Research* 78: 201 (2005), 311–53; Geoffrey K. Nuttall and N.H. Keeble (eds), *Calendar of Correspondence of Richard Baxter, Vol 2: 1660–1696* (Oxford: Clarendon Press, 1991), letter 710, 'From Joseph Glanvill 21 January 1662/3'.

59 Thomas Hill (c.1612-1671), another graduate of Magdalen Hall, recorded as coming from Salisbury, was rector of Writhlington, a couple of miles north of Hemington, between 1639 and 1641. He matriculated at the age of seventeen in 1629. Two Thomas Hills, sons of Thomas Hill, born about seventeen years earlier, appear in the baptismal records of the church of St Thomas, Salisbury – one dated 22 January 1612/3, the other 7 May 1611. Having gained BA (1632) and MA (1635) qualifications at Magdalen Hall, he held the Writhlington living before returning to Oxford for, seemingly, an academic career, becoming, in 1642, a Bachelor of Divinity. However, according to the university's records, in 1648 he was expelled 'by parliamentary visitors.' With the Restoration in 1660, Thomas Hill secured the position as rector at Wylye, about ten miles away from Brookway Gate. In 1664 he exchanged this for the living of Bishopstone just outside his home town of Salisbury. Here he remained until his death in 1671. The religious controversialist and author Samuel Hill ministered to the congregations of Kilmington in 1687 and Buckland Dinham from 1688 and became master of Bruton Free School in 1700, but he is known to have been born in South Petherton in 1648. Foster, *Alumni Oxonienses*, 713; Frederic William Weaver, *Somerset Incumbents* (Bristol: C.T. Jefferies and Sons, 1889), 117; ODNB, 'Hill, Samuel'.

60 Hunter, *Historical Research* 78: 201 (2005), 311–53.
61 Glanvill, *Saducismus*, 333.
62 *Ibid.*, 333–34.
63 Barry, *Witchcraft and Demonology*, 55.
64 On this point I disagree with Owen Davies, who concluded, 'They met at the house in which the supernatural activity was centred'. Davies, *Popular Magic*, 80.
65 Darren Oldridge, 'Light from Darkness: The Problem of Evil in Early Modern England', *The Seventeenth Century*, 27:4 (2012), 396.
66 Ferris Greenslet, *Joseph Glanvill: A study in English thought and letters of the Seventeenth Century* (Columbia: Macmillan, 1900), 144.

67 Notably Stanley Redgrove and I.M.L. Redgrove, *Joseph Glanvill and Psychical Research in the Seventeenth Century* (London: William Rider & Son, 1921).
68 Moody E. Prior, 'Joseph Glanvill, Witchcraft, and Seventeenth-Century Science', *Modern Philology*, 30:2 (1932), 168.
69 Prior, 'Joseph Glanvill', 192.
70 Michael McGarvie, *Marston House* (Frome: Foster Yeoman Ltd., 1985), 13.
71 Elmer, *Witchcraft*, 219.
72 Redgrove, *Glanvill*, 64.
73 Greenslet, *Glanvill*, 223.
74 Roger Latham and William Matthews, *The Diary of Samuel Pepys* Vol. VII (London: G. Bell, 1970), 382.
75 DNB, 'Glanvill, Joseph'.
76 Joseph Glanvill, *A Blow at Modern Sadducism in some Philosophical Considerations about Witchcraft* (1668), 90.
77 *Ibid.*, 2.
78 Sadducism: the rejection of belief in spirits and thus, by implication the soul's immortality.
79 *Ibid.*, 5.
80 *Ibid.*, 13.
81 *Ibid.*, 14–15.
82 *Ibid.*, 33–34.
83 Clark, *Thinking with Demons*, 299.
84 *Ibid.*, 306.
85 Glanvill, *Modern Sadducism*, 25.
86 Glanvill, *Saducismus*, 11.
87 Glanvill, *Modern Sadducism*, 25.
88 *Ibid.*, 43.
89 *Ibid.*, 44.
90 *Ibid.*, 46.
91 *Ibid.*, 29.
92 *Ibid.*, 32–33.
93 'Generation, Corruption, Alteration, and all the Vicissitudes of Corporeal Nature are nothing else but Unions and Dissolutions [...] of little Bodies or Particles of differing Figments, Magnitudes, and Velocities'. Henry More cited in Michael Hunter and Simon Schaffer (eds), *Robert Hooke: New Studies* (Woodbridge: Boydell Press, 1989), 18.
94 Clark, *Thinking with Demons*, 299.
95 Notably Peter Elmer and Malcolm Gaskill.
96 Gaskill, 'The Pursuit of Reality', 1072.
97 Henry More, *An Antidote to Atheism* (1653), 164.
98 Glanvill, *Modern Sadducism*, 'Preface'.
99 B. D. Bennington (ed.), *The History of Parliament: the House of Commons*

1660–1690 (Suffolk: Boydell and Brewer, 1983).
100 Walter Scott, *Letters on Demonology and Witchcraft* (London: Routledge, 1884), 215.
101 Barry, *Witchcraft and Demonology*, 17.
102 An argument reiterated by Elmer, *Witchcraft*, 218.
103 Elmer, *Witchcraft*, 8.
104 Joseph Glanvill, *Some Philosophical Considerations Touching Witches and Witchcraft* (1666).
105 Barry, *Witchcraft and Demonology*, 19.
106 *Ibid.*, 47.
107 *Ibid.*, 48; see also Julie Davies *Science in an Enchanted World: Philosophy and Witchcraft in the Work of Joseph Glanvill* (Routledge, 2018), Chapter 2.
108 Now a part of the Somerset Heritage Centre in Taunton.
109 Barry, *Witchcraft and Demonology*, 22.
110 Glanvill, *Saducismus*, 7–8.
111 John Beaumont, *An Historical Physiological and Theological Treatise of Spirits, Apparitions, Witchcrafts, and Other Magical Practises* (London: 1705), 39.
112 *Ibid.*, 264.
113 Michael Hunter, 'The Royal Society and the Decline of Magic', *Notes and Records of the Royal Society of London*, 65:2 (2011), 112.
114 Schiff, *The Witches*, 66.
115 Wallace Notestein, *A History of Witchcraft in England from 1558 to 1718* (Washington DC: American Historical Association, 1911), 1.

3
A BOOK OF EXAMINATIONS

Fig. 3-1 *Detail from the frontispiece of* Saducismus Triumphatus *(1681) depicting the levitation of Richard Jones.*

[Assuredly] was nothing so true in politics, *no bishop, no king*, as this is in metaphysics, *no spirit, no God.*
– Henry More, 1653.¹

THE FIRST LOCAL witchcraft case Joseph Glanvill related concerned the trial of Jane Brooks of Shepton Mallet in 1658.² It conforms to several witchcraft stereotypes but also contains a few surprises. The victim of her *maleficium* suffers from fits, which might indicate some form of epilepsy. The familiar details of bewitching the victim by touch and the gift of an enchanted apple are both there, conforming to the tradition that was certainly in place when Bernard wrote his *Guide* thirty years before in nearby Batcombe. So too is the popular belief that the witch's spell can be lifted by drawing her blood ('scratching the witch'). Implicit in the story is the tension between youth and age, and an inversion of the woman's role as the mother who nurtures the child. This is central to the early modern witchcraft paradigm for, as Ryan Stark has put it, 'In its most basic manifestation, witchcraft functions upon the principle of inversion'.[3] Richard Bernard had warned would-be witch-hunters against counterfeit, and the modern reader, seeking a 'rational' explanation, is bound to consider the possibility here that the boy's behaviour might have been, in part, a pretence. It is listed as 'Relation II' in the *Saducismus* following on from Glanvill's account of the Tidworth poltergeist.

Richard Jones first met Jane Brooks one Sunday afternoon in November 1657. Richard, 'a sprightly youth about twelve years old', saw her peering in through the windows of the Jones family home. He opened the door to her and, in return for a piece of bread, she gave him an apple and then, ominously, 'stroked him down on the right side, shook him by the hand, and bade him good night'. As Chadwick Hansen did with the Salem cases in *Witchcraft at Salem* (New York, 1969), it is tempting to find a psychosomatic explanation for the boy's subsequent ailments – psychological processes impacting upon his physical health and the malfunction of his motor systems.[4] Francis Hutchinson in 1718 concluded 'that filling people's heads with stories of devils, and spirits, and witches, corrupts the mind, and brings them under those frights and afflictions that are usually thought, and may, for ought I know, sometimes be diabolical'.[5] The accusation, prosecution and execution of supposed witches, he insisted, increased the evil. The stories might be a fiction, but the harm they could cause was real enough. Edward Bever has noted that even without a belief in witchcraft 'any strong negative emotion caused by another person's attitude or actions can cause, or contribute to, physical disorder';[6] indeed, this scientific fact could be an important reason *for* belief in magic as much as it might be a consequence of it. Furthermore, Bever has cited a German case from the duchy of Württemberg in which a woman admitted she had rubbed on to her victim a prepared substance in order to cause the person harm.

'Ingredients in the hallucinogenic ointments that people in the region are known to have used', Bever writes, 'are known to have contained alkaloids that interfere with neurotransmitters in both the central and peripheral nervous systems; small doses applied locally could have caused a loss of sensation and possibly control of a limb'.[7]

Apart from a slight baptismal record throughout the 1650s the parish register record for Shepton Mallet is fairly complete for the seventeenth century after 1609 and it substantiates some of the trial evidence. Richard Jones ('Joans'), the son of Henry, was baptized in Shepton Mallet on 24 April 1647. It is most likely that he is the Richard Jones ('Joans') who died in the parish on 4 February 1658/9. Just one other record for a person of the same name appears in the register for the whole of the second half of the seventeenth century – a burial at St Peter and St Paul's in Shepton Mallet on 8 October 1696, the year in which our Richard Jones would have just turned fifty had he survived.

A Henry Jones, probably the boy's father, had married Alice Plush at St Peter and St Paul's, the same church in which Richard was baptised, in 1636. At first sight the account implies that the Jones family was a comparatively important one within the community and one with the clout to galvanise its discontent into a full-scale and successful witch-hunt. It is likely they were involved in the local woollen cloth industry – perhaps Henry Jones was the ancestor of a later Richard Jones who, in his will of 1763, is recorded as having been a clothier. If so, the family was not sufficiently wealthy in 1641/2 to be liable for taxes on land or goods when the protestation returns and lay subsidy rolls were compiled but, equally, no Jones was sufficiently hard-up in 1670 to be exempt from paying the hearth tax. It is tempting to think, though seemingly not provable, that this was a family that was on the rise and one beginning to distance itself from its poorer neighbours.

As for Jane Brooks, 'of the same town', there is no sign of her at all in the local registers. In fact, the name 'Brooks' is entirely absent from the surviving records although the name 'Brooke' is comparatively abundant; at least eleven men over the age of eighteen with this surname are listed in the protestation returns and lay subsidy rolls for Shepton and adjoining Whitstone. One, Richard Brooke, was assessed for the payment of £2 on land he held. Hearth tax exemption certificates were awarded in 1670 to seven people with the surname of Brooke or Brook.

The Somerset session rolls of 1656 report the 'Informations of Robert Brooke sexton, Richard James overseer, and Robert Webb constable, of Shepton Mallet, concerning the very disorderly conduct of Benjamin Mansell of that place, who on the last Lord's day persisted in sitting in the church during the sermon and prayers with his hat on'.[8] It is probable that Jane Brooks was connected to at least one of these.

The narrative continues with an account of the first signs of Richard's bewitchment: 'When his father and one Gibson left him earlier the boy was perfectly well but, on their return, which was within an hour or thereabouts, they found him ill, and complaining of his right side, in which the pain continued the most part of that night'.[9] Elsewhere in the source Richard refers to Gibson as 'cooz Gibson'. Who was this 'cousin' Gibson? A good number of Gibsons appear in the Shepton register between 1637 and the end of the century. One stands out above the rest: the marriage of George Gibson and Elizabeth Brooke on 30 August 1639. Although Richard Jones may have recognised her he did not know Jane Brooks's name when she begged at his door, but it is possible that she had some kind of relationship, perhaps a familial one, with the Jones family. Conceivably, Gibson's wife was the third Brooks sister mentioned in the text, the others being Jane and Alice.

On the Monday evening Richard Jones roasted and ate the apple Brooks had given him and promptly became extremely ill. Again parallels can be drawn between this case and those from Württemberg in which the trials amply demonstrated 'angry or embittered villagers had access to [...] poisons'[10] and women were accused, for example, of poisoning their victims with tainted bread. When he was sufficiently recovered to be able to tell his father of his encounter with the unknown woman, an identity parade of sorts was arranged: 'Jones was advised to invite the women of Shepton to come to his house, and the child told him that if the woman should come in when he was having a fit and was not able to speak, he would give him a sign by a jog, and asked his father then to lead him through the room, for he said he would put his hand upon her, if she were there'.[11] Women were presented before him on a daily basis including, the following Sunday, Jane Brooks, two of her sisters, and several other local women.

The boy identified Brooks as the woman who had given him the apple and his father promptly scratched the supposed witch on the face, drawing blood, in the hope that this traditional remedy would lift her curse. Sure enough the lad soon recovered and was well for a week thereafter. However, after meeting Alice Coward, Jane Brooks's sister,[12] who said to him 'How do you do, my honey', he became ill again. In his sickness he would see the apparition of Jane Brooks and her sister and could describe the clothes they were wearing at the time with considerable accuracy. On one occasion he urged 'cousin' Gibson to strike the wall with a sharp knife where Jane Brooks had manifested and then declared he had wounded her in the hand. Sure enough, on arriving at her home, in the company of a constable (Robert Webb?), Gibson and Henry Jones found Brooks with a bloody hand; 'twas scratched with a great pin'[13] was her explanation. These terrifying experiences troubled the boy for three months: 'Between the fifteenth of November and the eleventh of January the two women appeared often to the boy, their hands cold, their eyes staring, and their lips and cheeks looking pale'.[14]

All of this was in Richard Jones's testimony, which was heard at Castle Cary on 8 December 1657 by Robert Hunt and another very active JP at this time, John Cary.[15] At the same hearings Jane Brooks and Alice Coward were examined. Jones appeared before them again in January in Shepton Mallet and also in February when 'many gentlemen, ministers and others' were also present. The case had caused quite a stir. In the courtroom, as on previous occasions, the lad put on a good show: 'The boy fell into his fit upon the sight of Jane Brooks, and lay in a man's arms like a dead person'. When Brooks was told to lay her hand on him 'he immediately started and sprang out in a very strange and unusual manner'. In case of fraud, one of the justices had the boy blindfolded and then 'called out for Brooks to touch him, but winked to others to do it, which two or three successively did, but the boy appeared unaffected'. However, when he called out for Jones's father to take hold of the boy, having 'secretly before arranged for one Mr Geoffrey Strode[16] to bring Jane Brooks to touch him as soon as he called out for his father' he 'sprang out in a very odd and violent fashion'. A similar ruse was tried several more times and only when touched by Brooks did he respond in the same way. His fits continued and when he was laid on a bed in the same room the people present could bow neither of his arms nor his legs.[17] Even more remarkable were the phenomena that followed:

On the twenty-fifth of February the boy was at the house of Richard Isles in Shepton Mallet. Between two and three in the afternoon Isles' wife followed him out of the room into the garden, and was within two yards of him when she saw him rise up from the ground before her, mounting higher and higher until he passed through the air over the garden wall, and was carried above ground for more than thirty yards before falling at last at one Jorden's door at Shepton, where he lay, as if dead for a time. Coming to himself again he told Jorden that Jane Brooks had taken him up by the arm out of Isles's garden, and carried him in the air as described. The boy on several occasions disappeared, and, after searching for him he was sometimes found in another room, as if dead, and sometimes suspended above the ground, his hands flat against a great beam in the ceiling, and all his body two or three foot from ground. He has been seen hanging in this position for a quarter of an hour before getting back to normal. He told the people that found him that Jane Brooks had carried him there and held him up. Nine people on one occasion time saw the boy hanging from the beam.[18]

The name Isles is absent from the parish registers for Shepton Mallet and its environs for the period 1580–1660 but a Richard and Jane Isles baptised a daughter in 1669 at St Peter and St Paul's. A Richard Giles also appears in the protestation returns and lay subsidy rolls for 1640/1. As for their neighbour, Jorden, we have very little to go on; however, it is interesting to find that one Mary Jorden married a Daniel Gibson in the parish on 16 November 1666. The hearth tax exemption records for 1670 list a Richard Isles and Thomas Isles senior and junior. Also listed are Joseph Jorden senior and junior. There too can be seen several Gibsons: George, Daniel, Grace and Joseph. These were poor families, close-knit and in similar straitened circumstances to the beggar, Jane Brooks. The evidence that Gibson, Isles and Jorden[19] provided doubtless contributed to the verdict when the case was heard at the Chard assizes: Jane Brooks was found guilty and hanged.

Just a few years before Jane Brooks was condemned, Robert Filmer had commented, in 1653, that, despite the draconian terms of the 1604 witchcraft act, judges 'condemn none for witches unless they be charged with murdering some person'.[20] The execution of Brooks on 26

March 1658, as recorded by Glanvill in 1668,[21] is surprising since her victim, Richard Jones, was still living. However, if there was an error of transcription[22] somewhere along the line and in fact she was executed in March 1659 the outcome is as one might expect. Given that the date in question – the first day of the new year according to the old calendar – an error is all the more likely. For example, if it should read 25 March 1658, the year, in modern terms, becomes 1659. If Richard was the 'Rechard Joans' who is recorded as dying on 4 February 1658/9 – a likely scenario is that Brooks and Coward received a year in prison for causing him harm and, following his death, this was transmuted into a death sentence. The fact that Alice Coward is not mentioned as sharing her sister's fate might well indicate her death in prison in the intervening months of their captivity.

The published account of the bewitchment of Richard Jones provides a highly detailed narrative of the events that can be summarised as follows:

> **Sunday 15 November 1657:** At 3.00 pm Jane Brooks begs bread from Richard Jones at his father's house; Richard receives from her an apple; Richard suffers pains one the right side of his body where Brooks had stroked him.
>
> **Monday 16 November 1657:** Richard roasts the apple in the evening and becomes extremely ill after eating just half of it.
>
> **17 November – 22 November 1657:** following the advice of an unnamed person or persons, Henry Jones 'invites' the women of Shepton Mallet to his home to be presented to his son with a view to discovery of the hitherto unidentified witch (Jane Brooks).
>
> **Sunday 22 November 1657:** Jane Brooks and two of her sisters are presented to Richard Jones who falls ill and cannot speak as soon as he sees her; Henry Jones scratches her on the face.
>
> **Sunday 29 November or Sunday 6 December ('A certain Sunday about Noon') 1657:** Jane Brooks is found with a bleeding hand after Gibson strikes her apparition (visible only to Richard Jones) with a knife.
>
> **Tuesday 8 December 1657:** Richard Jones, Brooks and Alice Coward are examined by JPs Hunt and Cary at Castle Cary.
>
> **Sunday 11 January 1657/8:** second examination of Jones, Brooks

and Coward by Hunt and Cary, this time at Shepton.

Tuesday 17 February 1657/8: Jones and Brooks are further examined at Shepton, this time with many gentlemen (including Mr Geoffrey Strode), ministers and others present.

Wednesday 25 February 1657/8: Richard Jones visits the home of Richard Isles and is seen to levitate in the garden by Isles's wife.

Tuesday 10 March 1657/8: Brooks and Coward are sent to gaol; Richard Jones recovers.

Friday 4 February 1658/9: death of Richard Jones.

Saturday 26 March 1658/9(?): Brooks is executed at the Chard assizes.

Gregory Durston has summarised the potential barriers along the way to a successful conviction, all of which the unlucky Jane Brooks passed through in the space of five months:

> Firstly, there had to be a potential suspect of the appropriate type, and a convincing incident of witchcraft that could be attributed to them. Then there had to be villagers willing to make a complaint, and, if these were not themselves people of some standing, other local men of influence willing to facilitate and support such a formal allegation. A sympathetic (to the reality of witchcraft) examining JP, was needed as was a similarly sympathetic Grand Jury (or at least a majority on it) willing to find a true Bill. Even at this stage it was still necessary to have a croyant trial jury potentially willing to convict (unanimously), and a trial judge who was not both hostile to such actions and capable of leading the jurors away from conviction, and also unwilling or unable to effect a post-conviction reprieve.[23]

Jane Brooks conformed to the witch stereotype just as Richard Jones's affliction corresponded to popular assumptions regarding forms of bewitchment. At least one of the two JPs, Robert Hunt, certainly believed in the reality of witches and witchcraft, and those sitting in court rooms so close to Batcombe, might have been especially sympathetic to the principles its former rector, Richard Bernard, had enshrined in his still influential *Guide*.

There were further barriers that stood in the way of those inclined to make accusations. In addition to the costs of potentially long journeys to give evidence wherever the case might be heard, complainants might be charged for the subpoenas and the drawing up of recognizances for witnesses, as well as with the cost of raising a warrant for the arrest of the accused in the first place. Various court fees might be incurred if the case was referred to an assize court. 'The total cost', Durston has concluded, 'could easily exceed £1; for many people this was several weeks' wages'.[24] If, as seems to be the case, the afflicted family in the case against Jane Brooks was not especially wealthy the question has to be asked whether they were the prime movers in bringing her to trial. Of particular interest is the identity parade of Shepton Mallet women at the Jones' home in the week after Richard Jones fell sick. Although the account tells us he was *advised* to proceed in this way and the women were *invited* to make a visit, it is tempting to see a parish constable's hand in this obliging of the women, very probably fulfilling the instruction of someone other than Henry Jones himself. Brooks and Coward, together with Richard Jones, made their first appearance before the magistrates at Castle Cary remarkably soon, just three weeks, after Brooks and Jones first met and the boy fell ill. Someone with significantly more influence than his father must surely have stepped in almost from the outset. There is no indication as to who this might have been but a member of the local gentry, such as Geoffrey Strode who was involved in the third examination, or perhaps a local minister, are obvious candidates. This case, along with others in the Selwood Forest region in the period, started in the squabbles and rivalries of lowly parishioners but escalated into a full-blown trial through the interest and involvement of those above. In many accusations and prosecutions the critical involvement of the local elite was because of the apparent bewitchment of one of their own; when this was not the case, as in this one, it can be supposed that some other imperative drove the hunt.

* * *

IN CHRONOLOGICAL TERMS the next of the cases associated with Selwood Forest is Glanvill's 'Relation VIII'[25] which concerns a trial at Taunton in 1663 during the summer after Glanvill and Mr Hill had made their trip to Tidworth. It is based on the record of October 1672 made by 'Mr Pool, a servant and officer in the court to Judge Archer, in his Circuits'. Glanvill's editor of the posthumous *Saducismus*, Henry More, knew this remarkable story would be challenged, particularly since the account on which it was based was written almost ten years after the trial ended. Despite its problematic provenance he defended its validity in the 'advertisement' which follows the narrative with the observation that 'Its credibility is assured by the fact he [Mr Pool] was an officer and servant of the judge and present in the court at the examination and trial, and there took notes, and wrote a narrative, when there were so many witnesses besides himself to the same things, and it would be offensive to him and those others present to attempt to disprove these claims'.[26]

Pool recorded the extraordinary tale of a seventy-year-old, pipe-smoking witch called Julian Cox who could turn herself into a hare[27] and who had a monstrous toad-familiar. The account of one witness sheds further light on the superstitious world in which these cases were set; when his cows were bewitched by Cox he took expert advice, probably from a white witch/cunning man/wise woman, in order to find a way of fighting magic with magic. She confessed to meeting the spirits of a deceased witch and a deceased wizard – an interesting distinction in a period in which both male and female practitioners were usually described as 'witches'. These witches flew through the air on broomsticks – one among

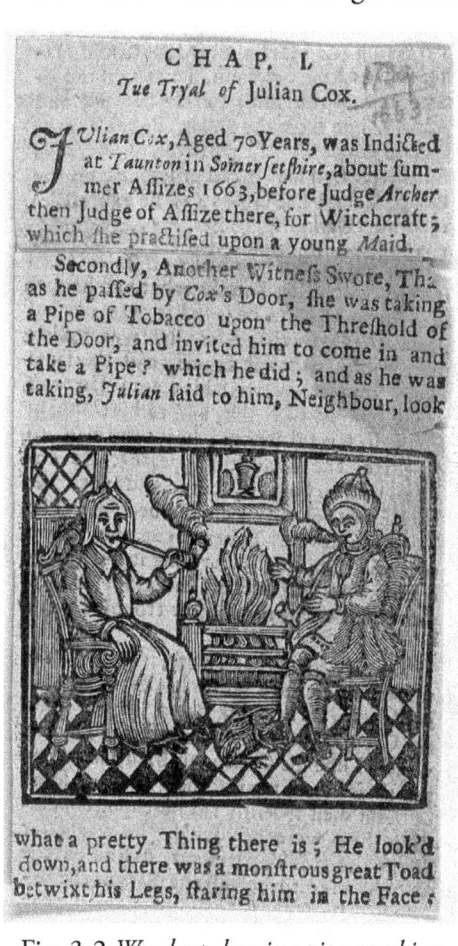

Fig. 3-2 *Woodcut showing pipe-smoking Cox, her toad-familiar and her astonished neighbour.*

a number of magical modes of transport that appear occasionally in the witchcraft accounts of sixteenth- and seventeenth-century Europe.

Cox was indicted for witchcraft 'which she practised on a young maid, whereby her body languished, and was impaired of health by reason of strange fits'. The evidence brought against her was divided into two parts – one 'to prove her a witch in general', the other 'to prove her guilty of the witchcraft contained in the indictment'.[28] Four witnesses made the extraordinary claims that she could shape-shift into a hare, that her imp was a toad, that she drove cattle mad, and that she could fly through the air. She helped to condemn herself with her confession of consorting with a witch, a wizard, and a third person, presumably a demon, 'in the shape of a black man',[29] even though, she insisted, she did not succumb to the temptation of forming a pact with the latter. In the pan-European tradition the Devil's colour was black – a designation that could refer to his clothing, skin colour or both.[30]

The name of the person bewitched is not given but she is identified as a servant and it is reasonable to presume that the family for which she worked initiated the proceedings. When she answered the door to Cox she incurred the fury of the old woman by refusing her alms. Cox told her she would regret her action before night fell. Shortly afterwards she began suffering fits and had visions of Cox from whom she implored others in the house to save her. The rest of the household became convinced she really was bewitched after the girl seized a knife and cut the leg of the witch, a manifestation that none but her could see. As in the Jane Brooks' narrative, Cox was found at her home with a freshly wounded leg she had recently bandaged.

After this the young woman claimed she was forced by the witch to swallow pins. For a whole day she was seen eating her invisible pins and by the evening she was in agony, screaming in pain, as 'in several parts of the girl's body great swellings appeared, and out of the head of the swellings several great pins' points appeared'.[31] Mr Pool declared thirty of these pins were presented before the court at Taunton, some of which he had handled himself.

Swallowed pins would soon play an important part in the trial proceedings at Bury St Edmunds concerning the bewitchment of seven children that led to the executions of Amy Denny and Rose Cullender in 1665. Their victims had fallen into 'swoonings' and

Fig. 3-3 *Detail from the frontispiece of* Saducismus Triumphatus *(1681) depicting Julian Cox in magical flight.*

suffered fits and, 'upon the recovery to their speech, they would cough extremely and bring up much phlegm, and with the same, crooked pins, and one time a two-penny nail with a very broad head'. As in the Cox case, these pins, 'amounting to forty or more', were produced in court.[32]

It seems likely that this developing tradition of pin-swallowing, briefly alluded to in Bernard's *Guide* and to occur again and even more spectacularly in the Beckington case of 1689, had much to do with the growing need for the witch-finders to acquire more convincing, tangible evidence of witchcraft in order to persuade an increasingly sceptical judiciary. This was of critical importance to Cox's accusers since, on this occasion, the witch refused to condemn herself by confessing to forming a diabolical pact. Nevertheless, the jury was convinced by other 'sufficient proofs' and she was executed in 1663. She had the misfortune to be presented before a judge who, though cautious and clear in what constituted proof, was sufficiently open-minded to put to the test the old tradition that a true witch would be unable to repeat the *Lord's Prayer*:

The prisoner was called up to the next bar to the court, and asked if she could say the *Lord's Prayer*. She said she could, and recited the prayer without difficulty until she came to that petition. Then she said 'And lead us into temptation' or 'And lead us not into no temptation' but could not say 'And lead us not into temptation', even though she was directed to say it after someone had carefully repeated it. But she could not repeat it except in the ways stated, even though she tried to do it near half a score of times in open court. After all of which, the Jury found her guilty, and judgement having been given, within three or four days she was executed without any confession of the fact.[33]

In an editorial postscript Henry More revealed the connection between this story, gleaned by Glanvill from the notes of Mr Pool, and those he took from Hunt's book of examinations. Hunt, it transpires, had examined Cox but she had refused to make a confession. The reason he used Pool's version and not Hunt's is made clear – More tells us Glanvill had written in a letter that 'he perused that examination in Mr Hunt's book, and there was not anything considerable therein'.[34]

Although her case was heard at Taunton it is erroneous to consider her 'the Taunton witch Julian Cox'.[35] The surviving account does not indicate in which part of Somerset she lived, but the fact that she was examined by Robert Hunt strongly implies she lived within the area of his jurisdiction – in other words in, or close to, Selwood Forest. It asserts that she was around seventy years old in the early 1660s. A search of several hundred parish registers for Somerset for baptismal records of a 'Julian Cox' or someone with a similar name has produced just three results for the period between 1680 and 1710. One of these is male, another, Julian Coxe, born in Bath in 1596, is female, and the sex of a third, Julian Coxe, born in Frome Selwood's neighbouring parish of Nunney on 6 June 1591, is unknown. If this Julian Cox(e) was still alive in the early 1660s he/she would have just turned seventy. Of course there is every reason to suppose our Julian Cox is remembered by her married name but a search of the parish records for marriages between 1605 and 1640 in the county of well over 200 men and women with Cox or Coxe in their baptismal surname does not produce a single one with the name

Fig. 3-4 *Woodcut depicting Robert Hunt and attendees.*

Julian or something similar (other than the occasional 'Anne'). Perhaps, like so many women in the period, she never did marry. The chances of the Nunney child being the witch in the account are slight but certainly not out of the question. There might even be some historical truth in the local tradition that Nunney's picturesque fourteenth-century castle was the setting of 'several witch trials' and that 'the spirit of a woman accused of being a witch and then put to death haunts the ruined corridors'.[36]

* * *

BARRY HAS TURNED up some interesting material, beyond Hunt's book of examinations, that sheds light on witchcraft beliefs in the period.[37] This includes a letter concerning the supposed bewitching of his daughter, Catherine, who married Richard Brodrepp of Mapperton, Dorset, in 1663. It post-dates the episodes recorded in *Saducismus Triumphatus* and, through its absence of consideration of 'natural' explanations, implies the writer's firm belief in the reality of malevolent witchcraft. Catherine was tormented for three weeks or more, with pains in her throat, heart, belly and back. The feeling that she was being pierced by invisible nails or needles forced her to rise each night at 2 am. At four o'clock one Sunday morning, she suffered a particularly violent fit, 'her eyes were stretched and swollen, her teeth clenched, her lips open, her chin gathered up like a button, her hands and arms turned backwards, and her legs and arms so stiff and distorted that they could not be bent'. In her agony she uttered the words, 'Alice Knight has made me giddy!' Knight was summoned to the Brodrepps' home and Catherine was seen to tremble as the woman approached the house. Here Knight was subjected to the old practice of a scratching – her blood drawn with a bramble in order to lift her curse. She was then forced to kneel 'and pray that neither the Devil nor any of his servants might do her any more harm'. Hunt remarked she had been well ever since. Several 'knackes' – trinkets – were found in her pillow, 'made up in feathers and bound with red silk'. Two were burned by members of the family but at least three more, now in Hunt's possession, were saved. This keeping of magical curios is reminiscent of the collection and preservation of nails vomited by Mary Hill in Beckington in 1689.

Hunt alluded to what seems to be another Selwood witchcraft case in a letter dated 26 February 1665 (i.e. 1666): 'a young mayde died at Killmington on Wednesday, bewitched by an apple, lay 3 weeks in great torment and dyed Wednesday, her body broake and her bowls came out'. Kilmington, a parish adjoining that of Brewham on its eastern side, is at the southern end of the forest. Hunt continued, 'The story is too longe for this paper. This unhappy business of witches hath given me very much trouble and they have done very much mischeife both to cattle & people, but I suppose some of them will receive their reward & they well deserve it'.[38]

1. Henry More, *An Antidote against Atheisme, or, an Appeal to the natural Faculties of Minds of Man, whether there be not a God* (1653), 164.
2. Glanvill, *Saducismus*, 339–44.
3. Stark, *Rhetoric*, 116.
4. Edward Bever, 'Witchcraft Fears and Psychosocial Factors in Disease', *The Journal of Interdisciplinary History*, Vol. 30, No. 4 (2000), 576–77.
5. Hutchinson, *An Historical Essay*, 229.
6. Bever, 'Witchcraft Fears', 581.
7. *Ibid.*, 586.
8. E. H. Bates Harbin (ed.), *Quarter Sessions Records for the County of Somerset, Volume 3: Commonwealth, 1646-1660* (London: Somerset Record Society, 1912), 291.
9. Glanvill, *Saducismus*, 339.
10. Bever, 'Witchcraft Fears', 587.

11 Glanvill, *Saducismus*, 340.
12 This is how she was described by Glanvill; in the seventeenth century the term 'sister' was also commonly used for a sister-in-law.
13 Glanvill, *Saducismus*, 341.
14 *Ibid.*, 342.
15 That the two men were working together at this time is confirmed by the Quarter Sessions records for 1657.
16 The influential Strode family of Shepton Mallet and Barrington Court near Ilminster was one of successful clothiers with Presbyterian/puritan leanings in the mid-seventeenth century.
17 Glanvill, *Saducismus*, 341.
18 *Ibid.*, 343.
19 The will of James Jordan of Shepton Mallet, 1764, like that of Richard Jones (1763), identifies its owner as a clothier.
20 Robert Filmer, *An Advertisement to Jury-men of England Touching Witches* (London: 1653), 18, in Gilbert Geiss and Ivan Bunn, *A Trial of Witches: A Seventeenth Century Witchcraft Prosecution* (London: Routledge, 1997), 25.
21 Glanvill, *Modern Sadducism*.
22 Barry has identified such mistakes by comparing the SRO manuscript with Glanvill's *Saducismus* – he considers Glanvill's thirty yards as the distance across which the levitating Richard Jones was carried on 25 February 1658 a mistaken transposition of the three hundred yards in the manuscript version; Ewen, as discussed below, identified the misspelling in *Saducismus* of a key witness in the Elizabeth Style case of 1665.
23 Gregory Durston, *Witchcraft and Witch Trials* (Chichester: Barry Rose Law Publishers Ltd, 2000), 224.
24 *Ibid.*, 311.
25 Glanvill, *Saducismus*, 387–92.
26 *Ibid.*, 392.
27 The witch-hare/witch-rabbit transformation tradition remained strong in popular folklore over the following two centuries, not least in the southwest. A researcher in County Antrim, Northern Ireland, in the late 1930s, claimed reports were heard 'in nearly every district [...] of the old dame who changed herself into a hare'. H.T. Browne in Sugg, *Supernatural Stories*, 198–99.
28 Glanvill, *Saducismus*, 387.
29 *Ibid.*, 389.
30 Roper, *Witch Craze*, 87.
31 Glanvill, *Saducismus*, 391.
32 Anon., *A Tryal of Witches at the Assizes held at Bury St. Edmonds in the County of Suffolk* (1682).
33 Glanvill, *Saducismus*, 391-92.

34 *Ibid.*, 395.
35 Davies, *Science in an Enchanted World*, Chapter 2.
36 'Paranormal Claims at Nunney Castle in Somerset', 30 August 2014, wiltshireparanormal.co.uk, accessed 10 August 2015.
37 Barry, *Witchcraft and Demonology*, 14–56.
38 *Ibid.*, 31.

4

A HELLISH KNOT OF WITCHES

Fig. 4-1 *The witches of Selwood engaged in image magic with the Devil.*
(Contemporary woodcut)

Atheism is begun in Saducism: And those that dare not bluntly say, 'There is no God', content themselves (for a fair step and introduction) to deny there are spirits or witches.
– Joseph Glanvill, 1681.[1]

RELATION III IN *Saducismus Triumphatus*[2] concerns the examination and confession of an elderly widow, Elizabeth Style of Stoke Trister, adjacent to Wincanton, in 1665. According to Glanvill she was found guilty when her case was heard at Taunton but she evaded execution by dying in gaol. Style was accused by her neighbours of causing inexplicable sicknesses in her community – fitting and wasting diseases; her case bears the hallmarks of the classic English witch trial.

Richard Hill, 'yeoman of Stoke Trister',[3] accused Style of causing his thirteen-year-old daughter's fitting sickness, which began around November 1664. Three local men, Francis White, Walter Thick and Robert Thick, 'willed her to complain to the Justice against him for accusing of her', but she rejected their advice declaring 'she would do worse than fetch a Warrant'.[4] For several nights, it was reported, the girl, Elizabeth Hill, suffered terrible fits during which 'holes would appear in her wrists, face, neck, and other parts of her body, which the informant and others that saw them thought were caused by thorns since they saw thorns in her flesh, some of which they hooked out'. When the fit passed she would declare, 'Widow Style had pricked her with thorns in those places'. William Parsons, Stoke Trister's rector, testified before Robert Hunt:

On Monday night after Christmas Day, he came into the room when Elizabeth Hill was suffering a fit, and found many of his parishioners being present and looking on. He saw the child forcibly held down in a chair by some of the people, struggling with an unnatural strength, foaming at the mouth and catching at her own arms and clothes with her teeth. This fit he believes lasted for about half an hour.[5]

This was affirmed by the testimony of Nicholas Lambert of Bayford, another yeoman, who saw Elizabeth Hill 'taken very ill and suffering fits that

Fig. 4-2 *The witchcraft of Elizabeth Style(s) of Bayford.*

were so strong that six men could not hold her down in the chair in which she was sitting'. Even more astonishing was her supernatural levitation: 'Although she was held down in a chair by four or five people, sometimes six, by the arms, legs, and shoulders, she would rise out of her chair, and raise her body about three or four feet high'.[6]

Quite probably the justice's house that Richard Hill rode to in order to receive the warrant for Style's arrest was Robert Hunt's at Compton Pauncefoot, about six miles away; when the hearth tax exemption certificates were drawn up for Stoke Trister in 1670 the list was signed off by Hunt and his colleague William Bull, his son-in-law's father. When the case came to trial Hunt's other examinees bringing evidence against Style included Elizabeth Torwood who searched her and found the Devil's mark:

She, together with Catharine White, Mary Day, Mary Bolster, and Bridget Prankard,[7] a little after Christmas last, searched Elizabeth Style, and that in her poll they found a little rising which felt hard like a kernel of beef. Suspecting it to be an ill mark, they thrust a pin into it, and having drawn it out, thrust it in again a second time, leaving it sticking in the flesh for some time, so that the other women might also see it. Despite this, on neither occasion did Style make any sign of feeling a thing. But afterwards, when the constable told her he would stick a pin into the same place, she made a show as if she did feel it saying, 'O Lord, you prick me!' when, in fact, no one was touching her. The examinant further says that Style has since confessed to her that her familiar used to suck her in the place mentioned, in the shape of a great miller or butterfly.[8]

Torwood was identified by Ewen[9] as Forward, using the Stoke Trister Hearth Tax exemption record for 1664. A poor woman named Elizabeth Forwod also crops up in the 1670 Hearth Tax records. In the SRO manuscript she is named 'Foarwood',[10] and an earlier Elizabeth Forwood was buried in the parish in 1629. William Thick, named as one of the two churchwardens in the 1670 record – the other was Thomas Thick – was one of three men directed to watch over Style after her arrest. Another was Nicholas Lambert, probably the person of the same name baptised there in January 1617/18, who clearly was an educated man – he stated in his confession he was reading *The Practice of Piety*,[11] sitting by the fire near Style, when, in the early hours of the morning,

Fig. 4-3 *Elizabeth Style makes her pact with the Devil who pricks her finger.*

he and his colleagues saw what they believed to be her demon-familiar:

The examinant, Thick and Read, believing that her familiar was with her, looked towards her poll, and, seeing her hair shake very strangely, lifted it up, and then a fly like a great miller flew out from the place, and pitched on the table-board before disappearing. Upon this the examinant and the other two looked again in Style's poll and found it very red and looking like raw beef. The examinant asked her what it was that had been in her poll; she said it was a butterfly and asked them why they had not caught it. Lambert said they could not. 'I think so too!' she answered.[12]

Although torture, strictly speaking, was not permissible in the handling of witches, this watching of Style through the night almost certainly amounted to a subtle torture through sleep deprivation. Each of the three men no doubt could slumber in shifts but it is likely Style was denied such a luxury. The blood-sucking fly-familiar, she later declared, went by the name of Robin and would sometimes appear in the form of a dog or a cat and, at least once, in that of a man. What actually went on in the room during the course of the watching of Elizabeth Style is unknown but a recent description of a similar case from East Anglia in the mid-1640s offers a likely scenario:

> Having taken the suspected witch, she is placed in the middle of a room upon a stool or table, cross-legged, or in some other uneasy posture, to which if she submits not, she is then bound with cords; there she is watched and kept without meat or sleep for the space of twenty-four hours for (they say) within that time they shall see her imp come and suck. A little hole is likewise made in the door for the imp to come in at; and lest it might come in some less discernible shape, they that watch are taught to be ever and anon sweeping the room, and if they see any spiders or flies, to kill them. And if they cannot kill them, then they may be sure they are her imps.[13]

David Jones has considered the psychological impact of the process on the watchers as well as the watched. 'It is quite probably the most exciting thing in which they would ever have taken part', he has written, 'the atmosphere within the room would have become powerfully charged, as people were keyed up and expecting to see something exceptional'.[14] The watchers were her near neighbours – Bayford men from that part of Stoke Trister that was home to Style.

A local butcher, Richard Vining,[15] claimed Style had bewitched to death his wife, Agnes, three years earlier. Agnes's illness, becoming all the worse after Elizabeth Style had persuaded her to eat 'a very fair red apple', began shortly after the two women had fallen out – according to the SRO manuscript, their dispute concerned 'eggs and poultry'.[16] Vining consulted Compton, the enigmatic physician and cunning man of Ditcheat, about ten miles away, who advised him accordingly, telling him 'he could do her no good for she had been hurt by a near neighbour – one who would come into his house and up into the chamber where his wife was, and then go out again without speaking'. Sure enough, the passage continues, 'After Vining came home, and while he was in the chamber with his wife, Style came up to them and then went out again without saying a word'. Unfortunately, it seems he was unable to supply any effective counter-magic for her ailments: 'His wife, Agnes, continued in great pain until the following Easter Eve and then she died. Before her death her hip had rotted and one of her eyes had swelled out'. Throughout her illness she insisted 'Elizabeth Style had bewitched her, and that she was the cause of her death'.[17]

Robert Hunt heard this testimony on 26 January 1664/5 at the town of Wincanton, a mile and a half away from Stoke Trister. It is notable that on the very first day he examined Style he was quick to condemn her as an 'old sinner' – his mind, probably, was already made up:

Whilst the justice was examining Style [...] he had noticed that Richard Vining was looking very earnestly at him. He asked Vining if he had anything to say to him and Vining answered that Style had bewitched his wife, and described how, as is in his deposition related. Upon hearing this Style seemed appalled and very concerned. The Justice said to her, 'You have been an old sinner' etc., 'You deserve little mercy'. She replied, 'I have asked God mercy for it'. Mr Hunt asked her that if this was so why did she continue in such ill courses?[18]

Fig. 4-4 *A black-faced man in black (note the clerical band around his neck) presents a witch with a demon-familiar.*

Up to this point it seems Style had made no confession of wrong-doing but now, bullied by Hunt and, doubtless, overwhelmed by the whole terrible experience, she broke down: 'She told him the Devil tempted her and then began to make some confession of his dealings with her'. Hunt sent her to the Bayford home of Mr Gapper,[19] the constable. The following morning he went there himself, accompanied by 'two highly regarded gentlemen, Mr Bull and Mr Court,[20] now both Justices of the Peace in the county'. In two further hearings, dated 30 January and 7 February, she made her full and shocking confession of her league with the Devil. The watching of Elizabeth Style at Constable

Gapper's house was probably in adherence with Hunt's direct order; he may also have arranged for the full body search of the old woman as a preliminary to the formal proceedings.

What sets this story apart is its extensive descriptions of sabbat meetings. Thomas Potts's account of the activities of the Pendle witches in 1612 included commentary on a 'special meeting' of the accused, and a fourteen-year-old girl, Grace Sowerbutts, in the same year described another meeting of witches in Lancashire, at Salmesbury, who feasted on the body of a recently buried child. A case in Devon in 1638 involved claims of witches meeting on a hill each Midsummer Eve where they met with the Devil who licked them.[21] The East Anglian cases of 1645–7 had further 'reinforced the idea that witches belonged to networks which could be broken'.[22] However, the Selwood Sabbat descriptions are unparalleled in the English tradition in the fullness of their accounts of feasting, dancing, and the ritual baptizing/naming of effigies made of wax and/or other materials (known in the period as 'poppets') which became the instrument of the coven's *maleficia*. Most importantly, they were convened by the Devil who, in the guise of a handsome man in black, led the proceedings:

> A little over a month ago the examinant [Elizabeth Style], Alice Duke, Anne Bishop and Mary Penny met at about nine o'clock at night on the common near Trister Gate. Here they met a man in black clothes with a little band,[23] to whom they did curtsy and gave due observance, and the examinant truly believes that this was the Devil. Alice Duke brought an image in wax representing Elizabeth Hill. The man in black took it in his arms, anointed its forehead, and said, 'I baptise thee with this oil', and some other words. He was godfather, and the examinant and Anne Bishop were godmothers. They called it Elizabeth or Bess. Then the man in black, the examinant, Anne Bishop and Alice Duke stuck thorns into several places, including, among others, the neck, wrists, and fingers of the wax figure.[24]

The Devil spoke in a low voice and sometimes made music on a pipe or a cittern. The sabbat was depicted as a very real experience with the witches often, though not always, present in physical form. Compared with contemporary continental accounts in which sabbat meetings were lurid, violent, depraved orgies, those described by Elizabeth Style are tame and without a hint of sex: the witches, she insisted, danced fully clothed:

> At their meeting they usually have wine or good beer, cakes, meat or the like. They eat and drink when they meet in bodily form, dance and have music. The man in black sits at the higher end, and Anne Bishop usually sits next to him. He says some words before they eat, and none thereafter.[25]

Sometimes those involved travelled distances of ten miles and more, gathering in several parishes on the Somerset–Dorset border. Style named thirteen others, both men and women, who gathered to participate in the baptism of poppets by the man in black, and the associated celebrations. Crucially, in relation to the validity of Glanvill's argument, Style's confession, according to a key witness – the rector, William Parsons – 'was free and unforced, without any torturing or watching, drawn from her by a gentle examination'. The piercing of poppets in the accounts leads directly to the agonies felt by the child-victims. By harming innocent children, the witches hurt their parents, the principal target of their *maleficia*. These included John, the child of Robert Newman of Wincanton, the focus of the poppet curse-ceremony carried out by Style and her two principal accomplices (witches so often, as in Shakespeare's play, did their magic in threes), Anne Bishop and Alice Duke. According to Duke's confession before Hunt in January and February 1664/5 the boy had died and, furthermore, they had done the same for an older brother, Peter, some five-and-a-half years before. This claim, in part, is substantiated by the Wincanton parish register – entries record the baptism of John Newman, son of Robert Newman, in May 1663, and his death in December 1664.

A late nineteenth-century historian, W. H. Davenport Adams, was unequivocal in his dismissal of Style's claims – it was just 'another case (if it be true) of the morbid self-delusion which in times of popular excitement makes so many victims'.[26] However, the alleged meetings, at places which probably were still unenclosed common grounds, could well have had at least something to do with traditional gatherings and activities such as dances on particular holy days.[27] One is identified as Trister Gate where the parish enters Selwood Forest, others were held at Leigh Common[28] on the northern edge of Stoke Trister, High Common near

Fig. 4-5 *The witches of Selwood; detail from the frontispiece of* Saducismus Triumphatus *(1681) depicting the baptizing of poppets by the man in black and the forging through the Devil's touch of a diabolical pact.*

Motcombe just over the Dorset border, and another 'at an open place near Marnhull' six miles or so to the south. The enclosure of Selwood Forest between 1627 and 1640 had provoked riots and the destruction of fences from the start of the 1640s up to the middle of the 1650s. Jonathan Barry has made a strong case for the possibility that 'all these locations [including the common grounds at Marnhull and Motcombe] evoked in the minds of the witches places of popular gathering, either to resist unwelcome authority or to celebrate customs targeted by reformers'.[29]

Style claimed she had met with 'John Combes, John Vining, Richard Diokes, Thomas Boster or Bolster, Thomas Dunning, James Bush (a lame man), Rachel King, Richard Lannen, a woman called Durnford, Alice Duke, Anne Bishop, Mary Penny and Christopher Ellen' in and around Stoke Trister and also at Motcombe and Marnhull. The names mentioned emphasise the close and sometimes familial links between the accusers of so-called witches, the accused, and their supposed victims. John Vining, for example, shares the name of the bereaved butcher, and also that of Dorothy Vining, another alleged victim of witchcraft.[30] A search of local marriage records identifies the marriage of John Vining in neighbouring Wincanton in 1651 to a woman by the name of Gartrud Still. If this surname is an alternative phonetic spelling of the name Style or Stile, that by which Richard Vining's persecutor is identified, it seems there is a strong chance that these neighbours, engaged in their deadly quarrels, not only knew each other well but were closely related. Incidentally, a John Cooms married Alice Dick (Duke?) in nearby Mere back in 1634.

Alice Duke of Wincanton, provided a detailed account of her own witchcraft (Relation IV).[31] Her age and socio-economic condition are uncertain but she was described as a widow and, it can be presumed, she was illiterate, signing her diabolical contract, using her own blood, with a simple mark. Her case sheds further light on the mystery of the means by which the witches were transported through the air to their sabbat meetings: her forehead was first 'anointed with a feather dipped in oil'; this greenish oil, it transpires, was Satan's gift. This reiterated Style's record of the anointing of foreheads and wrists with 'an oil the spirit brings them (which smells raw)'. This oil, combined with magical words, 'Thout, tout a tout, throughout and about', carried them to their meetings. Once again the examinant was keen to point out that they were there in person, fully dressed. In passing, a fascinating period detail is provided concerning the costume of one of the witches: 'a green apron, a French waistcoat and a red petticoat' – a cheerful contrast to the black widow's weeds of the modern witch stereotype.[32] When the Devil departed at the end of the witches' meetings he left a stink behind: a further reinforcement of the principle that he could adopt a physical form.

Duke provided interesting details about how she was initiated into the coven by Anne Bishop, who 'appears to have been the chief personage under the Devil, in other words the Officer',[33] as Margaret Murray noted. She and Bishop had walked backwards three times around the church in Wincanton. On the first circuit the man in black appeared; on the second a large black toad leapt up at them; on the third a rat-like creature ran past them. The man in black then spoke to Ann Bishop and shortly afterwards Alice Duke was accepted into the coven, the Devil pricking the fourth finger of her right hand to make his mark on her. Style, recalling her own initiation, said that she had traded her soul for money and for twelve years of pleasure on Earth, signing a pact to this effect with her own blood. The Devil had then given her sixpence and disappeared. She confessed to having a familiar which 'doth commonly suck her right Breast, about seven at night, in the shape of a little Cat

[...] and when she is suckt, she is in a kind of trance'.³⁴

Duke's confession reiterated, almost word for word, much of what had gone before regarding the sabbat meetings. Of course, much of what is recorded as her own words could in fact be those of her interrogator – 'yes' and 'no' answers to leading questions written up as detailed confessional statements in which the question itself is embedded. Barry has suggested Bernard's *Guide* might well have been the text that informed Hunt's questions.³⁵ Of her own personal acts of *maleficia* Duke confessed to a number of guilty secrets, including taking revenge for the trivial offences. Her curse is strikingly mild – 'Pox on you!' – but, in her imagination, it had dreadful consequences for which, on at least one occasion, she was sorry. The 'Pox on you!' curse can be regarded as her personal code for summoning her demon. Most pitifully she lamented being promised by the Devil 'she should want for nothing, but ever since she has continued to need everything as before'. She bewitched the cows of Thomas³⁶ Garret 'because he refused to write a Petition for her', provoked, she cursed Mr Swanton's first wife who subsequently died, and she caused the sickness of Edith Watts, the daughter of Edmond

Fig. 4-6 *Witches and demons dancing.*

Fig. 4-7 *Witches and demons feasting.*

Watts, having cursed her and touched her 'for treading on her Foot'.[37] She punished Thomas Conway by gifting him a pewter dish in which to prepare a balm to soothe his nursing daughter's breast. When his wife, Mary, treated her daughter's nipple she suffered such extreme pain that Mary threw the cursed dish into the fire where it was destroyed and, remarkably, not a trace of it remained. The same treatment warmed in a spoon and not a bewitched dish had no detrimental effect; it was also noted in the record of Mary Conway's examination that Thomas Conway, shortly after receiving the dish, 'was taken ill in all his Limbs, and held him for a long time in a very strange Manner'.[38] A manuscript version of the account once owned by the famous Dorset poet, William Barnes, and now in the Somerset Record Office, also mentioned her bewitching of William, the son of William Botwell of Wincanton, and the harm she caused the daughters of Thomas Gilbert, Grace and Magdalen, 'by giving them two apples'.[39]

Despite the frustrating absence of records for the 1650s,[40] the surviving evidence for Stoke Trister and Wincanton provides opportunities to locate these tall tales in the lives of real people. Rose Swanton, the wife of a gentleman, Mr Francis Swanton, was buried at Wincanton on 12 March 1663/4 – just under a year before Duke was examined by Robert Hunt. The Swantons, Barry has noted, were, like Hunt, barristers of the Middle Temple, and politically engaged in both Somerset and Wiltshire. This supposed bewitchment of the elite was bound to attract attention and, Barry has speculated, could have been 'what led to its suppression by "higher authority"'.[41] Edith, the daughter of Edmunde and Edith Watts was baptized in Wincanton on 18 November 1654 – she was about ten years old when she made the mistake of stepping on Alice Duke's foot. Marye Hauching married Thomas Conway in Wincanton in 1642; they had two daughters, Mary and Alice, the second of whom, married to a man named Robert Pitman, was almost certainly the bewitched mother who was nursing her first child, Jane, born 7 February 1663/4. There is no sign of the Botwell child in the Wincanton register but the Gilberts are very evident. Thomas married Magdalen Winbolt on 26 December 1655 at St Peter and St Paul's, Wincanton. Their daughters, Grace and Magdalen were baptized there on 12 October 1662 and 14 January 1660/1 respectively and Magdalen, aged four-year-old Magadalen was buried there a few months after Duke was examined by Hunt.

In both Style's and Duke's confessions, Anne Bishop was named as being a, perhaps *the*, principal witch at their night-time assemblies and ceremonies presided over by the man in black. Surprisingly, she was not one of those examined – perhaps she had died or maybe the investigation was suppressed before she was caught in the witch-finders' net. A burial of a widow by the name of Anne Bishop took place at St Peter and St Paul's Church at Wincanton in 3 June 1685. Alice Duke is recorded by Hunt–Glanvill as also being known by the alias 'Manning'. There is no trace of the burial of an Alice Duke of Wincanton but an Alice Manning was buried there on 28 November 1685; she was probably the same Alice Manning whose name can be found in the 1670 Hearth Tax exemption record, signed off by Robert Hunt and his fellow magistrate William Bull. In both cases, given the absence of Anne Bishops and Alice Mannings/Dukes buried elsewhere in Somerset in the period, these appear to be the Wincanton witches and they are records of lives that in a different context might well have been cut short by over twenty years.

As for Elizabeth Style, I have not found a trace of her in the records of Stoke Trister, although three people with the same surname were baptised there between 1593 and 1599 and a child was buried in 1611. However, she might have been the 'Eliz. Stile widow' who appears in the 1664/5 Hearth Tax exemption records for a place then known as Brook in the Stourton with Gasper civil parish close to Stoke Trister – a poor woman who, like the Elizabeth Style in the Hunt/Glanvill narrative, must have longed for the money and the 'pleasure of the World for twelve years' promised by the Devil in 1664. There is a possibility that she had been brought before a judge on a witchcraft charge earlier in her life. A record for the assize held at Chard on 7 March 1635/6 reads as follows:

> Whereas Elizabeth Stile, widow, was indicted at this assizes for witchcraft and upon her trial was acquitted, and forasmuch as it appeared to this court that she was maliciously prosecuted by her adversaries, it is ordered by this court at the humble request of the said Elizabeth that she shall be admitted *in forma pauperis* to bring her action against Nicholas Hobbes and all or any other of her prosecutors. And Mr Glanville [John Glanville, recorder of Plymouth], Mr Rolles, Mr Fynche, and Mr Morgan are assigned to be her council, and Mr Champion to be her attorney therein.[42]

I can find no sure sign of this impoverished woman's malicious accuser, Nicholas Hobbes, in the records of the period although Hobbes was quite a common name in neighbouring Wincanton. The extraordinary step of the judge in directing four eminent lawyers to defend the woman has led Malcolm Gaskill to conclude that it is not surprising 'that even when magistrates were willing, accusers declined to take the risk' of pursuing a prosecution.[43] The available data for the decade before the Civil War implies considerable judicial resistance at circuit level to accepting as sufficient the sort of 'proofs' of which Bernard had written in the late 1620s. The witch-hunts and successful prosecutions of the Civil War era and thereafter were 'a spectacular reversal after almost twenty bloodless years on the Home Circuit'.[44]

Style's trial at Taunton and death in prison – 'she prevented her Execution by dying in Gaol'[45] – are mentioned by Glanvill but the fate of the rest of her 'hellish Knot' is unknown. However, Jonathan Barry has found evidence that might indicate that her allies and acolytes were also tried at Taunton. A letter by James Hickes, dated 17 March 1665, noted how it was reported that:

> The prisoners being all taken out of the gaol [at Ilchester] to go to Taunton to their trial, the under-keeper desired the old witch to show the people one of her pranks before she went thence, which desire she readily complied and the people bidden to stand around the yard, the old witch took up her coats round and immediately the under-keeper fell down of his knees and kissed her britch round with such an ardent affection that there was much ado to get him up.[46]

Perhaps these prisoners included more of Style's supposed coven; it is quite likely that the 'old witch' was Style herself. The episode underlines the inversion element of the seventeenth-century witchcraft paradigm – the sexualisation of an old woman and the magical seduction and subjugation of her gaoler.

* * *

Glanvill's Relation V is set in the Selwood Forest parish of Brewham, about two miles north of Stoke Trister. It comprises Hunt's 'Examination and Confession of Christian Green, aged about thirty three years, Wife of Robert Green of Brewham' which took place on 2 March 1664/5.[47] Christian (née Ittery) married 'Robert Cornish of Broueme, Somerset' at nearby Mere across the county border in Wiltshire, presumably her home parish, on 25 November 1655 – the same place where John Cooms married Alice Dick (Duke?) in 1634. Robert Green's burial record for November 1686 survives and it confirms his (and hence her) alias: Cornish.

She claimed that she first met the Devil at 'Mr Hussey's Ground in Brewham Forest',[48] otherwise known as 'Hussey's Knap', a knap being the crest of a hill. Exactly where this place was is unknown but it might well refer to the wooded ridge on the south-east edge of the parish, close to Alfred's Tower, the well-known local landmark built a century later. Lyndal Roper has remarked that 'at the height of the witch craze', when witches spoke of their night-time meetings, 'the sites they described were often tucked away locally', usually in some 'isolated area or at the edge of habitation; or in the woods'.[49] 'Mr Hussey' could well have been William Hussey of Brewham who is recorded in a minor case presided over by Robert Hunt ten years later on 26 April 1675:

> Evidences given by Richard Perry of Doulting, Husbandman, John Sheppard of North Brewham, and William Hussey of Brewham, against William Morrice of Henstridge and Robert Ryall of Stourton, Wiltshire, that they swore in court that Thomas Morrice of Henstridge paid Richard Perry money owed to him, that the jury gave a verdict against Richard Perry as a result, and that Richard Perry was not present on the day the money was allegedly paid. JP: Robert Hunt.[50]

This gentleman, his status confirmed by the insertion of the 'Mr' title in the parish register, buried two daughters there in the 1680s. Barry has noted that the Husseys were a well-established Dorset family, some members of which were known recusants. They owned manors in both Marnhull[51] and Henstridge.[52] The self-confessed Brewham witches also claimed to have met at Brewham Common and a place called Redmore. The 1811–1817 series Ordnance Survey map identifies Brewham Common as constituting the area directly to the north of the later settlement of North Brewham.[53] In 1662 there were between 200 and 300 acres of common in the parish.[54] Redmore was an extra-parochial district of Brewham in the vicinity of Brewham Lodge, below the source of the River Brue, where the Selwood ridge, to the north of Alfred's Tower, 'falls westwards to 110 m. (360 ft.) where the Brue, which formed the district boundary for a short distance, joined a tributary, also a boundary'.[55] Redmore Lake was recorded in the sixteenth century, probably identifying the pool formed where the two water courses met.

At Hussey's Knap Green made her covenant with the Devil, 'in the shape of a Man in blackish Cloths', having been persuaded that in so doing she might evade her present state of acute poverty. Such were the promises he made in return for her body and soul, and her commitment to 'suffer him to suck her once in twenty-four hours'. This condition blurs any distinction between the demonic 'Man in black' and the witch's demon-familiar. He left his mark on her body, sealing the deal by pricking 'the fourthe Finger of her Right-hand, between the middle and upper Joints'. The tell-tale mark could still be seen at the time of her examination. After giving her 'four-pence-half-penny', with which she brought bread in Brewham, he vanished 'leaving a smell of Brimstone behind'. Thereafter each day at around five in the morning, mostly in a trance, she allowed her familiar, in the form of a hedgehog, to suckle her left breast which gave her considerable pain.[56]

Green was the first of six Brewham people examined by Hunt between March and June 1665, the statements of the other five appearing in *Saducismus Triumphatus* as Relation VI.[57] Those with her 'in Covenant with the Devil' – her coven – included two more Brewham women, Catharine Green and Margaret Agar, and, 'three or four times', Mary Warberton also of Brewham. 'That rampant Hagg' Agar's supposed crimes are the main focus of these testimonies. She had been sent to prison some time before 3 June 1665, probably by the time Green made her own confession on 2 March 1664/5.[58] Her examination for some reason was not included in Glanvill's relations; perhaps another JP heard her case and had her arrested while Hunt sought evidence among her Brewham allies, acolytes and victims prior to the next assizes. The researcher of seventeenth-century Brewham is greatly inconvenienced by the virtual absence of register evidence for the two decades between 1640 and 1660 but the surviving record, nevertheless, still sheds light on its history of witchcraft: Agar, it appears, survived the ordeal and was buried in the parish on 20 September 1670. Warberton appears in the Hearth Tax exemption records for North Brewham in 1670 and again, now listed as a widow, in 1674, and she was buried on 23 January 1676/7.

They met the Devil again at Hussey's Knap and also on Brewham Common. Christian provided a concise description of the mode of their witchcraft at these meetings:

> Margaret Agar brought [...] an Image in Wax for Elizabeth the Wife of Andrew Cornish of Brewham,[59] and the Devil in the shape of a Man in black Cloths did Baptize it, and after stuck a Thorn into its Head; [...] Agar stuck one into its Stomach, and Catharine Green one into its side. She further saith, that before this time, Agar said to her this Examinant, that she would hurt Eliz. Cornish, who since

the Baptizing of the Picture hath been taken and continues very ill.[60]

Shifting the blame onto her associates, she told Hunt how her mother-in-law, another Catharine Green, had fallen sick five or six years ago: 'One day one Eye and Cheek did swell, another day another, and so she continued in great pain, till she died'.[61] The woman was convinced she had been bewitched by her own sister-in-law, Christian Green's fellow-covenanter, Catharine Green, and Christian believed the same. Her mother-in-law died shortly before Hunt commenced his examinations and, according to the parish register, she was buried on 10 December 1664. Green also accused Catharine of cursing to death three horses belonging to Robert Walter[62] of Brewham.

Elizabeth Talbot reiterated Green's account of how Agar, a year earlier, had bewitched to death her father Joseph Talbot, the Overseer of the Poor who 'made her Children go to Service, and refused to give them such good Cloths as she desired'. Elizabeth Talbot described the suddenness of her father's illness and its severity, 'as if he had been stabb'd with Daggers'; after 'four or five days in great pain' he died.[63] Joseph Smith, described as a husbandman, was another witness in the affair and one who claimed he had heard Agar curse Talbot, swearing 'by the Blood of the Lord' he had not long to live, that soon his body would be carried to its grave on the four men's shoulders, and that once he was buried she 'should tread on his Jaws'. Mary, the wife of William Smith, complained Agar had called her an 'old Whore' and declared, 'I shall live to see thee rot on the Earth before I die, and thy Cows shall fall and die at my feet'. Sure enough, three of her cows died shortly afterwards, two at the door of Agar's home. Mary herself had fallen sick, 'her Body and Bowels rotting', and she was convinced Agar's witchcraft was the cause.[64] She outlived the alleged witch by just four months and was buried in Brewham at the start of February 1670/1.

Catharine Green, alias Cornish, confirmed Mary Smith's claims and also the part Agar played in Talbot's death. In addition, she confessed to participation in a meeting at Hussey's Knap with the 'little man in black Cloths' at which image-magic was deployed to cause the illness of Elizabeth Cornish.[65] Mary Green, described as a single woman, confessed to her involvement in the night-time meetings at Hussey's Knap and Redmore, and, in addition to corroborating much of Christian and Catharine Green's accounts, she also listed several more participants: a fourth Green named Alice, Dinah and Dorothy Warberton, Joan Syms, Margaret Clark, and Henry Walter. The little man in black she described as wearing a hat, speaking 'low but big', and answering to the name 'Robin'.[66] Their evil deeds included, two years before Mary Green's examination, the murder by witchcraft of Richard/Dick Green. The names of most of these characters can be found in the parish records. Alice, wife of George Green, was buried there at the start of February 1673/4; for Dorothy Warberton there seems to be no trace but a Dinah Warberton was baptized in the parish in 1617 and she or her namesake was buried on 28 April 1675; a Joane Symes was baptised there in 1602, and Joan, wife of Henry Symes, was buried there in March 1668/9; Margaret Clark (Clerk/Clarke), a widow whose husband had died many years before, was buried at St John's, Brewham, in April 1666; Henry Walter went to his Brewham grave in March 1687/8. The evidence strongly suggests that at least three of the five women in Mary Green's list were in their fifties or sixties at the time of their accusation. Their supposed victim, Richard Green alias Cornish, had been buried in the village at the end of April 1663. As for Mary Green herself it seems likely she too was part of the Cornish family and closely related to the other Greens and Cornishes in the accounts. She may well have been the Mary Cornish baptized in the parish in 1621. A Mary Green, an impoverished widow, appears in the 1664/5 Hearth Tax record for neighbouring Brook (now known as Gasper) – the parish which has been identified above as possibly being Elizabeth Style's place of residence. However, it was a common name: five people called Mary Green were buried in Brewham between 1666 and 1689.

The witches from this small village on the south-eastern edge of Selwood Forest conformed to the established stereotype – 'a herd of poor quarrelsome, bickering females who went from house to house seeking alms' as Notestein put it.[67] They seemed to engage in fewer magical practices than their Wincanton counterparts. At their meetings the Devil ('the Fiend'[68]) as a man in black is depicted as the centre of attention but there is no mention of feasting or music and dancing. Their *maleficia* was enacted through curses and the piercing of a wax doll – no poison apples or bewitched dishes, no touching of the victim, and just one reference to familiars. Furthermore, there is no hint of magical transportation to their meeting places, all of which seem to have been within easy walking distance of their homes. More striking is the clear evidence, as in many other cases,[69] of the close and familial relationship between the accused, their accusers and their alleged victims. Whatever else was going on there can be no doubt that this was the product of vicious, internecine feuds in a remote rural community, some involved living on the margin, hopelessly dependent on, or in competition with, their neighbours.

Table 1 *The accused and their alleged victims in the Brewham witchcraft cases of 1664-5.*

Accused	Victims
Margaret Agar	Catharine Green, mother-in-law of Christian Green, sister-in-law of Catharine Green (death by witchcraft)
Margaret Clark	
Alice Green	
Catharine Green, alias Cornish	Elizabeth, wife of Andrew Cornish (physically injured by witchcraft)
Christian Green, alias Cornish (wife of Robert Green alias Cornish)	
Mary Green (alias Cornish?)	Richard Green, alias Cornish (death by witchcraft)
Joan Syms	Mary Smith (physically injured by witchcraft)
Mary Warberton	
Dinah Warberton	Joseph Talbot, Overseer of the Poor (death by witchcraft)
Dorothy Warberton	
Henry Walter	Robert Walter (property injured by witchcraft)

* * *

GLANVILL DECLARED HE had 'shortened the examinations' in Hunt's book and 'cast them into such an order' as he considered 'fittest for the rendering of the matter clear and intelligible'. As with the Jane Brooks case, there is enough information to summarise the events, through a synthesis of the statements of the many witnesses and those accused, as a detailed chronological narrative. Some of Hunt's examinations seem to have been formal court-room proceedings, notably the hearings at Wincanton on Monday 26 January 1665, but some were probably conducted more informally elsewhere – sometimes at Hunt's home in Compton Pauncefoot. Between 23 January and 15 March he heard the statements of at least thirteen people across thirteen days of interrogation. The sequence of the hearings suggests that his interest in illicit meetings in Stoke Trister somehow prompted similar allegations in Brewham – just as he was completing his Stoke Trister enquiries, the Brewham ones began. Perhaps the impoverished widows living at Brook in 1664, Elizabeth Style and Mary Green, who shared the names of alleged witches in each place respectively, had something to do with the reason for why Hunt's attention moved a few miles to the north in his continuing search.

Late November 1664: start of thirteen-year-old Elizabeth Hill's illness.

***c.*11 December 1664:** Richard Hill, yeoman of Stoke Trister, accuses Elizabeth Style of bewitching his daughter; three Stoke Trister men (Francis White, and Walter, and Robert Thick) urge Style to make a complaint to the justices but she declines.

Late December 1664: following the sabbat meeting of Style and three companions (Alice Duke, Anne Bishop, Mary Penny) with a man in black near Trister Gate, a wax doll, 'which was for Elizabeth Hill', is anointed and pierced with thorns. The man in black leads the ceremonies and provides wine, cakes and roast meat. They meet again a second time at the same place and direct their *maleficium* against Robert Newman's child, a man who was first targeted five and a half years before. They and 'several others' meet or have met (for at least the past five and a half years) at other places including Marnhull.

Monday 29 December 1664: Elizabeth Hill suffers the first of five or six severe fits in which thorns are found in her flesh and six strong men struggle to hold her in her chair; this is witnessed by several people including Rector William Parsons of Stoke Trister, and Nicholas Lambert, a yeoman; at around this time ('a little after Christmas') Style is subjected by five women to a full body search.

Friday 23 January 1665: Richard Hill is interviewed by Robert Hunt. This is probably the occasion when Hunt gives Hill a warrant 'to bring Style before him'; as he rides home from Hunt's home at Compton Pauncefoot Hill's horse proves very reluctant to make the return journey.

Monday 26 January 1665: at Wincanton, butcher Richard Vining and Elizabeth Style are examined before Robert Hunt. Vining claims Agnes, his wife, who fell out with Style about three years earlier, was bewitched to death by her (probably in 1663) after Agnes had eaten 'a very fair red apple' she had given her. Hunt declares Style is an 'old sinner' and one deserving 'little mercy'; Style is placed in the custody of the constable, Mr Gapper, at his home in Bayford.

Tuesday 27 January 1665: Hunt, together with JPs Mr Bull and Mr Court, visit Gapper's house; Style is watched through the night of 26/27 by the Bayford yeoman, Nicholas Lambert, and two of his neighbours, William Thick and William Read; Style's familiar appears in the form of a fly.

Friday 30 January 1665: Lambert testifies before JP Hunt to what he has witnessed; Style is further examined and makes certain confessions; first examination before Hunt of Alice Duke; examination of Walter Thick (mentioned in SRO manuscript but not *Saducismus*) who accuses Style of having bewitched two oxen and a cow – an act of revenge because he denied her request for Pease.

Monday 2 February 1665: second examination of Alice Duke before Hunt.

Saturday 7 February 1665: Style is examined again before Hunt and makes further confessions; Rector Parsons provides a sworn witness statement to the validity of Style's recorded confessions; Elizabeth Torwood is examined and testifies to the findings of the search of Style's body; this is validated by the other four women engaged in the search; third examination of Alice Duke.

Tuesday 10 February 1665: fourth examination of Alice Duke before Hunt.

Thursday 12 February 1665: examination before Hunt of Thomas Conway regarding Duke's alleged bewitching of his daughter.

Saturday 21 February 1665: fifth examination of Alice Duke before Hunt.

Friday 6 March 1665: examination before Hunt of Mary, wife of Thomas Conway, regarding Duke's alleged bewitching of their daughter; also of Edward Watts who claims his daughter, Edith, is also bewitched by Duke.

Monday 2 March 1665: Christian Green, thirty-three-year-old wife of Robert Green, examined before Robert Hunt, confesses to being persuaded, in the summer of 1663, by Catherine Green (alias Cornish) to meet the Devil appearing as a man in blackish clothes at Hussey's Ground in Brewham Forest with whom she makes a diabolical pact; she also declares Margaret Agar told her she had bewitched Joseph Talbot to death, and that she believes her sister-in-law, Catherine Green, murdered her mother-in-law, also called Catherine Green, who fell ill five or six years ago, using witchcraft.

Saturday 7 March 1665: Elizabeth Talbot is examined before Hunt concerning the supposed death by witchcraft of her husband, Joseph Talbot, Overseer for the Poor, in February 1664.

Sunday 8 March 1665: Mary Smith, wife of William, is examined before Hunt and claims she has been bewitched by Margaret Agar.

Sunday 15 March 1665: Joseph Smith is examined before Hunt who brings evidence incriminating Agar concerning the death of Joseph Talbot.

Monday 16 May 1665: Catherine Green (alias Cornish), a Brewham widow, is examined before Hunt concerning the supposed recent bewitchment of Elizabeth Cornish, and the death in the previous year of Joseph Talbot.

Tuesday 3 June 1665: Mary Green, a single woman of Brewham, is examined before Hunt concerning the death of Talbot; she provides details of meetings with the man in black spread over the previous two years, and explains how Richard Green was killed by witchcraft.

These accounts raise a number of important but unanswerable questions. Are the recorded examinations accurate transcriptions of actual proceedings? Did the accused engage in any kind of magical practices? Did they ever meet in a secret place to participate in secret rituals? Was there an actual 'man in black' co-ordinating their activities? Were their confessions entirely imagined – the fantasies of the powerless, the isolated, and the oppressed?[70] Were they guided to the 'correct' answers by a series of carefully worded leading questions? The maverick writer and historian Montague Summers, the man who published, in 1928, the first English translation of the famous German fifteenth-century witch-hunter's manual, the *Malleus Maleficarum*, answered these questions with an unswerving conviction of the reality of these sabbat meetings:

> In his *Displaying of Supposed Witchcraft*, 1677, John Webster had suggested with reference to Margaret Agar, and other 'deluded Haggs' of the Brewham coven, tried at Taunton during the June Assizes of 1665, that the 'little Man in black Clothes with a little band' who presided over the meeting at Hussey's Knap, a coppice near the hamlet, and who instructed the crew in moulding wax figurines and pricking them with thorns was the local Grand Master, a man-Devil, and Burns Begg points out that the witches on occasion 'seem to have been undoubtedly the victims of unscrupulous and designing knaves who personated Satan'. This, however, is no palliative of their crimes, and they are not one whit the less guilty of sorcery and devil-worship if they obey and adore a representative of Satan, rather than the demon himself. Nor do I think that the man who personated Satan at these horrid assemblies was so much an unscrupulous and scheming knave as himself a demonist, believing intensely in the reality of his own dark powers, wholly and horribly dedicated and doomed to the service of evil.[71]

This concept of a 'Grand Master' impersonating Satan is one that must be considered a possibility, albeit a most unlikely one. What is less acceptable for most investigators in the first quarter of the twenty-first century is Summers's conviction that the Devil himself sometimes made an appearance:

> It is certain that he can do so, that he has done and yet does so very frequently, and the number of cases in the records of trials which are to be explained in no other way, that is to say where the devil manifests himself in some shape, appears to and has most intimate connections with his besotted worshippers, are extremely numerous, and from what I know I am persuaded that we may safely avouch that today the demon is more frequently himself present at the modern

day sabbats than he functions through a deputy.[72]

By Summers's reckoning the witches who gathered for their sabbat meetings in clearings in Selwood Forest in the mid-seventeenth century were part of a 'definite and disciplined organisation of the infernal cult of Satanism, which is one and the same the world over'. Writing in the era of Aleister Crowley, the infamous practitioner of magic, he believed this early modern cult could well be the direct ancestor of 'the London Sabbats of the present day'.[73]

As for the claims of witchcraft victims such as Richard Jones of Shepton Mallet and Mary Hill of Beckington, Summers was certain that 'angels, be they blessed spirits or demons, have the power to move matter. The levitation of sorcerers is effected by the agency of evil forces, devils who bestow this favour upon an auxiliary and a companion'.[74] Juliette Wood has suggested that the continuing popular interest in Summers's witchcraft-related output is the 'air of delicious decadence' in his analyses which, equally, helps explain why he has been 'dropped by serious witchcraft scholars'. Indeed, Wood continues, 'Summers' influence on popular culture [novels, films etc.], in particular gothic horror, is undoubtedly more significant than his influence on witchcraft historiography'.[75]

However, the later twentieth-century 'witch as victim' model can also be challenged for over-simplifying, if not mythologizing, matters. Gaskill has asserted 'most witches were innocent in the sense that they had not attempted *maleficium* or even thought themselves capable of it', even if they confessed to maleficence retrospectively, but recognises that they, like their accusers, almost certainly believed in magic.[76] Although historians have been reluctant to state it, the logic of this argument is that there is no reason *not* to suppose that at least some individuals or, conceivably, small groups of people, actually practised black magic. Gaskill provided a few possible examples,[77] even though, in his opinion, the feasts in the confessions of the Selwood witches in 1664 were fantasies. Witchcraft in early modern mentalities was 'a potential source of power by which the weak [could have] sought to free themselves from the constraints of daily life and re-route their destinies'.[78]

Summers's contemporary, Margaret Murray, was also convinced that these statements of those interviewed in Somerset and recorded by Glanvill were sure evidence of witchcraft assemblies. Like Summers she identified an organised religion, concluding that 'All the Covens of Somerset, 1664, were evidently under one Chief'. She noted one curious, repeated detail (mentioned above) in the testimonies of the witches:

> The Somerset witches, in 1664, were marked on the fingers; it was stated of Elizabeth Style that the Devil 'prickt the fourth Finger of hir right hand, between the middle and upper joynt (where the sign at the Examination remained)'; of Alice Duke, that 'the Devil prickt the fourth finger of her right hand between the middle and upper joynt (where the mark is yet to be seen)'; and of Christian Green, that 'the Man in black prickt the fourth finger of her Right-hand between the middle and upper joints, where the sign yet remains'.[79]

This, she supposed, was the ring finger and thus it marked the 'marriage' of witch and Devil. Murray noted too the exceptional detail the Somerset cases provided regarding the application of magical flying ointment, the ritual of making and pricking wax or clay figurines of the witches' victims, and the sabbat feast for which the Somerset trials 'give more detail than any of the other English cases'.[80] Murray was absolutely correct in identifying the importance of the Selwood Forest cases but entirely wrong in making them fit a pre-conceived model of an aberrant pagan cult. This fiction had a lasting impact upon popular culture in the twentieth century through the multiple reprints between 1929 and 1968 of her seminal essay on the subject in the *Encyclopaedia Britannica*.[81]

1 Glanvill, *Saducismus*, 62.
2 *Ibid.*, 345–58.
3 A child named Richard Hill was baptized in the village in 1606.
4 Probably all of Style's advisors were men of standing in the village – tythingman White drew up the hearth tax exemption record for the village that year, and the Thicks shared the same surname as its two churchwardens, William and Thomas Thick.
5 Glanvill, *Saducismus*, 346.
6 *Ibid.*

7 The names Day, Boulster and Prankett all appear in the short list of hearth tax exemptions for Stoke Trister in the same year.
8 Glanvill, *Saducismus*, 357.
9 Ewen, *Witchcraft and Demonianism*, 344.
10 Barry, *Witchcraft and Demonology*, 24.
11 Lewis Bayly, *The Practice of Piety, directing a Christian how to walk that he may please God* (1611) – a highly influential guide to a godly life, widely read, written by the puritan Bishop of Bangor.
12 Glanvill, *Saducismus*, 357.
13 John Gaule, *Select Cases of Conscience* (1646).
14 David L. Jones, *The Ipswich Witch: Mary Lackland and the Suffolk Witch Hunts* (Stroud: The History Press, 2015), 132.
15 The hearth tax exemption record for that year includes one Richard Viminge who was too poor to be rated; a Richard Vining was buried in the village in 1667, a couple of years after these events.
16 Barry, *Witchcraft and Demonology*, 37.
17 Glanvill, *Saducismus*, 349.
18 *Ibid.*, 350.
19 He might have been recently bereaved – Thomas Gapper and his wife Elizabeth buried a daughter in the parish in 1663.
20 William Bull was Hunt's son-in-law and Edward Court was Bull's son-in-law.
21 Sharpe, *Instruments*, 76–77.
22 Malcolm Gaskill, 'Witchcraft, Politics, and Memory in Seventeenth-Century England', *The Historical Journal*, Volume 50, 2 (2007), 289–308.
23 The clerical style of dress in which the Devil is portrayed in the accompanying woodcut of this meeting suggests the 'band' (i.e. neckband) is the simple 'dog collar' he is shown wearing around his neck.
24 Glanvill, *Saducismus*, 352.
25 *Ibid.*, 353.
26 William Henry Davenport Adams, *Witch, Warlock and Magician: historical sketches of magic and witchcraft in England* (New York: J. W. Boughton, 1889).
27 Barry (2012) gives the example of such festivities on Holy Rood Day in Motcombe – one of the places named in the Elizabeth Style case as a meeting place of witches.
28 Barry (2012) has noted that William Barnes (1801–86), the Dorset poet,

heard that a corner of Leigh Common was known locally as 'Witches' Corner'.
29 Barry, *Witchcraft and Demonology*, 39.
30 Alice Duke confessed 'That she hurt Dorothy the Wife of George Vining, by giving an Iron slate to put into her steeling Box'. Glanvill, *Saducismus*, 361.
31 Glanvill, *Saducismus*, 358–64.
32 Popular Somerset tradition dressed witches (and fairies) in red hooded cloaks. 'Ol Mother Redcap' is recorded as a nickname for a 'wise woman'; Michael Howard, *West Country Witches* (California: Three Hands Press, California, 2010), 188–9.
33 Margaret Murray, *The Witch-Cult in Western Europe: a Study in Anthropology* (Oxford: Clarendon Press, 1921), 188.
34 Glanvill, *Saducismus*, 361.
35 Barry, *Witchcraft and Demonology*, 47.
36 'Richard' Garret in the Barnes version, according to Barry.
37 Glanvill, *Saducismus*, 361.
38 *Ibid.*, 363.
39 Barry, *Witchcraft and Demonology*.
40 In addition there is a gap in Wincanton's record of baptisms, marriages and burials for the period 1610-1619.
41 Barry, *Witchcraft and Demonology*.
42 Thomas G. Barnes, *Somerset Assize Orders, 1629–1640* (Somerset: Somerset Record Society, 1959), 28.
43 Malcolm Gaskill, 'Witchcraft and Evidence in Early Modern England', *Past and Present*, 198 (2008), 45–46.
44 *Ibid.*, 48.
45 Glanvill, *Saducismus*, 345.
46 Barry, *Witchcraft and Demonology*, 17.
47 Glanvill, *Saducismus*, 364–66.
48 In 1839 three distinct areas of woodland in the parish were identified: Brewham Forest, Brewham Wood and Pinkwood. (VCH, 'Brewham', Somerset, Vol. 7.)
49 Roper, *Witch Craze*, 109.
50 SRO Q/SR/126 Sessions roll for 1675.
51 It may be no coincidence that Elizabeth Style identified Marnhull as a place where she met for a ceremony with thirteen others.

52 Barry, *Witchcraft and Demonology*, 39.
53 'The Common' identified today by signs on the green in present-day South Brewham is part of what was formerly known as Shave Common. The site of Brewham Common constituted land going up to the top of James's Hill across the road from the Old Red Lion inn.
54 VCH, 'Brewham', Somerset, Vol. 7.
55 VCH Somerset, Vol. 7, 15-16.
56 Glanvill, *Saducismus*, 365.
57 *Ibid.*, 366–70.
58 Mary Green declared in June 1665 that Margaret Agar had been absent from meetings with the man in black ever since she was sent to prison; Glanvill, *Saducismus*, 370.
59 Probably the Andrew Cornish who was baptised in the Brewham on 19 January 1639/40.
60 Glanvill, *Saducismus*, 365.
61 *Ibid.*, 366.
62 Buried 21 February 1691/2.
63 Glanvill, *Saducismus*, 366-67.
64 *Ibid.*, 367.
65 *Ibid.*, 368.
66 *Ibid.*, 369–70.
67 Notestein, *Witchcraft in England*, 525.
68 Glanvill, *Saducismus*, 369.
69 These themes, with copious examples, have been explored by Malcolm Gaskill; Gaskill, *Crime and Mentalities* (2000), 54-78.
70 On this David Underdown has remarked: 'It may seem odd to place the witch in the category of independent women, the typical suspect being usually old and powerless. But witchcraft fantasies were often a response of the powerless to isolation and oppression that were both social and sexual in origin'. Underdown, *Revel, Riot, and Rebellion*, 40.
71 Montague Summers, *Witch Covens and the Grand Masters* (c.1930; reprinted by Read Books, 2011), 12.
72 *Ibid.*, 13–14.
73 *Ibid.*, 34.
74 *Ibid.*, 44.
75 Juliette Wood, 'The reality of the witch cults reasserted: fertility and Satanism' in Jonathan Barry and Owen Davies (eds), *Witchcraft*

Historiography (Basingstoke: Palgrave Macmillan, 2007), 69–90.
76 Gaskill, *Crime and Mentalities*, 71-2.
77 Ibid., 72-74.
78 Ibid., 78.
79 Murray, *Witch-Cult*, 309.
80 *Ibid.*
81 Malcolm Gaskill considered Murray's writing the seed of some of the most persistent and damaging of witchcraft-history myths, 'nurtured by pagans and feminists' fifty years after she developed them in the 1920s (Gaskill, 'The Pursuit of Reality', 1078). My own experience of teaching for almost thirty years at an institution a mile or so from Glastonbury has revealed that they remain robust in contemporary 'alternative' culture.

5

PANDAEMONIUM

Fig. 5-1 *Devils bewitching Monmouth's army in Somerset in the summer of 1685. (Contemporary playing card)*

The Devil is with you wherever you are, he watches you wherever you go.
— Richard Alleine, 1694.[1]

THESE WERE ANXIOUS times; fears that the plague that had raged in London through the summer months of 1665 must have reminded some of the older inhabitants of Beckington of the terrible outbreak that had hit the region hard in 1625. One nineteenth-century account, referring to 'a very old history of Somerset', speaks of the virtual extinction of the populations of Kingsbury, Muchelney and Long Sutton.² That same year strangers had brought the plague to nearby Frome; the town was saved only by the cruel wisdom of shutting those infected in a remote house where, subsequently, they all died.³ Such disasters were prone to divine explanation 'in a world that most continued to perceive as governed by the hand of a vengeful and providential God'.⁴ Furthermore it was one in which the Devil and his witch-acolytes were also at large.

This was an age of social, political and religious turmoil, and one in which all kinds of real and imagined dangers haunted the lives of those who lived through it. Post-medieval existential doubts manifested as fears of witchcraft and reinvigorated concerns about ghosts and poltergeists.⁵ Beckington's rector from 1668, May Hill, who was instrumental in recording the 1689 witchcraft episode in the village, was born at a point between March 1643 and March 1644, and his earliest memories were of the era of England's most devastating civil war. His youth was passed in the chaotic age of Cromwell's Protectorate, the Interregnum as it would come to be known, his early manhood coincided with the restoration of the monarchy under Charles II, and his middle age with the Monmouth Rebellion, crushed in 1685 in the heart of Somerset, and the Glorious Revolution that overthrew James II in 1688. The witchcraft panic in his parish the following year was set against a background of recent, savage civil war and the dismal prospect of more to come.

It was the gloomy conclusion of Lawrence Stone that the early modern village was 'a place filled with malice and hatred, its only unifying bond being the occasional episode of mass hysteria which bound together the majority in order to harry and persecute the local witch'.⁶ Three miles north-east of Frome on the Somerset–Wiltshire border the rectory of Beckington and its church lay within the diocese of the Bishop of Bath and Wells. On the eastern bank of the River Frome, it had emerged in the Middle Ages as a prosperous centre of woollen cloth manufacture, noted for its blankets.⁷ Indeed, in the seventeenth century it was regarded as a town rather than a village. Its fine church had been endowed by wealthy clothiers such as John Compton, 'Clothman, of Bekyngton', who, when he died in 1484, gave £8 to the church and 50 marks (just over £33) for a chaplain to pray for his soul in Purgatory for the space of five years.⁸ The pre-eminent land-owning clothier family by the late sixteenth century

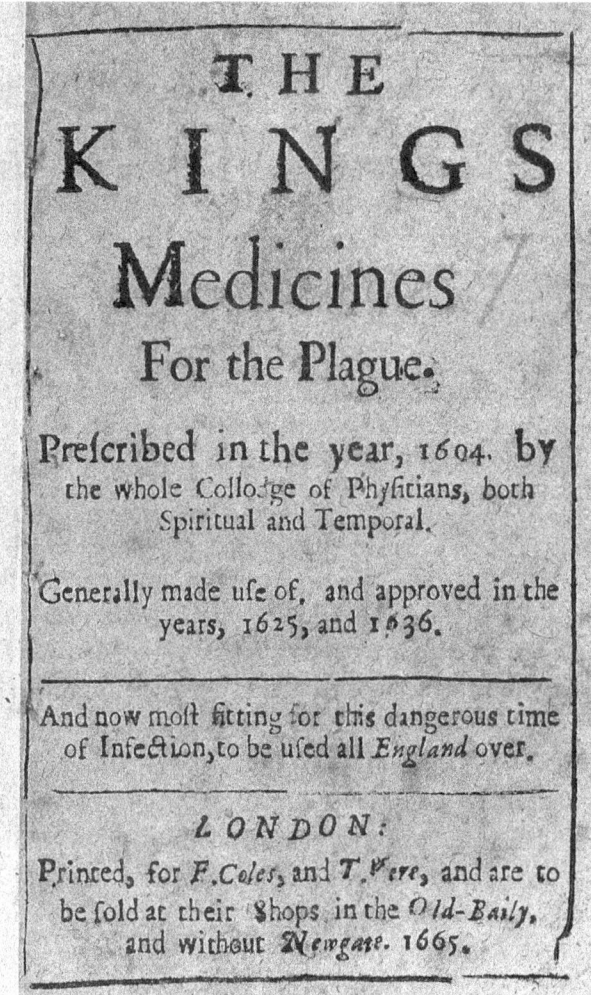

Fig. 5-2 *Pamphlet illuminating the constant and universal fear of plague in seventeenth-century England.*

and into the seventeenth was that of the Webbs. Samuel Daniel, who, Collinson claimed,[9] was Edmund Spenser's successor as Poet Laureate in the reign of Elizabeth I, died in the village in 1619 and a monument in his honour was set up in the church.[10] The village was also the birthplace, in about 1390, of the influential Thomas Bekynton, Bishop of Bath and Wells and political adviser to the inept Henry VI.

In 1689 Frome was entering its manufacturing boom years as a great woollen cloth town. Daniel Defoe observed at the start of the next century that the town had 'prodigiously increased within these last twenty or thirty years [...] now reckoned to have more people in it, than the city of Bath, and some say, than even Salisbury itself'.[11] Beckington was just one among 'innumerable villages, hamlets, and scattered houses, in which, generally speaking, the spinning work of all this manufacture is performed by the poor people; the master clothiers, who generally live in the greater towns, sending out the wool weekly to their houses, by their servants and horses, and, at the same time, bringing back the yarn that they have spun and finished, which then is fitted for the loom'.[12]

By the time Collinson published his history of Somerset in 1791, over a hundred years after the witchcraft episode of 1689, Beckington's own heyday had passed:

> Beckington is a village of several streets, situated in the turnpike-road between Bath and Frome, from the former of which it is distant ten miles, and from the latter three. It was formerly a town of considerable importance, and carried on a large manufacture of woollen cloths, of which at this day about seven hundred are made here yearly.[13]

Ten years later the 1801 census recorded a population of 1469 for the village.[14] It was one of those small communities, of which Edward Bever has written, in which 'contact with strangers is limited, and the bonds that exist are tight' and, in turn, it was a place in which parties in dispute with one another could avoid each other only with difficulty – a place in which hostility, dramatic or subtle, might provoke a crisis.[15]

Beckington's new curate in 1665, May Hill, served the parish in conjunction with its long-established rector, Alexander Huish. The rectory, now a private house, was built at some time in the seventeenth century and, without doubt, was home to Hill if not Alexander Huish.[16] Huish would be remembered for his significant contribution to Bishop Bryan Walton's great polyglot Bible (in nine languages including Hebrew, Greek and Latin), published in 1652. Born in the parish of St Cuthbert's in Wells in about 1594, he went up to Oxford in 1609, transferring from Magdalen Hall to the new Wadham College at the request of its founder, Dorothy Wadham, in

1613. Thus, having completed his BA studies in 1614, he has the distinction of being Wadham's first graduate. He was elected Fellow of Wadham, made Master of Arts in 1616, served the College in a variety of positions, and became a Bachelor of Divinity in 1627. In 1629 he resigned his fellowship, having taken up the Beckington living on 21 December 1628.[17] The parish would soon prove to be for Huish a troublesome 'nest of Puritans'.[18] He and his wife, Deborah,[19] had two daughters, Deborah and Anne, the latter marrying Hill in 1675.[20] Huish died in April 1668 having 'done extraordinary benefit for the common good'.[21] Hill, by now a Perpetual Vicar and preacher at the archdeaconry of Wells, succeeded him and remained the incumbent of St George's until his own death in April 1700.

Huish supported the views of William Laud, the High Church scholar (and another Oxford man) who was rewarded with the archbishopric of Canterbury in 1633. Laud's insistence on the reinstatement of certain traditional Catholic practices, and his hard-line treatment of those who opposed him, made him the focus of a vociferous puritan opposition. That Huish should prove himself a committed Laudian is not surprising – his bishop for the diocese of Bath and Wells, at the time of his appointment to Beckington in 1628, was Laud himself.[22] By this time the reign of Charles I had begun (1625) and Laud's opinions, which challenged those of the popular puritanism of the times, began to have a significant influence upon clerical preferment. In a list he compiled for the king, who shared Laud's enthusiasm for episcopal order, discipline and ritual in the English Church, the names of prominent clerics were identified with an 'O' for orthodox and 'P' for puritan to help guide the king in his patronage.[23]

For puritan, or merely conservative, congregations, the most obvious Laudian abuse was the relocation of the communion table from the centre of the choir, its typical position in most parish churches, to the east end in the style of the cathedrals and the king's own chapel. In 1635 Rector Huish found himself in conflict with his Beckington churchwardens, John Frye and James Wheller, when they refused to remove the communion table in St George's 'where it stood in the chancel fairly encompassed with wainscot'.[24] For failing to carry out this instruction – which Huish had of his bishop, William Piers of Bath and Wells – Frye and Wheller were excommunicated for a year. When in 1636 Thomas Homes and Thomas Dunnings were directed by Piers to remove the table they too objected and, according to subsequent parliamentary proceedings, 'told him they thought they could not answer it to a parliament'. Allegedly, the bishop jeered, 'What tell you me of a parliament – when the sky falls we shall catch larks'. A riot of some kind ensued which led to arrests and assize court proceedings. Allegedly, one of the judges at the subsequent trials, Lord Finch, replaced a jury appointed by the sheriff with one comprising 'young ignorant men', and some of the rioters were imprisoned for six months and ruined by a fine of £2,000. The man testifying against them and accusing them of sedition was Alexander Huish. It was later reported that Huish 'and the rest that assisted him', once the rioters were dispersed, 'cut up the wainscot about the communion table'. Assize records reveal that another rioter, Thomas Jones, 'made his humble submission to his lordship' in advance of the assizes of 1639.[25] When Parliament met in 1640, sitting for the first time in twelve years, a petition from Beckington detailing Huish's innovations in services at St George's resulted in his arrest and a period of imprisonment at Chalfield[26] near Bradford-on-Avon.[27] He was described in the proceedings of the Long Parliament's opening session in December 1640 as 'a most wicked popish fellow' and 'the wicked parson of Beckington'. His removal from the parish is evident in the almost total absence of entries in the parish register between 1642 and 1647 when, in a different hand, they resume.[28] He was formally dispossessed of the parish in 1650 and replaced by John Aster. The civil registration of births, marriages and deaths was maintained by John Horsman who lived in the village on Bath Road at the house now known as The Cedars. At much the same time the manor of Beckington was purchased by the fabulously wealthy John Ashe, clothier of Freshford.[29] The Beckington altar squabble is remembered as the most famous of grass-roots Laudian-era ecclesiastical disputes.[30] The survival of nonconformist tradition within the parish is evident in its having an independent Baptist church by the time of the Restoration.[31]

Huish was reinstated in 1660 and John Aster was removed. Although Aster departed for London many ejected ministers in the region stayed put, some stubbornly continuing to provide spiritual services for their congregations in illicit meetings ('conventicles'). In May 1688 James

II was informed that there were 108,678 Protestant dissenters in his kingdom.³² The Conventicle Act of 1664 had forbidden religious meetings, outside the Church of England, of more than five people. Hence dissenters, avoiding arrest, met in out-of-the-way places, out of doors and at night. Thousands of nonconformists were incarcerated in squalid prisons, where many died.

Selwood Forest in the Restoration era was especially well-known for the prevalence of its nonconformism where meetings, it was recorded in 1670, were held 'in by-corners and in woods and edges of counties or hundreds'.³³ Henry Butler, who, after his ejection at Yeovil in 1662, retired to Witham Friary, very close to both Stoke Trister and Brewham, preached in private homes or, for greater safety, 'Sir Edward Seymour's woods'.³⁴ At much the same time the Bishop of Salisbury railed against the 'divers great and outrageous meetings' held around Warminster.³⁵ Conceivably those named in confessions of meetings of witches were in fact dissenters attending conventicles where all 'did obeisance to the man in black, who was at every one of their meetings'.³⁶ Historians concerned with the demonization of nonconformists after 1660 speak of 'surrogate witches' and dissenters as 'a far more visible enemy of the state'³⁷ than the traditional malefic witch. Conceivably the Stoke Trister/Brewham cases combined the old with the new.

Barry has identified some of the local dissenting ministers who could have been the men (in black clerical garb) leading religious ceremonies that others construed as witches' sabbats. One of these was Edward Bennett, born in South Brewham in 1618. After serving as curate to nearby Batcombe's Richard Bernard, whose *A Guide to Grand-Jury Men* was first published when Bennett was a ten-year-old, he held a living in Dorset from which he was removed in 1662. In 1665, the year in which the Brewham witches were tried, he spent a couple of months in Ilchester gaol before, ultimately, returning to Brewham. Here, in 1672, he was licensed to use his home as a Presbyterian meeting house.³⁸ In 1672 Philip Bennett, the son of Philip Bennett of Brewham (who had married Mary Shute of Bayford/Stoke Trister), is recorded as serving as Somerset's Clerk of the Peace; Barry has considered the possibility that it was he who suppressed Hunt's investigations in the mid-1660s. Allegations concerning clandestine and illegal religious meetings in the parish might well have had very serious implications for members of the Bennett family, not least Edward.

Rector John Batt, born at Kingston Deverill in 1613, was ejected from his Stoke Trister living in 1662. According to Edmund Calamy he seldom preached thereafter and died in 1684 at the age of seventy-one,[39] however he was certainly living in the village at the time of the witchcraft scare – his name is listed in the 1664/5 hearth tax exemption record having 'beaten up one [hearth/chimney] and pulled down one'.[40] Another nonconformist, John Bolster, who ran a grammar school in the parish, preached in and around the village, and 'strangers from all parts' preached in private houses in the locality.[41] Bolster, it is worth recalling, was the surname of both one of the women who searched Style for physical evidence of her diabolical pact and also one of those identified as part of the community attending nocturnal meetings with the man in black. The 'amiable, diligent and pious preacher' William Parker was ejected from Bruton[42] and Bernard's successor, Richard Alleine, was ejected from Batcombe.[43]

In 1648 the 'presbyterial' religious administration of Somerset was divided into several 'classes'.[44] The Somerset part of Selwood Forest was part of the Wells and Bruton class. Each parish within the class was to be provided with 'able Ministers and Elders'. The ministers, some of whom would be ejected, demonized even, at the time of the Restoration, included Robert Balsum (Shepton Mallet), Richard Alleine (Ditcheat), his son, Richard Alleine (Batcombe), William Parker (Bruton), Richard Faircloth (Mells), and William Wright (Frome). The elders named for these parishes, and those to which Presbyterian ministers were yet to be appointed, included Sir John Horner (Mells), Sir Robert Gorges (Redlynch), John Sanders (Bruton), John Keene (Wincanton), Francis Plympton (Wincanton), John Accort (Rodden), John Prankett (Bayford), William Bennett (Brewham) and George Millard (Shepton).

It is tempting to think there is a connection between the alleged meetings of witches in and around Selwood Forest, exposed in early 1665, and the passing of the 1664 Conventicle Act designed to suppress the meetings of dissenters.

Table 2 *Ejected ministers with Selwood Forest associations.*[45]

Minister	Parish	Post-ejection
Henry Albin (1624–1696)	West Camel; Donyatt	Ejected from West Camel in 1660 and Donyatt in 1662. Returned to native parish of Batcombe and continued preaching there and at the home of Thomas Moore at Spargrove; became a licensed preacher in 1687, active at Frome Selwood, Shepton Mallet, Bruton, and Wincanton.
Richard Alleine (1610/11–1681)	Batcombe	Ejected 1662. Retired to Frome Selwood following the introduction of the Five Mile Act where he preached privately until his death 22/12/1681; brief spell in prison for refusing to pay a fine for illicit preaching; licensed to preach as a Presbyterian in Beckington from 1672; published several tracts post-1662.
John Aster	Beckington	Ejected 1662. Moved to London.
Francis Bampfield (c.1615–1683)	Sherborne	Ejected 1662. Arrested for preaching in Shaftesbury (1663) and imprisoned for a time at Dorchester.
John Batt (1613–1684)	Stoke Trister	Ejected 1662. Lived and occasionally preached at the home of a farmer, John Prankett, in Stoke Trister/Bayford in 1665;[46] John Prankett was listed as an elder for Bayford in the 1648 list.
Edward Bennett (1618–1673)	Dorset	Ejected 1662. Formerly curate to both Richard Bernard and Richard Alleine at Batcombe. Returned to South Brewham in 1665 where William Bennett was named as an elder in the 1648 list; active nonconformist preacher; home licensed for Presbyterian meetings in 1672; buried at South Brewham.

Minister	Parish	Post-ejection
Henry Butler (c.1624–1696)	Yeovil	Ejected 1662. Continued to preach in and around Yeovil for a time after 1662 and was often convicted and fined; according to Calamy, 'At length he settled at a place in [Somerset] called Witham Friary, about five miles from Frome, where he was pastor of a congregation [...] meeting his people, either in private houses, or in Sir Edward Seymour's woods, as was thought most safe'.[47]
John Humfrey (c.1621–1719)	Frome	Ejected 1662. Settled in Kingswood, Somerset, where he was licensed to preach in 1672; eventually moved to London where, in 1700, he established a Congregational church at Duke's Place (later relocated in Petticoat Lane); maintained connections with Selwood Forest; prolific writer of tracts post-1662.
William Parker	Bruton	Ejected 1662. Post-ejection career unknown.
Humphrey Phillips (c.1633–1707)	Sherborne	Ejected 1662. Curate to Francis Bampfield. Imprisoned in 1663 (with Bampfield) for eleven months; reported preaching to congregations of 200–300 at various places in Somerset in 1669; licensed to preach in 1672; settled, sometime after 1672, at his estate in Beckington where he continued preaching and was living at the time of the 1689 witchcraft case.

Minister	Parish	Post-ejection
John Sacheverell	Wincanton	Ejected 1662. Arrested with Francis Bampfield at a meeting in Shaftesbury and imprisoned for three years at Dorchester.

The Oxford Act, or Five Mile Act, of 1665, in the words of Samuel Palmer, the eighteenth-century historian of nonconformism, 'restrained all dissenting ministers (on the penalty of £40) who would not take a most unreasonable oath therein specified, from coming within five miles of any city, town corporate, or borough, or any place where they had exercised their ministry'.[48] Those who dissented were kept under the strictures of the earlier legislation. The plight of the ejected after the passing of the act was described by Richard Baxter in his autobiography. One significant observation was his comment on the refusal of some to adhere to its strictures:

> By this Act the case of the ministers was made so hard that many thought themselves necessitated to break it, not only by the necessity of their office, but by a natural impossibility of keeping it, unless they should murder themselves and their families [49]

In 1669 a great meeting of nonconformists was held near the River Frome in a barn at Clifford, on the outskirts of Beckington. Here at least 500 people gathered to hear Edward Hancock preach. This was the greatest congregation that attended his meetings in the locality that year, when he also preached to a hundred at Monkton Combe, a hundred more at a barn in Batheaston, 300 at a sheep-house in Dunkerton and around 300 or 400 at Charlton in Wiltshire.[50] Hancock, clearly a very popular minister, had been ejected in 1664. An investigation into the conventicle at Beckington was conducted by a local JP, George Horner, in 1670.[51]

The effects of senility, the subtle torture of sleep deprivation, and interrogators' leading questions must all be considered when trying to explain cases in Robert Hunt's 'Book of Examinations'. However, the highly detailed accounts of illicit meetings of historically identifiable people at very particular places in and around Stoke Trister and

Brewham at the time of the imposition of the Conventicle Act points to the strong possibility that they had something to do with the meetings of nonconformist congregations, akin to those recorded by Calamy as having taken place in the woods in Brewham's adjoining parish of Witham Friary. In the religious propaganda of the times such meetings might easily be construed as blasphemous, even diabolical. Even so, the confessions of malevolent image magic by the chief protagonists in these tales, Elizabeth Style and Christian Green (closely corroborated by Alice Duke, Catharine Green and Mary Green), remain a problem for those seeking a rational explanation. While there is no reason to suppose, as Margaret Murray once did, this is evidence of the survival of an ancient pagan cult, the dabbling in magical practices by at least some members of those undeniable nonconformist congregations is quite probable given our present understanding of the prevalence of 'cunning folk', popular assumptions regarding the supernatural (fairies, familiars, spectres and the like), and widespread belief in 'magic' in the period. In, what one historian has called 'this climate of fear and accusation',[52] the exposure of the supposed deviance of any one member of a congregation was a valuable weapon in the demonization of the rest – a strategy fully deployed by those engaged in the contemporary campaign to destroy Quakerism. Magistrate Hunt's persecution of the witches of Selwood served a higher purpose – not that of rooting out Satan but that of securing regime change and enforcing conformity in the most volatile period of England's post-medieval history, a time of recurring crisis, compounded in the mid-1660s by the widespread fear of religious 'Fanaticks' conspiring to assist an imminent Dutch invasion.

* * *

THE UNPRECEDENTED WITCHCRAFT activity in and around Selwood Forest since 1657 must have had a profound impact upon May Hill who, years later, would reveal himself in print as a man convinced of its reality. In the remaining seven years of Glanvill's Frome ministry it is most likely that the two men met – indeed, they probably knew each other well. When Hill wrote about the bewitchment in his own parish in 1689 it is reasonable to suppose he had read Glanvill's thoughts on the subject, perhaps in the latest edition of the *Saducismus* that was published in the same year. Although the 1665 trials were exceptional, between 1670 and 1687 there were at least fifteen further witchcraft indictments in Somerset during the years of Hill's ministry in Beckington. In all of these cases, where the outcome is known, the accused was acquitted.

As reasonable as it is to assume that Hill knew Glanvill and that he might well have been familiar with Bernard's *Guide*, it is also highly likely that during the 1680s he would have encountered the arguments of another Somerset man of letters, and a champion for Glanvill, Richard Bovet. Bovet's *Pandaemonium, or, The Devil's Cloyster* (1684)[53], 'being a further blow to modern sadduceism', was published just three years after

Fig. 5-3 *Illustration showing various forms of sorcery in Richard Bovet's* Pandaemonium *(1684)*.

Glanvill's *Saducismus Triumphatus* and a year before what was probably the last execution in England for witchcraft was carried out in Exeter. Pandaemonium was Milton's name for the Devil's palace in the middle of Hell – 'the high capital of Satan and all his peers'.[54] Bovet's 239-page book, 'a weakened solution of Glanvill' as Notestein put it,[55] follows Glanvill's model in being divided into two parts, the first of which is a general and philosophical discussion of demonism and witchcraft, the second of which catalogues a wide range of supernatural happenings and presents these as evidence for the real presence of the Devil in the world. Though a lesser work than the *Saducismus*, *Pandaemonium*, in Sharpe's reckoning, 'demonstrated that an awareness of the new natural philosophy was not inconsistent with serious argument in support of the reality of witchcraft'.[56] It is virulently anti-Catholic, written in the wake of the Exclusion Bill introduced in 1679, and published on the eve of Monmouth's attempt to remove the Catholic king, James II. There is a strong case for reading it as a demonological text with an overtly political agenda at a time when rebellion and a return to civil war threatened.[57] In the struggle against sedition, the biblical dogma 'rebellion is as the sin of witchcraft'[58] was invoked in the demonization of political and/or religious dissenters. While Glanvill (and More) might be seen as 'seeking to walk a line between popery and nonconformist enthusiasm and using witchcraft and the spirit world to vindicate Anglicanism against both threats', Barry (and Bostridge) finds in Bovet 'a devastating contrast between the evils of the Restoration regime' and the republican experiment, the 'good old cause', that preceded it.[59]

Hill's mode of constructing his argument as a list of numbered conclusions, in the account of the Beckington case he delivered to Richard Baxter in 1690, seems to follow the design of Richard Bovet's *Pandaemonium*. Bovet's tale of 'the strange manner of fits which seized the children of Mr Meredith of Bristol', which bears striking resemblances to the Beckington affair, concludes with five numbered points summarising the author's reasons for suspecting bewitchment.

There is uncertainty regarding exactly who Richard Bovet was but it seems he was either Richard Bovet of Bishops Hull near Wellington, or his close relation (son or nephew), Richard, who was born in 1641 and educated at Wadham College, Oxford, and was a writer of poems and other literature. Both men were anti-Jacobite. Richard senior, Colonel Bovet, led one of the regiments formed to support the duke of Monmouth's rebellion in 1685. Both the colonel and his brother Philip were executed in the same year, victims of the dread Judge Jeffreys. The brothers had served in parliament and Richard was MP for Taunton in 1659.

Summers[60] identified the author of *Pandaemonium* as the younger Richard Bovet, a 'country-squire' who lived in South Petherton, twenty miles to the east of Bishops Hull. His account concerning the family of Mrs Aysh of South Petherton appears to confirm the author's familiarity with the place and its inhabitants. Barry, on the other hand, finds Colonel Bovet an equally credible candidate for its authorship. The potentially hazardous writing of such a provocative anti-papal diatribe at this moment in time does seem to chime with what we know of the life of the vigorous parliamentarian who was not averse to taking risks. Associated with numerous post-Restoration plots, according to Barry,[61] his career ended on the battlefield of Sedgemoor a year later. From 1653 to 1659 he served as a JP. He was in attendance at the General Sessions held in April 1653 at Ilchester, named among nine. One of the cases presented at these sessions concerned the alleged witchcraft, the details of which are unknown, of Dorothy Chapple.[62] Another of the magistrates at Ilchester in 1653 was John Cary who, as well as working alongside Bovet, heard evidence at various times in conjunction with Glanvill's informant Robert Hunt, including the Shepton Mallet witchcraft case in 1657, Glanvill's 'Relation II' in *Saducismus Triumphatus*.

Pandaemonium contains a dedication to Henry More, Glanvill's collaborator and fellow member of the Royal Society. It was based on the following premise:

> It is evident, that the Prince of Darkness has a very large dominion among the sons of men; that he has his temples, altars, and sacrifices. Though under new and different names, he continues to attract poor bigoted wretches to pay at his impious shrines that honour, homage, and adoration which is only due to the Most High. There are besides these, another sort of infernal disciples who give themselves up immediately to the conduct and disposal of the Apostate Angel by entering into a league and covenant with him, and giving themselves up to those black and illegal mysteries, which justly are punished with death, both by divine and human law. These have their familiars of the dark region, that assist them in the execution of their hellish purposes; by this means they attain to performances vastly transcending the capacity of human agents, as much as can be supposed that spiritual, and angelical beings exceed in subtlety, agility, and power, beyond anything that can be attempted by mere mortals.[63]

Writing in the same pan-European tradition as Richard Bernard, Bovet recognised the existence of both 'white' and 'black' witches, all of whom were engaged in a diabolical relationship, despite the one having powers to undo the work of the other. Of this apparent contradiction Gregory Durston has noted that Bovet was of the opinion it may have come from 'a form of diabolical apathy, or a rare show of common decency by Satan; as a result '…by a Diabolical Complaisance, or good nature, [they] are to uncharm and give ease to those the other [black witches] have afflicted."[64] Nevertheless, Bovet warned, recourse to 'cunning folk' to counter maleficent witchcraft was itself an exceedingly dangerous engagement with dark arts that were equally satanic. This was a long-established assumption and one clearly stated in William Perkins's *A Discourse of the Damned Art of Witchcraft* first printed in 1608: 'Now howsoever both these be evil, yet of the two the more horrible and detestable monster is the good witch; for look in what place soever there be bad witches that hurt only, there also the Devil hath his good ones, which are better known than the bad, being commonly called wisemen or wise-women'.

The second part of *Pandaemonium*, 'an account of divers most remarkable witchcrafts [...] demons, and spectres, never before published', includes a number of Somerset cases, some close to the Bovet family's Wellington home as well as that of the younger Richard Bovet's home in South Petherton. In these, despite the conviction of doctors that some of the conditions described had natural causes, Bovet searched for, and found, supernatural explanations informed by his reading of Glanvill's *Saducismus Triumphatus*. Once again we hear of victims of witchcraft who levitate and vomit pins. The Seavington[65] episode is another classic 'charity-refused' case of bewitchment. In the same story the witch's familiar is a monstrous toad, reminiscent of that in the story of Julian Cox. Another case involves a manifestation of the Devil in the house of 'Sir J.F.' which is described as being 'near Sherborne', just over the Somerset border into Dorset. In this account a naïve falconer raises the Devil by reading a book containing supernatural, dangerous and unlawful material.

Following Glanvill's example, Bovet seemed quite satisfied to accept any kind of spectral evidence so long as it had been witnessed by sober, respectable folk such as the neighbours of old Mr Ansty, who used to regale them with the terrifying tale of his dead-of-night encounter with a demon in West Coker, near Yeovil in Somerset, on his way home to South Petherton from Woodbury Fair. A fairies' fair is the focus of Bovet's tale of strange happenings near Pitminster on the edge of the Blackdown Hills. As in many English witchcraft cases, such as that of the Pendle witches in 1612, the condition now known as a stroke but then called a 'lameness' is given a supernatural explanation: the punishment for a man who dared to interfere in the affairs of fairies.

Bovet's account of apparitions in South Petherton provides some fascinating insights into popular beliefs in seventeenth-century Somerset. It focuses in particular upon the magical practices associated with Midsummer Eve. The 'watchers' who, he maintained, gathered in church porches to observe the passing of the spectral forms of those who would die in that parish during the following year has echoes of the mythical outdoor, dead-of-night sabbat meetings. While modern historians have rejected the views of earlier twentieth-century writers that witch persecution in the period was that of a demonic or pagan cult, it is quite reasonable to suppose that on special occasions ordinary folk *did* meet up in groups, if not covens, to engage in certain traditional rituals. It is certain that the spirit world was a reality for most of those alive in England at the time. Doubtless many more then than now spent time engaging with it in a variety of authorised and other ways.

Summers, for whom his relations bore 'the hall-mark of truth',[66] considered Bovet's work 'one of the most extraordinary works in the immense library of occult research'.[67] He was writing, Summers further noted, at a time when the county of Somerset 'was imbued with the most intense Protestantism', which 'it would not be too much to say' was 'the centre of a furious and fiercely unreasoning fanaticism as regards religion'.[68] At such times of extreme political crisis, some historians have argued, 'godly magistrates were far more likely to invoke the threat of witchcraft' and their authority was strengthened by the purge of witches and other representatives of subversion and disorder.[69] In such contexts, as Malcolm Gaskill has put it, the persecution of witches was 'a livid symptom of social and political turmoil'.[70]

* * *

WITHIN A YEAR of Bovet's publication, Somerset was torn apart by the Monmouth Rebellion. It was at Taunton that the duke of Monmouth, when he arrived in the West Country in the summer of 1685, was most lauded and proclaimed king by his ardent Somerset supporters. And it was in the heart of Somerset, at Sedgemoor, that his rebellion was quashed a month later. Terrible retributions throughout Somerset came in the wake of defeat.

Fig. 5-4 *Contemporary playing cards illustrating the impact of the Monmouth rebellion upon Frome Selwood.*

Although the claim that on the eve of the battle of Sedgemoor James II spent a night in Beckington in the home of the schoolmaster Mr Hudson proves to be apocryphal,[71] Beckington was *en route* for the rebel army, as it retreated to Frome following a bloody skirmish that June at Norton St Philip, and, ultimately, to defeat at Sedgemoor. Following his trial by Judge Jeffreys at Taunton Castle, William Haynes of Beckington was transported from Bristol to Barbados on 24 October 1685 for his part in the rebellion. After a long crossing aboard the *John Haynes* he was sold to a planter named Henry Quintyne. Another Beckington rebel, a clothier named William Selfe, was tried at Wells and transported to Jamaica.[72] His fellow clothier from the parish, John Jesse, spent some time in gaol at

Newgate for his involvement in the uprising but, repentant, it seems he was wealthy enough to secure a pardon. A monument to a John Jesse who died in 1710 at the age of fifty-three, also commemorating his wife and two sons, is probably that of the one-time rebel.[73] One of the witnesses to the Beckington witchcraft case of 1689 was a member of the Jesse family, Francis Jesse, one of Rector Hill's churchwardens.

* * *

Brian Levack has identified nine social and economic factors that underpinned witch-hunting in early modern Europe: 'Overpopulation, an unprecedented rise in prices, a decline in real wages among the poor, chronic famine and dearth, especially during years of climatic severity, periodic outbreaks of plague, extraordinarily high levels of infant mortality, migration of the poor from the countryside to the town, pestilence among people and beasts, and the social dislocations that resulted from widespread domestic and international warfare'.[74] Some of these were age-old problems, but several were specific to the early modern period. The era has been construed as an age of anxiety and fear – one in which the old order, together with the assumptions and certainties of former times, was in a state of disintegration.

'First among the destabilizing forces', David Underdown has observed, 'was demographic growth'.[75] During the second half of the sixteenth century there was an increase of around 45 per cent in the population of England and Wales, from less than 3 million to more than 4 million. It is estimated that this grew by roughly 5.25 million in the first half of the seventeenth century. Furthermore, Underwood continues, 'it was most marked in the industrializing wood-pasture regions' – a denomination that exactly describes Selwood Forest in the early modern period. The estimated population increase for Somerset in the hundred years between 1600 and 1700 is 21 per cent and 27 per cent for Wiltshire.[76] This growth in population inflated grain prices and led to a 'disastrous decline in real wages for the labouring poor'.[77] Underdown has further concluded that it was in the cloth-manufacturing wood-pasture districts of the West of England that the 'gentry and middling sort of the new parish elites' were most inclined 'to use their power to reform society according to their own principles of order and godliness'.[78] Charismatic preachers in the region, notably Richard Alleine, cultivated anxiety through their hellfire and brimstone sermonising. As mentioned above, Alleine had been Richard Bernard's assistant at Batcombe before succeeding him as rector. Following his dismissal, he was licensed to preach in Beckington from 1672. That his dire warnings in promoting *Godly-Fear* had some effect locally seems evident in his remarks probably directed to his Beckington congregation:

> Beloved, while we are comforted over you, and rejoice that there is so much done upon many of you as there is, that there are so many praying ones among you who were wont to neglect prayer, that there are so many of you to be found at a sermon who were once more likely to have been found in an alehouse – blessed be God that there is such visible reformation among you, both of yourselves and your families. [...] Yet beware how you venture your souls upon this, though hopeful, yet I doubt but partial reformation; and, all this notwithstanding, fear lest you should [...] fall short of the Grace of God at last.[79]

In an earlier collection of sermons (1668) Alleine urged constant vigilance against the subtle intrusions of the Devil: 'Brethren, who is there with you at this house? Here you are before the Lord, but who is there with you? Search every room, look into every corner; is there none within that should not be there? Is there no messenger of Satan, hath the world no agitator at work within you?'[80] 'The Devil', he once warned another congregation, 'is with you wherever you are, he watches you wherever you go'.[81] Elsewhere he conjured up images of demonic armies, Hell's 'black regiments', the Devil's 'instruments',[82] hunting the souls of worldly sinners. Witchcraft he listed with adultery, drunkenness, sodomy, buggery, blasphemy, idolatry and atheism, as abominations encouraged by Satan.[83]

By the time of the Beckington case of 1689, conditions generally may have been improving. The initial population explosion of the early modern period had passed after the middle of the seventeenth century, inflation had slowed and real wages had risen. Improvements in agriculture, such as the creation of water-meadows, increased the food supply; England became more or less self-sufficient in corn by the later seventeenth century. The Thirty Years War in central Europe ended in

1648, and England's Civil War, which severely affected the counties of Wessex, concluded in 1651. Rural poverty in the second half of the seventeenth century was being addressed in many regions by a more systematic form of communal provision.[84] With such developments social tensions between neighbours are likely to have lessened. Plague, which had raged in the West in 1625,[85] was also in decline; the last epidemic in England, largely confined to London, was in 1665.

However, as Alan Macfarlane has pointed out, it would be very difficult to show that disease and loss declined significantly after the middle of the seventeenth century.[86] And, at a local level, the inhabitants of Beckington, like those in many other places, suffered as severely in this respect in the late 1680s as at any other point in their recent history. Indeed, the 1680s for Beckington, which culminated in the witchcraft panic of 1689, was by far, in terms of mortality, the worst decade of the second half of the century. 'In a society with no effective medicine, high infant mortality and an average life expectancy below forty', Oldridge has remarked, 'the 'secret working hand' of God offered explanation, comfort, and the promise of better things to come'.[87]

Table 3 *Number of Beckington burials 1660-1709 recorded in the extant parish registers.*
1660-1669: 251 **1670-1679:** 250 **1680-1689:** 658 **1700-1709:** 290

Exactly twenty years on from the Great Plague of 1665, London, from the early spring of 1685, was again afflicted by the scourge of a fever 'that proves very mortal, and gives great apprehensions of a plague'.[88] This was the most significant health scare since the Great Plague and, for a time, it looked as if it might be as catastrophic. On this occasion, thankfully, the fever did not bring plague in its wake but it had a devastating impact upon many communities, including, it seems, Beckington. Like the plague, it was especially severe in the summer and early autumn. It followed two years of excessive drought and hard winters; the Thames at London froze for most of the winter of 1683–4. The deleterious effect of these conditions upon public health doubtless weakened resistance to the ensuing fever.

Contemporary observations suggest that the fever of 1685–6 was a form of typhus, described at the time in bills of mortality as 'spotted fever':

The early symptoms of the 'new fever' were alternating chills and flushings, pain in the head and limbs, a cough, which might go off soon, with pain in the neck and throat. The fever was a continued one, with exacerbation towards evening; it was apt to change into a phrensy, with tranquil or muttering delirium; petechiae and livid blotches were brought out in some cases, and there were occasional eruptions of miliary vesicles. The tongue might be moist and white at the edges for a time, latterly brown and dry. Clammy sweats were apt to break out, especially from the head. If the brain became the organ most touched, the fever-heat declined, the pulse became irregular, and jerking of the limbs came on before death.[89]

Furthermore, its 'effects were felt far more in other places'[90] than in London. The register for burials in wool in Beckington in the period indicates the arrival of the epidemic there in the spring of 1686. If May Hill's parishioners in Beckington were resorting to wise women or cunning men to find cures in 1686, it is evident from the mortality data that they were ill-served. Perhaps it is no coincidence that before the end of the decade three elderly women in the village would be accused, possibly not for the first time, of witchcraft.

Table 4 *Burials in wool, Beckington Register, 1681–7.*

Month	1681	1684	1685	1686	1687
JAN	1	7	3	6	1
FEB	1	5	0	3	3
MAR	3	2	7	6	3
APR	2	3	2	19	4
MAY	1	3	3	9	2
JUN	2	3	2	17	5
JUL	3	0	0	16	1
AUG	1	9	3	25	2
SEP	1	4	4	14	1
OCT	3	2	3	8	3
NOV	3	2	5	4	1

DEC	4	4	0	1	2
TOTAL	25	44	32	128	28

1 Richard Alleine, *A Rebuke for Backsliders and a Spur for Loyterers* (1694), 110.
2 Comment of a Langport medical officer in *Report on Sanitary Condition of the Labouring Population of Great Britain, 1842*.
3 Charles I sessions xxii.
4 Elmer, *Witchcraft*, 230.
5 Ronald C. Finucane, 'Historical introduction: the example of Early Modern and Nineteenth-Century England' in James Houran and Rense Lange (eds), *Hauntings and Poltergeists: Multidisciplinary Perspectives* (Jefferson: McFarland, 2001), 9–10.
6 Lawrence Stone in Sharpe, *Instruments*, 165.
7 Michael McGarvie, *St George's Church, Beckington* (Beckington: Beckington Parochial Church Council, 1990), 25.
8 *Ibid.*, 7, 23.
9 John Collinson, *The History and Antiquities of the County of Somerset* (Bath, 1791), Vol. II, 201.
10 *The National Gazetteer of Great Britain and Ireland* (London: Virtue, 1868).
11 Daniel Defoe, *A Tour Through England and Wales*, Vol. 1 (London: J.M. Dent, 1928), 280.
12 *Ibid.*
13 Collinson, *History*, Vol. II, 198.
14 VCH, 'Beckington', Somerset, Vol. 8.
15 Bever, 'Witchcraft Fears', 582.
16 English Heritage, 'The Old Rectory, Beckington', *British Listed Buildings*, ID: 266983.
17 DNB, 'Huish, Alexander'.
18 David Underdown, 'A Reply to John Morrill', *Journal of British Studies*, 26:4 (1987), 474.
19 Deborah Hill was previously married and, as Deborah Bryant, had two sons, Thomas and Robert Bryant. (Sources: DNB, 'Huish, Alexander'; wills of Deborah Hill and Alexander Huish.)
20 A record of marriage licences issued by the Vicar-general of the Archbishop of Canterbury reveals that on 14 September 1675 May Hill, Rector of Beckington, a bachelor aged about thirty, was married to Anne Huish of St Giles Cripplegate, London, a spinster also aged around thirty. Their marriage was at the parish church of Chobham in Surrey. The Cripplegate connection is explained elsewhere in this book but the Chobham connection remains a mystery. (George Armitage, *The Publications of the Harleian Society for Marriage Licences Issued by the Vicar-General of the Archbishop of*

Canterbury (1892), 149.)
21 John Walker, *Sufferings of the Clergy* (London: 1714), 76.
22 PRO E331 Bath and Wells 3.
23 DNB, 'Laud, William'.
24 Proceedings in the Opening Session of the Long Parliament, House of Commons, 12 December 1640.
25 Assize and General Delivery held at Chard, Monday 11 March, 14 Charles I, 1638/9 before John Finch (Somerset Record Orders, 1620–1640).
26 The remarkable Tudor manor house at Great Chalfield, a National Trust property, is very likely to have been Huish's place of imprisonment.
27 DNB, 'Huish, Alexander'.
28 One marriage is recorded for September 1643.
29 McGarvie, *St George's Church, Beckington*, 30.
30 Kenneth Fincham, 'The Restoration of Altars in the 1630s', *The Historical Journal*, 44, 4 (2001), 919–40.
31 Underdown (1985), 247; the present Baptist Chapel on the Frome Road dates back to 1786.
32 Gordon, *Freedom*, 188.
33 VCH, Wiltshire, Vol. 3, 109.
34 Edmund Calamy, *An Account of the Ministers, lecturers, masters and Fellows of Colleges and Schoolmasters, who were Ejected or Silenced after the Restoration in 1660* (second edition, 1713), 612.
35 VCH, Wiltshire, Vol. 3, 109.
36 Glanvill, *Saducismus*, 354.
37 Elmer, *Witchcraft*, 233.
38 VCH, 'Brewham', Somerset, Vol. 7.
39 Edmund Calamy, *The Nonconformists' Memorial*, edited by Samuel Palmer (London: 1725), 377.
40 E. Dwelly, *Dwelly's National Records, Vol. I: Hearth Tax for Somerset 1664-5* (Fleet: E. Dwelley, 1916), 94.
41 VCH, 'Brewham', Somerset, Vol. 7.
42 Calamy, *Memorial*, 352.
43 DNB, 'Alleine, Richard'.
44 William Prynne, *The county of Somerset divided into several classes, for the present settling of the Presbyterial government* (1648).
45 Various sources including Calamy and Alexander Gordon (ed.), *Freedom After Ejection: A Review (1690–1692) of Presbyterian and Congregational Nonconformity in England and Wales* (Manchester: Manchester University Press, 1919).
46 Barry, *Witchcraft and Demonology*, 40.
47 Calamy, *Account*, 612.
48 Samuel Palmer, *A Brief History of the Nonconformists* (London: third edition, 1774), 15.

49 N.H. Keeble (ed.), *The Autobiography of Richard Baxter* (London: J.M. Dent and Sons, 1931, 1974), 196–97.
50 Gordon, *Freedom*, 113.
51 Somerset Heritage Service Q/SR/114a/1.
52 Rebecca Rideal, *1666: Plague, War, Hellfire* (London: John Murray, 2016), Chapter 8.
53 The full title of Bovet's book is *Pandaemonium, or, The Devil's Cloyster being a further blow to modern sadduceism, proving the existence of witches and spirits, in a discourse deduced from the fall of the angels, the propagation of Satans kingdom before the flood, the idolatry of the ages after greatly advancing diabolical confederacies, with an account of the lives and transactions of several notorious witches: also, a collection of several authentic relations of strange apparitions of dæmons and spectres, and fascinations of witches, never before printed.*
54 John Milton, *Paradise Lost* (London: 1667).
55 Notestein, *Witchcraft in England*, 578.
56 Sharpe, *Instruments*, 21.
57 Barry, *Witchcraft and Demonology*, Chapter 4; Ian Bostridge, *Witchcraft and Its Transformations, c.1650-c.1750* (Oxford: Oxford University Press, 1997), 90.
58 1 Samuel 15:23; Elmer, *Witchcraft*, 233
59 Barry, *Witchcraft and Demonology*, Chapter 4.
60 Summers, who died in 1948, edited the 1951 reprint of Bovet's *Pandaemonium* (Aldlington: Hand and Flower Press).
61 Barry, *Witchcraft and Demonology*, Chapter 4.
62 Bates Harbin, *Quarter Sessions Records Volume 3*, 203, 206.
63 Bovet, *Pandaemonium*, 98-99.
64 Durston, *Witchcraft*, 35.
65 Seavington St Michael is a village in South Somerset, three miles east of Ilminster.
66 Summers, *Pandaemonium*, xx.
67 *Ibid.*, ix.
68 *Ibid.*, xiv.
69 Elmer, *Witchcraft*, 8.
70 Malcolm Gaskill, *Witchcraft: A Very Short Introduction* (Oxford: Oxford University Press, 2010), 13.
71 McGarvie, *St George's Church*, 32.
72 Shirley Toulson, *Somerset* (London: Pimlico, 1995), 107.
73 McGarvie, *St George's Church*, 32.
74 Brian Levack, *The Witch-Hunt in Early Modern Europe* (London: Pearson, 2006), 274.
75 Underdown, *Revel, Riot, and Rebellion*, 18.
76 J. H. Bettey, *Wessex from AD 1000* (London: Longman, 1986), 206.

77 Underdown, *Revel, Riot, and Rebellion*, 18.
78 *Ibid.*, 40.
79 Richard Alleine, *Godly-Fear* (1674), 211–12.
80 Richard Alleine, *The World Conquered or A Believers Victory over the World* (1668), 238.
81 Richard Alleine, *A Rebuke for Backsliders and a Spur for Loyterers* (1694), 110.
82 Richard Alleine, *The Godly Man's Portion and Sanctuary Opened in Two Sermons Preached August 17 1662* (1662), 33–4; this fascinating book includes a succinct point-by-point guide to achieving the mid-seventeenth-century puritan lifestyle (125–36). He mostly avoided the derogatory term 'puritan', substituting for it the word 'precision' to define those who were precise in their reading of the scriptures: 'Whosoever is not truly a person of a precise life, is certainly in the state of damnation' (*Vindiciae Pietatis*, 1664, 91).
83 Alleine, *Sermons*, 49.
84 Levack, *Witch-Hunt*, 274–75.
85 E. H. Bates Harbin (ed.), *Quarter Sessions Records for the County of Somerset: Charles II 1625–1639* (London: Somerset Record Society, 1908), xxi.
86 Macfarlane, *Witchcraft*, 202.
87 Oldridge, 'Light from Darkness', 405; the 'hand of God' allusion references Thomas Whitfield's *A Treatise tending to Shew that the Just and Holy God may Have a Hand in the Unjust Actions of Sinfull Men* (1652).
88 Excerpt from a letter dated 12 March 1685, in Charles Creighton, *A History of Epidemics in Britain*, Vol. II (Cambridge: Cambridge University Press, 1894), 22.
89 *Ibid.*, 27.
90 *Ibid.*

6

THE BEWITCHING OF WILLIAM SPICER

Fig. 6-1 Seventeenth-century woodcut depicting stereotypical witches and their familiars.

> These miserable wretches are so odious unto all their neighbours, and so feared, as few dare offend them, or deny them anything they seek.
> – Reginald Scot, 1584.[1]

GREAT NEWS FROM *the West of England,* published in 1689, presented before the general public for the first time the remarkable 'true account' of bewitchment in the 'town' of Beckington ('Beckenton'), 'about two miles from Frome and seven from Bath'.[a] It was attested (26 October 1689) by May Hill (who almost certainly wrote it); the village's two churchwardens, Francis Jesse and Pollidore Mosse; the Overseers of the Poor, Christopher Brewer and Francis Francke; and the two constables, William Minterne and William Cowherd. In essence it can be presumed to be a version of the formal written testimony delivered by these men preliminary to a court hearing. Accordingly, while her alleged victims are named, the witch in the case is not. On whose initiative the account was published is less apparent. The testimony was derived from the experiences of two of the witch's alleged victims who, very probably, had been interrogated in accordance with the advice given by the local authority on such matters, Richard Bernard:

> The afflicted party, if he or she can come to give testimony [...] is to be questioned in these things:
> How, when and where, and upon what occasion the pain happened to him or her.
> How their fits affect them.
> What understanding or memory they retain, and with what apparitions their minds are troubled.
> How the fit ends, and how they are afterwards. (By these questions may be gathered the natural or supernatural quality of the disease.)
> Whether they have had the judgement of some learned and judicious physician concerning the nature of the disease.
> Why they should think the disease to come by witchcraft, and not rather either to be a natural disease, or Satan's work, through God's permission, without any league with a witch.
> And, lastly, who it is they suspect, and upon what good grounds.[2]

In the opening preamble to the account the author upheld Glanvill's position on the subject and reiterated his argument that the denial of witchcraft and diabolism amounted to atheism. This was the great fear of many English theologians, particularly since Thomas Hobbes began to articulate his distinctly secular philosophy, challenging the notion of incorporeal spirits, around the time of the Civil War.[3] It was probably no coincidence that Hobbes' provocative publications coincided with the seventeenth-century reissues of Scot's *Discoverie of Supposed Witchcraft* (1584) in 1651 and 1654, and the production of the new works by contemporary sceptics such as *A Candle in the Dark* (1655) by Thomas Ady. On the subject of witches, Hobbes had written in what would become his most famous work, *Leviathan* (1651): 'I think not that their witchcraft is any real power; but yet that they are justly punished, for the false belief they have that they can do such mischief, joined with their purpose to do it if they can; their trade being nearer to a new religion than to a craft or science'.⁴ To such claims the anonymous writer of *Great News* retorted: 'I know there be persons in the World, who will not believe there are witches; that is, such persons, who, by a league and confederacy with the Devil, do get him to enter, possess, and torment the bodies of children, and others: but whosoever shall read this ensuing narrative, if he be not an atheist in his heart, as well as in his practice, may be easily convinced – and see the necessity of keeping close to God, in a constant performance of his duty – that God may keep close to him in his daily preservation and safety'.

The other account of the case, and the one that can be attributed with certainty to Hill, was written in Beckington on 4 April 1691, and given to Richard Baxter.⁵ Ejected in 1660, Baxter (1615-91) was the most eminent of the nonconformist clergymen of the Restoration: 'Towering among them rises the gaunt and giant figure of Richard Baxter, the first to eject himself, with a call to the consciences of his brethren who soon follow him, twenty five hundred strong', as Alexander Gordon put it in his discussion of dissent at the time of the Beckington witchcraft trials.⁶ Regarding his interest in this and the other cases he collected, it has been observed: 'There was a natural affinity between [a belief in the supernatural] and the idealistic yet gloomily dualistic preaching of the Presbyterians. Baxter's *Certainty of the Worlds of Spirits* is the great work of this school'.⁷ Baxter was the principal spokesperson for several decades of a community of dissenting, excluded nonconformists who, in alliance with sympathetic latitudinarian churchmen, including Glanvill, advanced 'a providential world-view in which belief in witches, demons, and spirits was prominent'.⁸

The Certainty of the Worlds of Spirits, in which Hill's account was published, is 250 pages long and written, like Bovet's *Pandaemonium*, in the tradition of Glanvill's *Saducismus,* a work Baxter much admired. It was designed to affirm the reality of the 'worlds of spirits' by relating numerous witchcraft and other supernatural 'histories'. Baxter had requested Hill's testimony, having met the rector and received from him certain physical evidence concerning the case. Although the Baxter–Hill version broadly reiterates the content of the 1689 pamphlet, certain details are left out, and some key ideas and other information are added. The two narratives combine into a single fascinating account.

Balthasar Bekker (1634-1698), Dutch pastor and demonologist, was deeply disturbed by the case when he read about it (presumably in Baxter's book), and it informed his repudiation of popular beliefs in spirits in his subsequent *The World Bewitched* – a hugely influential work published in four volumes between 1691 and 1694.[9] This second version also appeared in William Turner's *A Compleat History of the Most Remarkable Providences* (1697), and was summarised by Francis Hutchinson in his influential *An Historical Essay Concerning Witchcraft* (1718).[10] Versions of the Baxter-Hill account cropped up in minor works in later centuries, for example Thomas Wright in 1851 had provided, in two sentences, a muddled précis of the narrative, arriving at the important conclusion that 'This case seems to have been the first check put upon the courts of law'. Howard Williams in *The Superstitions of Witchcraft* (1865) cited the case, somewhat inaccurately, in his consideration of factors in the decline of witch-hunting:

> The great revolution of 1688, which set the principles of Protestantism on a firmer basis, could not fail to effect an intellectual as well as a political change. A recognition of the claims of common sense (at least on the subject of diabolism) seemed to begin from that time; and in 1691, when some of the criminals were put upon their trial at Frome, in Somersetshire, they were acquitted, not without difficulty, by the exertion of the better reason of the presiding judge, Lord Chief Justice Holt. Fortunately for the accused, Lord Chief Justice Holt was a person of sense, as well as legal acuteness.[11]

In fact, the trial was not conducted at Frome but it did reach the assizes held at Taunton that year; more importantly, Williams depicted it as a landmark event, a turning point, even, as one of the two witchcraft cases[12] heard at the start of his service by the influential Judge Holt (1642-1710)[13] who, in April 1689, became Lord Chief Justice. He was regarded as a 'godly judge' since the 1650s, a latitudinarian, and a close friend of Richard Baxter.[14] The full Baxter-Hill version was transposed and published in Ashton's *The Devil in Britain and America* (1896), a substantial collection of sources 'bringing to light very many cases never before republished'.[15] In this it is accompanied by an undated and unreferenced engraving, in the style of the period, purporting to show a bewitched girl vomiting.

However, when in 1907 George Kittredge acknowledged the considerable contribution of Lord Chief Justice Sir John Holt in hastening the end of witch-hunting in England through 'the acquittal of a dozen witches between 1693 and 1702' he neglected entirely the Beckington hearing of 1690.[16] The case was included in truncated form, together with the corroborative gaol delivery record, in Cecil Ewen's great compendium, *Witchcraft and Demonianism* (1933). The folklorist, Ruth Tongue, included an erroneous version in her *Somerset Folklore* (1965) based upon Cuming Walters' account in *Bygone Somerset* (1894).[17] This retelling, in turn, has informed more recent references to the case in both popular and scholarly studies.[18] Until very recently,[19] the fascinating *Great News* broadsheet seems to have eluded the close attention of historians and yet most of the protagonists, including the witches and the bewitched, can be identified in contemporary documents.

Great News begins with a commentary on the behaviour of William Spicer, 'a young man about eighteen years of age'. William is readily identifiable in the parish registers as the son of William and Margaret Spicer, who was baptised in St George's on 28 August 1670. He had a younger sister, Margaret (born 1673), and three older siblings, Joseph (born 1667), Hannah (born 1664) and Mary (born 1662). His father ('Willyam Spicer the younger') had married Margaret Vinney, also at St George's, on 25 June 1661. The record of the burial for a Margaret Spicer in 1687 strongly suggests that he had very recently lost his mother when he became bewitched in, or shortly before, 1689. The woman swearing the affidavit to her burial in wool was Anne Belton, a woman who would play a significant part in the witch-hunt two years later.

The Spicers were not wealthy: William's father is listed among those with hearth tax exemption certificates for 9 March 1670. He was born in 1637, son of William and Mary Spicer, and was lucky to survive: five of his siblings died before he was ten years old. Two men called William Spicer were buried in 1705 and 1714 respectively, probably the father and the son. A single leaf bastardy examination that has survived provides a glimpse of what seems to be William's subsequent history. It is dated 7 August 1694 and records 'Evidence given by Margaret Deverill of Beckington, single-woman, that William Spicer of Beckington had carnal knowledge of this examinant's body and is father of her bastard female child'. Margaret Deverill was born in the parish on 19 February

1667; at the time of her examination she was twenty-seven and William had just turned, or was about to turn, twenty-four.[20] The allegation may well have been proven for, on 22 December 1695, a Margaret Spicer, daughter of William, was buried at St George's – she was probably Margaret Deverill's illegitimate child.

There is no record in the parish of a subsequent William Spicer marriage. Joseph, his brother, reappears, having married Anne Sainsbury on 8 September 1706, shortly before his twenty-ninth birthday. Anne died after giving birth to their daughter, Margaret, in May 1707 (she was buried four days after the infant's baptism). Joseph remarried, becoming the husband of Anne Spincers in 1714. William's sister Hannah is likely to be the same Hannah Spicer who died, unmarried, in 1695; an affidavit confirming her burial 'in woolen' was given by William Spicer, presumably her elderly father.

In the village alms-house there lived a woman, 'about four-score', named in the Baxter–Hill account as Elizabeth Carrier, and William Spicer was in the habit of calling her a witch. This great age for the accused is not unusual in witchcraft cases: Anne Bodenham, for example, tried at Salisbury in 1653, also was in her eighties. This particular octogenarian can also be identified, tentatively, in the parish baptismal records as the Elizabeth Carrier entered for 27 July 1603 who would have been in her mid-eighties in 1689. There is no record of her marriage within the parish and it is notable that she is described as an 'old woman', but not as a widow, in both versions of the case. Furthermore, no Carrier men in this or a neighbouring parish are recorded as marrying a woman by the name of Elizabeth at any point between the marriage of Stephen Carryer and Elizabeth Craye, most probably her parents, in 1600, and Thomas Carrier and Elizabeth Duland in 1701.

The pioneering demographic historians E. A. Wrigley and R. S. Schofield concluded that for the period 1575 to 1700 between 13 and 27 per cent of women never married before their forties. The peak of non-marriage rates for women came towards the end of the seventeenth century. Amy Froide, through her close analysis of the Married Duty Tax records for eight Southampton parishes,[21] discovered that in the 1690s between a third and a half of adult women living there were single, the majority of whom had never married. The Married Duty Tax, imposed to help fund war with France, was in place between 1695 and 1706 and it represents the nearest thing to a complete pre-nineteenth-century census even though perhaps as much as 10 per cent of the population evaded registration. In 1696, of those registered, 56.6 per cent of females in Southampton, including children, were single, 9.5 per cent were widows, 5.2 per cent, for which the record is less obvious, were either unmarried or widows. Just 28.7 per cent were married. Having taken children out of the equation, Froide calculated that 25.6 per cent of the adult females in Southampton in 1696 were single, 16.3 per cent were widows, and 8.9 per cent were either widows or unmarried. Less than half, 49.2 per cent, were married. Of those that were single the majority had never married. Furthermore, because 'a number of adult single women are likely to be hidden [in the record] behind the words 'daughter' or 'child',[22] these striking figures are likely to be an underestimation of the actual situation; plenty of single women of adult age, one can presume, were living in the parental home. Comparisons with other communities reveal that the figures for the number of adult single women in Southampton are not exceptional – in fact they are lower than elsewhere. Clearly Elizabeth Carrier's single-woman status was not at all unusual but it probably made her more vulnerable to the abuse she suffered as she came towards the end of her very long life.

The Carrier family was poor. Dwelly's record of hearth tax exemption certificates include (in 1670) Stephen Carrier (1606–?1681), probably Elizabeth's brother; and in 1674 John Carrier, who is likely to have been her 21-year old nephew, the son of her younger brother Roger (1608–?1675). Three Elizabeth Carriers appear in the burial records: in 1683, the 10-year old daughter of Stephen and Dorcas Carrier, in 1694 the 10-year old daughter of Joseph and Margaret Carrier; and on 24 November 1700 one who might have been the alleged witch.[24] If this was the case – and our Elizabeth Carrier cannot otherwise be accounted for – she was 98 years old, an exceptional but not impossible age. Alternatively, if Carrier was her married name she might be the widow who was buried in neighbouring Frome in 1696.

Elizabeth Carrier's presence in the parish of Beckington in the later 1680s is very evident in the considerable number of affidavits in her name confirming the burial of her deceased Carrier relatives, and others, 'in woolen'. Her own affidavit, if indeed she was the person of that name buried in 1700, was sworn by Joseph Carrier four days after the burial.

In the same year her old adversary, Rector May Hill, was also laid to rest.

These affidavits were made in accordance with the 1678 Woollen Act.[23] The first legislation, 'intended for the lessening the importation of linen from beyond the seas and the encouragement of the woollen and paper manufactures of this kingdom', was passed in 1667 but seems to have been largely disregarded. From 1678 records of affidavits for each parish were required by law and kept among the registers of baptisms, marriages and burials. Burial 'in any shirt, shift, sheet or shroud or anything whatsoever made or mingled with flax, hemp, silk, hair, gold or silver, or any stuff or thing other than what is made of sheep's wool only' would result in a £5 fine – effectively a tax on those who continued to bury their dead in linen. The law also extended to any material used for lining the coffin. The affidavit had to be made before the church minister or his representative within eight days of burial. Failure to do so would also result in a fine of £5, payable by the deceased's heir or next of kin. If the death was by plague, penalties were not incurred.

The winding[24] of the corpse in its burial shroud was an unpleasant duty often undertaken by a poor woman in the community; sometimes it might be done by a neighbour.[25] The person responsible for this task would usually have been the same who swore and signed the affidavit that wool had been used.[26]

One of the most tantalising details contained in the parish registers is the revelation that during Beckington's epidemic of 1686, time and again the person recorded as swearing an affidavit that the deceased was buried in wool is Elizabeth Carrier. In the period between September 1684 and October 1686 her name appears in sixty-one separate entries. Between the start of April and the end of September 1686 she provided affidavits for forty-two of the hundred recorded. This included twelve of the fourteen listed for August, and in the closing weeks of the epidemic she was the *only* person fulfilling this role. How can this be explained? It might well indicate some kind of quarantine measure whereby those close family members who would usually see to the laying out of the body were evading contagion by surrendering this traditional practice to another. Alternatively, it might indicate a cessation of attendance at church, where the affidavit would be sworn, as the villagers closed their doors to their infected neighbours and avoided all unnecessary contact. If this was the case, one can imagine the lonely work of the rector, or his representative, burying the dead with just the sexton and this ancient woman for company. At the very least it can be presumed that Carrier viewed each corpse in its woollen shroud before it was laid to rest. If we can suppose that she received some form of remuneration for her vital work, she was uniquely placed to benefit directly from the bereavement of her neighbours. Her last recorded affidavit was made on 24 September 1688, at around the time of the start of her troubles concerning William Spicer and Mary Hill.

Anne Laurence made some illuminating observations on the role of women like Carrier during a plague epidemic at Norwich in 1630. She noted how 'After members of the household, the most important part in the care of the sick was by local women who had a reputation for knowledge in medical matters'. The parish in such contexts would pay for their services as did the Norwich Corporation which employed Mrs Sandcroft 'to make provision for the infected poor in the pest house and to make them water, for which she was paid 7d.'. The women probably were very poor and perhaps in receipt of parish relief themselves. Laurence further remarked, 'How far such women were separate from [...] the women who came to lay out corpses is not always clear'. Still, this interesting account points to the strong possibility that our old, impoverished woman in Beckington in the 1680s both laid out corpses *and* had a reputation for healing. If so, her reputation as a witch is all the more explicable.[27] It is reasonable to suppose similar strictures were imposed in Beckington in 1686 to those in London in 1665, in line with the Plague Orders of 1646. These have been summarized in Rebecca Rideal's recent account of the Great Plague:

> they stipulated that no clothes or bedding were to be removed from the houses of the infected, no family or friends were to witness the burial of the plague dead and no one was to leave an infected house [...] The most revolting task fell to the 'searchers', women of 'honest reputation' who were to examine the dead and report 'to the utmost of their knowledge' whether they had died of plague.[28]

These 'searchers' might well also have served as nurses allocated to each afflicted family. They were not always trustworthy; one contemporary physician, Nathaniel Hodges, complained, 'these wretches out of greediness to plunder the dead, would strangle their patients and charge it to the distemper in their throats'. Worse still, he maintained, some were thought to 'secretly convey the pestilent taint from sores of the infected to those who were well'.[29]

It was during May Hill's ministry in Beckington when a separate register for recording the buried in wool affidavits was created. Prior to this these details were included in the main register. Although written in the same hand as the parish register, there is a curious and critical difference between the two records – they do not match. The front page of the second register reveals that it was written in 1696 by Francis Jesse, one of Hill's two churchwardens named in the *Great News* account. The information relating to burials contained in the main register is duplicated together with the names of those swearing affidavits. However, all entries for the period 1682–90 are incorrectly dated: in the 1696 document the list of entries for each year is out by two. So, where the register for the death of someone we can presume is William Spicer's mother, Margaret, is listed under the subheading 1687 in the main register, it appears under 1689 in the second register. The confusion seems to be entirely Jesse's error in transcription or, possibly, an erroneous correction made by a later hand: a close examination of the date entry that reads '1687' in the book looks very much as though a previous number has been scratched out where the '7' now appears.

The place in which the aged Elizabeth Carrier was living in 1689 might well have been the almshouse, marked by a plaque, in Goose Street. There had been an almshouse in Beckington at least as early as 1502. In that year Robert Parnell bequeathed 'for the sustentation of the alms folk there' a woollen blanket, no doubt locally made, 'there to abide as long as it will endure'.[30] The Goose Street almshouse seems to have opened its doors in 1670 as the bequest of John Ash.[31]

In addition to calling Carrier 'witch', young William Spicer 'would tell her of her buns'. 'Bun' in the period was a colloquial term for a squirrel and, as now, a rabbit; in this context it indicated a demon-familiar. Rabbits and, less frequently, squirrels are listed in accounts of early modern witches and their familiars. In 1645, for example, black rabbits were identified by one witness in the trial of Anne West in Chelmsford. Bernard recalled in his *Guide to Grand-Jury Men* that 'There was a boy at Bradley, which a spirit in the form of a toad called

Bun [...] told him, that to kill a man's horse [...] he must get the owner to give him something such as bread and cheese before he could kill him'.[32] In one of the earliest English witchcraft tracts, *The Examination of John Walsh* (1566), which records an episode on the Somerset-Dorset border, 'Bonne' is identified, together with 'Browning' and 'Tom Twit', as a typical name for a witch's toad-familiar. Two infamous witches in earlier times, Elizabeth Stile in 1579 and Agnes Pepwell in 1605, sometimes referred to their familiars by the nickname 'bun'.[33]

William Spicer's taunts are the only clear indication that the Beckington case was informed by the popular assumption that witches derived their powers from demons and diabolical pacts. The old woman was so enraged 'that she threatened him with a warrant, and accordingly did fetch one from a neighbouring Justice of the Peace'.[34] Alarmed, Spicer apologised and promised to leave her alone.

Although on this occasion the accused witch resorted to the law and not a curse to counter her enemy, it is possible that Carrier really *was* a practising witch. The parish records suggest she was unmarried, from a poor family, and in her mid-eighties at the time of her accusation. Perhaps she maintained herself using her inherited knowledge and folk-magic to provide a service for some and, possibly, a threat against others. Her involvement in the laying out of the dead indicates that she was more engaged in the darker aspects of life's mysteries than many of her neighbours. While it is impossible to prove Notestein's contention in the early twentieth century that 'a large proportion, after the Restoration, as in any other period of those finally hanged for witchcraft, had in fact made claim to skill in magic arts',[35] it is likely that at least some of the people accused in the Selwood Forest region traded in magic and exploited the superstitions and fears of others. More recently Edward Bever has concluded that 'Even though the majority of suspects in European witch trials were entirely innocent, some of the suspects were clearly guilty, perhaps not of witchcraft as defined by demonologists, but definitely of witchcraft as commonly understood'.[36]

Given her great age it might well be the case that Carrier had acquired a reputation for deviance over a considerable period of time. The records that survive from witchcraft cases, as Sharpe has noted, often must be merely the tip of an iceberg of narrative. What else had she been accused of during the course of her long life, one wonders? When Elizabeth

Johnson was accused of killing a child in Kent in 1582 she found herself facing further charges for *maleficia* against other women in 1566, 1569 and 1576: deeds she was believed to have committed over a period of sixteen years.[37]

A common theme running through the Selwood Forest accounts, replicated in numerous other cases, is that of the aged woman using witchcraft against youth. Although men and women of all ages, including children, were accused in the period, it is likely that most were women over fifty years old. The age of most of the accused was not recorded, but it has been suggested that in Geneva the median age was sixty, and those in Essex typically fell into the fifty to seventy age bracket. The reason why older women were targeted was, in part, perhaps to do with a common perception of their diminishing value to society at large as they grew older. Barbara Walker has suggested they 'could be called witches and destroyed, like domestic animals past their usefulness [...] The old woman was an ideal scapegoat: too expendable to be missed, too weak to fight back, too poor to matter'.[38] In earlier times the wisdom that comes with age had added value; in the 'witchcraze' era their supposed knowledge, their 'cunning', was sometimes enough to condemn them. A woman like Carrier who probably had never married was especially susceptible. Through his studies of witchcraft accusation in Somerset, Owen Davies concluded, 'the social status of widows depended considerably on the financial state of their offspring, and their relations with those offspring'. While children 'could and did support their widowed mothers',[39] spinsters were that much more likely in their destitution to resort to begging and other activities that might attract the hostility of their neighbours. Robin Briggs has considered the possibility that the targeting of mature females is linked to the universal and subconscious fear of the 'bad mother' – a concept that, according to Kleinian psychoanalytical theory,[40] terrorises the infant child: 'Every individual's fundamental experience of love and hate is with a woman, in the mother–child relationship, or whatever surrogate takes its place'.[41] That menopausal and post-menopausal women were particularly vulnerable to accusation has been linked by Lyndal Roper to deep-seated concerns regarding the fertility of people, animals and the land in a period of heightened anxiety and stress in the context of challenging demographic and climatic developments.[42]

The objections to such allegations that Carrier raised before the unnamed magistrate were listened to, and the warrant, accordingly, was issued. As the Selwood Forest cases heard by Robert Hunt clearly demonstrate, the attitude of the JP towards witchcraft was of paramount importance in the history of almost every witchcraft accusation case – 'the main legal variable in witchcraft trials' in the opinion of legal historian Gregory Durston.[43] Hunt shared common ground with the witch-fearing JPs who heard the case brought against witches in Essex and Suffolk in 1645, and with Roger Nowell who presided over the Pendle witch trials of 1612. Such men, ready to accept the truth of the supernatural charges brought before them, especially when their opinions were shared by respected and influential clergymen in their vicinity, were instrumental in fashioning a local culture of witchcraft suspicion and accusation within and without the courts.

In bringing the case to the magistrate's attention, Carrier must have made sufficient complaint at a local level, presumably through the local constables and, perhaps, the rector. In so doing she provoked further bad feeling within the village; very rapidly, it seems, the complainant herself became the subject of the general animosity of her neighbours. Although the warrant was enough to persuade William Spicer to leave the old woman alone, her troubles in fact had only just begun.

William began to exhibit some startling behaviour:

> Within a few days this young man fell into the strangest fits that anyone has ever seen, and these, by turns, held him about a fortnight. When the fits came upon him he would often say that he could see this old woman standing against the wall in the room he was in, and that sometimes she would shake her fist at him, sometimes bare her teeth, and sometimes laugh at him in his fits. He was so strong in these fits that three or four men could scarcely hold him down. When he was given some small [i.e. weak] beer to drink he would be sure to throw up some crooked pins; between the first and the last times this happened these amounted to at least thirty.[44]

The three elements of the young man's bewitchment – seizures, manifestations of the witch visible only to her victim, and the evacuation of pins – can all be found in narratives of witchcraft in the books written by the Somerset demonologists Bernard, Glanvill and Bovet. Bernard advised the jurymen of Somerset (and elsewhere) against the risk of mistaking natural disorders for magical ones: 'It is the general madness of people to ascribe unto witchcraft anything they don't understand'.[45] He provided examples of disturbing conditions that a 'learned physician'[46] found to have a medical explanation. These included the afflicted biting their tongues, making 'fearful and frightful outcries and shrieking', being 'violently tossed and tumbled from one place to another', frothing at the mouth and gnashing their teeth 'with their faces deformed and drawn awry', rolling their eyes, and having their limbs 'suddenly with violence snatched up and carried aloft, and by their own weight [...] made to fall again'.[47]

Nevertheless, convulsive fits were sometimes interpreted as a symptom of witchcraft, as in the Shepton Mallet case of 1658 and the Julian Cox case of 1663. Robert Hunt's own daughter, as detailed above, endured the same. While Bernard advised against assuming that witchcraft explained seizures, he regarded convulsions as a typical, and detectable, part of the Devil's work. 'Sometimes', he wrote, 'with a natural disease Satan may also intermix his supernatural work to hide his and the witches' practices under such natural diseases when they work together'.[48]

Like others before him, William Spicer also displayed extraordinary strength during his convulsions: 'three or four men could scarcely hold him down'. For both the Rector of Stoke Trister in 1664 and May Hill, Rector of Beckington, in 1689, this was powerful proof for the unnatural cause of the sufferer's condition.

The third element of William Spicer's enchantment, the throwing up of pins, was a phenomenon of witchcraft persecution already well established by the time Bernard published his *Guide* in 1627. In this, invoking the claims of John Cotta published ten years before,[49] he declared that one of the signs of bewitchment is 'When the diseased vomits up crooked pins, iron, coals, brimstone, nails, needles, lead, wax, hair, straw, or suchlike'. Another physician, John Webster (1611-82), Glanvill's most outspoken critic in the Royal Society and author of *The Displaying of Supposed Witchcraft* (1677), was deeply sceptical of Dr Cotta's assumptions. That cases of strange vomiting were of concern to him is evident from the start: his dedicatory 'epistle' to the Yorkshire judiciary identified 'vomiting of preternatural and strange things' as 'counterfeit' and 'juglings', 'for malice, revenge or some other base ends'.[50] In the previous century the Elizabethan sceptic, Reginald Scot, had written a detailed account of the sleight of hand trickery that could convince onlookers they had witnessed the regurgitation of indigestible objects.[51]

In 1684 Richard Bovet recorded a little-known tale of bewitchment that closely parallels that of William Spicer of Beckington. In this the children of Mr Merideth, who gave him the account first-hand, all fell ill with violent convulsive fits and one of the children vomited pins. For Bovet this was the detail that clinched it – a phenomenon of this kind could only have a supernatural explanation:

> But what can possibly be thought of the vomiting of pins? If there could be imagined any natural condition that could create brass wire in the body, it would be hard to imagine how they should come to be pointed and headed, without a manufacturer. This sort of torture is so commonly practised upon the bodies of people under those sad circumstances, that if there were no other mark of the black art, this alone would be enough to remove all doubt.[52]

In another account, also received from contemporary eye-witnesses, Bovet described how, many years before, the seventeen-year-old son of a teacher living at Seavington near Ilminster was, like eighteen-year-old William Spicer, horribly troubled by fits and the vomiting of pins:

> A little time after she moved to the second house, her son came from Winchester, aged about seventeen. He was a strong, and healthy youth but had not been there above two or three months, before he was taken after a most dreadful manner, in raving, and frantic fits, so that five or six men could not hold him. He would spring out of their hands, and leap up with his head banging the ceiling, and sometimes he would catch up a knife, pen-knife, or razor, and endeavour to cut his own throat with it, or do himself some other mischief, roaring out in a most frightful manner that the suspected woman was by him and commanded him to do it, threatening to strangle him or choke him with pins, and such like. All knives, scissors, razors, and anything else which might prove dangerous to him on such occasions, were

carefully put away. Nevertheless, even though they had cleared his pockets of such weapons at the first sign of a fit coming on, they would see in his hands, and find in his pockets, various of those sharp tools they had just removed. After these fits, he would cast out of his mouth pins and needles in great abundance, and, being extremely weakened, he would be forced to stay in bed for several days.[53]

In 1665 *Daimonomageia: A Small Treatise of Sickness and Diseases from Witchcraft* was published, anonymously, in London. It opens with seven 'Signs Diagnostical' of witchcraft, the very first of which deals with the affected person's expulsion of foreign bodies: 'I. If the sick voids things that naturally cannot be bred in the body, nor put therein from without, distrust witchcraft'. Such objects passed 'by stool' included 'rose-briars a hand length, sticks, thorns, and bones'. The author cited a case he had heard of from 'A physician of my acquaintance' who received eye-witness accounts of 'a maid bewitched' who vomited 'wood, hair, needles, pins, etc.'. He provided details of cases heard at the assize courts; these included someone who threw up 'thorns of the sloe tree' as well as hooks, another who 'vomited cloth, pieces of iron, stones, and bones', and a girl who 'voided downwards pitch and soap, stones, and pieces of bones, which also she cast up by vomiting'. Eventually the emaciated maid died. Quite understandably, the author continued, 'Those that vomit, or void by stool, with greater or less torments, knives, scissors, briars, whole eggs, dogs' tails, crooked nails, pins, needles [...] bundles of hair, pieces of wax, pieces of silk, live eels, large pieces of flesh, bones and stones, and pieces of wood, hooks, and pieces of saltpeter conclude they are bewitched'.

The second diagnostic sign in the unknown author's list is 'Strange and wonderful convulsions, indomitable and inexpressible torments' – the other condition that characterised William Spicer's bewitchment.[54] In 1616 the frequently sceptical physician, John Cotta, was satisfied that the vomiting of 'crooked iron, coals, brimstone, nailes, needles, pinnes, lumps of lead, waxe, hayre, strawe, and the like, in such quantity, figure, fashion and proportion, as could never possibly passe downe, or arise up throw the natural narrownesse of the throat, or be contained in the unproportionable small capacity, natural susceptibility and position of the stomache', when witnessed by reliable observers, 'prove a supernaturall Author, cause or virtue, because they are manifest supernaturall effects'.[55] Not all of the well-known English writers on the subject of witchcraft during the period were as impressed by pin-related magic: Thomas Ady's famous attack on 'witch-mongers', *A Candle in the Dark* (1655), ignored it entirely.

Pins have a rich folklore and in different contexts are associated with both good luck and misfortune. In cases of witchcraft they are particularly linked to the magical tradition of witches pushing pins into the wax or clay figurines symbolising the victim of their *maleficia*. Such was the practice of the Selwood Forest witches recorded by Glanvill in *Saducismus Triumphatus*. In these cases thorns were substituted for pins. In counter-magic pins also had a place. Pins and other items have been found in seventeenth-century 'witch-bottles', carefully concealed to protect people from witchcraft or to undo witches' spells. These might be very small, no more than three inches in height, though some are bigger, notably when the famous German 'bellarmine' wares of the period, decorated with the face of a bearded man, were employed. The distinctive broad-bellied shape of these vessels used in this way is thought to have symbolized the witch's bladder. Attracted to the material in the bottle derived from the bewitched – urine, hair, nail parings and the like – it followed that the witch would be injured by the sharp objects it also contained.[56] In the 1860s a bottle containing over 200 bent pins was recovered from under a hearth in a cottage in Sussex.[57] In his *Astrological Practice of Physick* (1671) Joseph Blagrave recommended the witch bottle as a sure way of undoing witchcraft:

> Stop the urine of the patient, close up in a bottle, and put, into it three nails, pins, or needles. With a little white salt, keeping the urine always warm. If you let it remain long in the bottle, it will endanger the witch's life: for I have found by experience, that they will be grievously tormented making their water with great difficulty, if any at all, and the more if the Moon be in Scorpio in square or opposition to his significator, when it's done.[58]

This uniquely British ritual (extending to colonial and post-colonial North America and Australia) is identified as originating in England in the early seventeenth century, and thus coincides with the escalation of reports of strange vomiting in witchcraft cases.[59] In a similar tradition such things as pigs' hearts pierced with pins and thorns, designed to ward off evil, were hidden in chimneys or other domestic apertures, examples of which can be found in several British museum collections. This 'sympathetic' magic combatted that of witches who invoked evil by piercing the images of their victims with pins and thorns.

Clearly there is a close connection between witch-bottle countermagic and the phenomenon of strange vomiting by the bewitched: the same indigestible material is associated with both vessels, the anthropomorphic and the human. As fears of bewitchment developed in the early modern period, and as more material was disseminated in print concerning bodily afflictions and witchcraft, the pins-and-needles metaphor took physical form. Witches, seemingly, tortured their victims with *actual* pins, needles and nails. A single well-documented case of strange vomiting, verified by experts and other respectable folk, was bound to bolster the myth.

1   Reginald Scot, *The Discoverie of Witchcraft* (London: 1584).
1a According to the *English Short Title Catalogue* there is just one known extant copy of this document which is held in the collection of the Huntington Library in California.
2   Bernard, *Guide*, 228–29.
3   Thomas Hobbes, *The Elements of Law, Natural and Politic* (London: 1650); Hobbes was born in Malmesbury, Wiltshire, not far north of Selwood Forest, in 1588. He preceded May Hill and his brother Stephen as a graduate of Magdalen Hall, Oxford.
4   Thomas Hobbes, *Leviathan* (1651), Chapter 2; W. Molesworth, *The English Works of Thomas Hobbes, Vol. 3* (London: John Bohn, 1839–45), 9.
5   Nuttall and Keeble, *Richard Baxter, Vol. 1, 1638–1660*, letter 1230.
6   Gordon, *Freedom*, 188.
7   Greenslet, *Glanvill*, 150.
8   Elmer, *Witchcraft*, 11.
9   Andrew Fix, 'Angels, Devils, and Evil Spirits in Seventeenth-Century Thought: Balthasar Bekker and the Collegiants', *Journal of the History of Ideas*, 50:4 (1989), 539. Fix, erroneously, refers here to 'published reports of the trial and execution of the so-called 'Beckington witch' in England' – in fact not one of the three women accused in Beckington in 1689 was executed.
10 Assuming, like Williams, that the trial was held in 1691, the year in which

Baxter's *Certainty of the Worlds of Spirits* was published, he named just one of the three witches, 'Moor' (i.e. Ann More), 'committed for supposed witchcraft upon Mary Hill of Beckington, by Frome, in Somersetshire'. He continued, 'one of them died in gaol; the other two were tried before the Right Honourable the Lord Chief Justice Holt, and were acquitted. And the maid that was thought to have been bewitched, in a little time did well, and was fit for service'. Francis Hutchinson, *An Historical Essay Concerning Witchcraft* (London: 1718), 42.

11 Howard Williams, *The Superstitions of Witchcraft* (London: Spottiswoode and Co., 1865), 249.
12 His first concerned the trial of Margareta Young and Christiana Dun for the bewitching of William Mundy heard at Salisbury on 13 July 1689; Ewen, *Witchcraft and Demonianism*, 445.
13 Described by Elmer as a 'loyal Whig, and arch-sceptic'; Elmer, *Witchcraft*, 278.
14 See Elmer, *Witchcraft*, 227.
15 John Ashton, *The Devil in Britain and America* (Adelphi: Ward and Downey, 1896), Preface.
16 George L. Kittredge, *Notes on Witchcraft* (Massachusetts: The Davis Press, 1907), 55.
17 Tongue's is a severe abridgement of Baxter's account which placed the case in the early eighteenth century. This was a slight improvement on Walters who located the 'quaint record' at some unstated point 'in the last century'. In both accounts the principal 'witch', Elizabeth Carrier, appears as 'Currier'; Ruth Tongue, *Somerset Folklore* (Glasgow: The University Press, 1965), 226; S. Burgess and E. H. Rann, 'Superstitions and Curious Events' in Walters, *Bygone Somerset*, 115.
18 For example, Roger Evans, *Somerset: A Chilling History of Crime and Punishment* (Newbury: Countryside Books, 2009), 29; P. W. Randell, *Crime, Law and Order in a Somersetshire Market Town: Bruton c.1500-c.1900* (Brighton: Pen Press, 2011), 184.
19 I first stumbled upon *Great News from the West of England* in my research for a gazetteer of witchcraft cases, compiled in conjunction with my brother, David, and first published as *Witch-hunting in England* (Stroud: Amberley, 2010). Malcolm Gaskill cited it briefly in *Crime and Mentalities in Early Modern England* (Cambridge: Cambridge University Press, 2000), 50-1; Jonathan Barry also referred to the source in *Witchcraft and Demonology in South-West England, 1640-1749* (London: Palgrave Macmillan, 2012), Chapter 2; it is mentioned again in Peter Elmer's *Witchcraft, Witch-Hunting and Politics in Early Modern England* (Oxford: Oxford University Press, 2016), 213, fn. 121.
20 SRO Q/SR/196/1.
21 Amy Froide, 'Hidden Women: Rediscovering the single women of early

modern England' in *Local Population Studies*, Number 68 (Spring 2002), 26–41.
22 *Ibid.*, 33.
23 John Raithby (ed.), *Statutes of the Realm: Volume 5: 1628–80* (London: the Record Commission, 1819), 885–86.
24 Alternative terms included shrouding, steiping, socking, laying, and stretching forth.
25 Clare Gittings, *Death, Burial and the Individual in Early Modern England* (London: Croom Helm, 1984), 112.
26 *Ibid.*, 113.
27 Anne Laurence, *Women in England 1500–1760: A Social History* (London: Phoenix Press, 1994), 138.
28 Rideal, *1666*, Chapter 2.
29 *Ibid.*
30 McGarvie, *St George's Church, Beckington*, 25.
31 Anon., *History and Description of the Public Charities in the Town of Frome* (Frome, 1833, printed by W.P. Penny), 12.
32 Bernard, *Guide*, 181.
33 James Sharpe, *The Bewitching of Anne Gunter* (London: Profile Books, 1999), 85. This unfamiliar term, he concluded, 'may have been peculiar local [i.e. Berkshire] terminology'; the Beckington case shows it was also established in the vernacular of the south-west as well as the south-east. This is reinforced by the evidence of *The Examination of John Walsh*: the cunning man, Walsh, was from Netherbury in Dorset and his 'master', a Catholic priest, was from Drayton in Somerset.
34 Anon., *Great News*.
35 Notestein, *Witchcraft in England*, chapter 11.
36 Bever, 'Witchcraft Fears', 589.
37 Sharpe, *Instruments*, 118.
38 Quoted in Anne Barstow, *Witchcraze* (San Francisco: Pandora, 1995), 29.
39 Owen Davies, *A People Bewitched: Witchcraft and Magic in Nineteenth Century Somerset* (Bruton, 1999), Chapter 2.
40 Melanie Klein (1882–1960), a great admirer of Freud, pioneered pyschoanalytical studies of infant development. She was born in Austria and studied at Budapest and Berlin before moving to London in 1926 where she remained for the rest of her life.
41 Robin Briggs, *Witches and Neighbours: The Social and Cultural Context of Witchcraft* (Oxford: Blackwell, 2002), 246.
42 Roper, *Witch Craze*.
43 Durston, *Witchcraft*, 245.
44 Anon., *Great News*.
45 Bernard, *Guide*, 11.
46 John Cotta, author of *The Tryall of Witch-Craft*.

47 Bernard, *Guide*, 11–15.
48 *Ibid.*, 26.
49 John Cotta, *The Tryall of Witch-Craft, shewing the true and right Methode of the Discovery with a Confutation of Erroneous Wayes* (London: 1616).
50 John Webster, *The Displaying of Supposed Witchcraft* (London: 1677), 'the Epistle Dedicatory'; Webster's original dedication, never published, was addressed to the Royal Society. See Michael Hunter, 'John Webster, the Royal Society and *The Displaying of Supposed Witchcraft* (1677)', Notes and Records, The Royal Society, 201.
51 Reginald Scot, *The Discoverie of Witchcraft* (1584).
52 Richard Bovet, *Pandaemonium, or the Devil's Closter. Being a further Blow to modern Sadduceism, proving the Existence of Witches and Spirits* (1684), 103.
53 *Ibid.*, 116.
54 Anon., *Daimonomageia: A Small Treatise of Sickness and Diseases from Witchcraft* (1665), 3–6.
55 John Cotta, *The Tryall of Witch-Craft* (London: 1616), 76-77.
56 Philip Carr-Gomm and Richard Heygate, *The Book of English Magic* (London: John Murray, 2009), 326; Ralph Merrifield, 'Witch Bottles and Magical Jugs', *Folklore*, 66: 1 (March, 1955), 195-207; Ralph Merrifield, *The Archaeology of Magic and Ritual* (London: Batsford, 1987), 163-75.
57 Jacqueline Simpson and Stephen Round, 'Witch Bottles', *A Dictionary of English Folklore* (Oxford: Oxford University Press, 2000).
58 Joseph Blagrave, *Astrological Practice of Physick* (1671), 154.
59 Brian Hoggard, 'Witch Bottles: Their Contents, Contexts and Uses' in Ronald Hutton (ed.), *Physical Evidence for Ritual Acts, Sorcery and Witchcraft in Christian Britain: A Feeling for Magic* (Basingstoke: Palgrave Macmillan, 2015), 104.

7

THE BEWITCHING OF MARY HILL

Fig. 7-1 Contemporary woodcut depicting a bewitched girl vomiting nails.

Everything whereof every man cannot give a reason is not therefore a miracle.
— John Cotta, 1666.[1]

WILLIAM SPICER'S SEIZURES, 'the strangest fits that ever mortal beheld with eyes', plagued him for a fortnight at some point in or around 1689. Another young person in the village, 'about the same age as this young man',[2] 'a maid of about eighteen years of age',[3] would suffer even more horribly than William. Her name was Mary Hill. While the account of William's bewitchment appears only in the 1689 pamphlet, the details of what Mary Hill experienced also survive in Richard Baxter's *Certainty of the Worlds of Spirits* in 1691. It was for the bewitchment of Mary that two Beckington women were brought before the circuit judge, Lord Chief Justice Sir John Holt, at the Taunton assizes in April 1690. The hearing post-dated by four years the final execution for witchcraft, that of Alice Molland at Exeter. It was fortunate for the women in the dock that this was the first witchcraft trial overseen by the recently appointed judge, a sceptical Whig, who went on to earn a reputation for leniency in such cases.

Mary Hill is also readily identifiable in the Beckington registers. Her parents were John and Mary Hill and she was baptised on 16 April 1671. Again the accounts are absolutely correct – she was, indeed, eighteen at the time of her bewitchment in 1689. Her siblings included an older brother, John, and sister, Margaret, and two younger sisters, Elizabeth and Joan. It seems likely that in 1689 she too was contending with grievous personal loss. Her mother, 'wife of John Hill', is recorded in the register as having been buried at St George's on 7 March 1676/7. The children's grandfather, John 'senior', died in March 1677/8, many years after his wife, Margaret, in 1663. On 6 June 1686,[4] their father was buried and the children were orphaned. When a gentleman from Castle Cary, Squire Player, visited Beckington at the time of Mary's bewitchment, 'he found the maid living only with a brother, and three poor sisters, all young persons, and very honest, and the maid kept at the charge of the parish'.[5] 'Honest' Mary might have seemed in relation to the possibility of counterfeit, but Rector May Hill in the same account was careful to assert that Mary had 'lived very much in the neglect of her duty to God' – perhaps he believed that the afflicted girl, to an extent, had herself let the Devil in through her own wanton ways. The eldest of the siblings, John, would have been about twenty-one years old at the time. The affidavit confirming John Hill's burial in wool was made by someone who, at first sight, seems to have had no relationship with the family at all: the name in the register is Elizabeth Carrier. Nevertheless, the old woman living in the almshouse might have known the orphans well. This was not the first member of the Hill family Carrier had made an affidavit for – six years before she had done so for the widower Richard Hill,[6] who was probably the children's elderly uncle and, quite possibly given his age, the absence of a son[7] and his family's poverty, was himself living off the parish, possibly as another incumbent of the almshouse. His wife, Katherine, is known to have died in 1675.

The Carriers and the Hills may have been closely related. The children's father, John, and mother, Mary, were married in around 1665 but there is no trace of their marriage in any of the surviving records for Beckington or the surrounding parishes. Thus Mary's maiden name cannot be identified – she is known through the baptismal records of her children and the notification of her burial in 1677. As explained below, there is a good chance that she was Mary Carrier, the daughter of Elizabeth Carrier's younger brother Roger, born in 1650,[8] and otherwise untraceable in the marriage and burial records for Beckington. If so, she married John Hill at the age of sixteen and, after giving birth to at least five children in quick succession (1666, 1669, 1671, 1673, 1676), she died aged about twenty-seven. This would make Elizabeth Carrier the children's great-aunt.

Mary Carrier's mother, Roger's wife, was Christian Penny, born in Beckington in 1616. The Penny family and the Carrier family were further connected through the marriages of Elizabeth Carrier's other brother, Stephen, and Judith Hall in 1634, and Judith's sister, Anne, to Christian Penny's brother, Thomas, in 1640. Back in 1582, one William Hall had married a Margaret Carrier. Although there is no obvious connection in the surviving records it is possible that the Hills were a branch of the Haull/Hale/Hall/Halle family of the late fifteenth-century and early sixteenth-century records. A younger Penny brother, William, married Anne Bull in 1654 and when their grand-daughter, Elizabeth Penny, died in infancy in 1680, Elizabeth Carrier swore the affidavit that he was buried in wool. She did the same following the burial of a Simon Penny, very likely baby Elizabeth's brother, in 1686. To these children, almost certainly, Elizabeth Carrier was a great-aunt.

Mary Hill provoked the wrath of the witch by offending her on three occasions. First, she demanded back a ring Carrier had borrowed from her and managed to get it from the old woman.[9] This confirms the well-established relationship between the two women, a pattern many times repeated in English bewitchment cases. The history of the squabble, of course, is unknowable, but, conceivably, the ring was that worn by the girl's deceased mother, the precious heirloom that the old woman had persuaded Mary to give over to her safe-keeping. Whatever the truth of the matter, the outcome would be dire: the old woman warned her 'that she had been better to have let her kept it longer'.[10] Whether or not the girl harboured a belief that Carrier had maleficent powers, the stress such a threat might have provoked could have induced the physical ailments she suffered thereafter.[11]

Mary's sickness – seizures, visions and vomiting – seems to have begun in mid-August 1689,[12] just a week after she had caused further offence by refusing to help the old woman find work. *Great News from the West of England* recorded how Carrier took her by the hand and asked her to accompany her to Frome to look for some spinning work, for no one in Beckington would give her any. Mary, being afraid, refused to go with her.

Why Carrier was unable to find work in her own village, described by Collinson a century later as 'a [manufacturing] town of considerable importance' that 'carried on a large manufacture of woollen cloths',[13] is open to question. This raises a further question: why should Carrier have expected Mary Hill to accompany her to Frome to find work, a round trip taking about two hours, and why was she so offended when Mary refused? This, one suspects, was over and above the reasonable neighbourly expectations of the period and implies that the older woman had some kind of hold over the younger, a familial connection for example, against which the eighteen-year-old had rebelled. About four days later Mary met the old woman again, who begged her for one of the apples she had just bought. The girl refused and her troubles began.

The following Sunday, she complained of a pricking in her stomach. On the Monday, as she was eating her dinner, something arose in her throat which seemed to be choking her and at the same time she started having violent fits, which held her until nine or ten o'clock at night. The fits were so strong and violent that four or five people were scarcely able to hold her down. In the midst of her seizures, she would tell how she could see Carrier standing against the wall, grinning at her. When struck at, this manifestation would step aside to avoid the blows. The following day Mary was taken with more fits, and again said she could see the old woman as before, and she declared that this was the person who had bewitched her.

The girl's severe illness, coming so soon after causing offence to the old woman, was the first of four types of evidence that would eventually be presented as proofs that she had been bewitched. In his *Guide to Grand-*

Jury Men, Richard Bernard had categorised forms of evidence in such cases under three headings: 'Weak conjectures, which are commonly alleged by the weaker sort, arising out of their own imaginations or the idle talk of others', 'Strong presumptions [...] which are much to be insisted upon', and 'Sufficient proofs'. Of these, he wrote, 'The proof of the first, if no further presumptions can be made, may cause a watchful eye over the suspect who deserves a sharp admonition', while 'The second sort, which are great presumptions, being justified by witnesses, are just cause of the suspect's imprisonment, and are worthy, after trial at the bar, though not of death, of very severe punishment'. Carrier was well on her way to 'trial at the bar' but whether the 'sufficient proofs' would be found that made 'the party or parties justly guilty of death' remained to be seen.[14]

* * *

That children and adolescents, such as William Spicer and Mary Hill, should so often exhibit such alarming symptoms in cases of bewitchment and demonic possession is intriguing. In his study of the feigned possession in 1604 of Anne Gunter of North Moreton near Oxford, James Sharpe observed, 'In the modern societies that anthropologists study, possession by spirits usually afflicts the weak and disadvantaged: it gives the relatively powerless a temporary notoriety and moral leverage'.[15] Mary Hill was certainly 'disadvantaged' and her condition made her the focus of village affairs for a while. Indeed, it empowered her to such a degree that three women much older than her would face court proceedings for the harm they had, allegedly, caused her. It is tempting to find a psychosomatic explanation for her behaviour. Citing Sasha Hindley, Laura Gowing and others, Jacqueline Pearson has noted: 'observers of ghosts (and, we might add, of other supernatural phenomena) in the seventeenth century were very often female, young or servants: the supernatural 'allowed the female and servant voice to be authorised outside of purely domestic concerns', and for 'subjugated knowledge' to be recognised by and influence the world of its superiors'. 'For low-status men', Pearson continues, 'and, more often, children and women, the suggestive language of the supernatural may also be a way of gaining their own voice'.[16]

On the Wednesday after she first fell sick, Mary Hill began to throw up crooked pins and continued to do so for a fortnight until about 200 could be counted. Next, she started vomiting nails as well as pins, and, after the abeyance of her affliction for a period of eight days, the handles of pewter and brass spoons, and pieces of iron, lead, and tin. In addition she threw up several clusters of crooked pins, some tied with yarn and some with thread. One lump of lead weighed two ounces and some of the twenty-two nails she produced were board-nails more than three and a quarter inches long. As one would expect, all of this material was expelled with an abundance of blood. The introduction to *Great News* implies Mary Hill and/or William Spicer voided material in a range of ways: 'by vomiting or otherwise passing out of their bodies'. In the Baxter version we learn how two women had hooked crooked pins, nails and pieces of brass out of her navel 'as she lay in a dead fit'.

This phenomenon of the bewitched vomiting objects made of metal and other materials occurs on occasion throughout the history of England's seventeenth-century witchcraft trials. One early and exceptionally well-documented example is that of the bewitchment of Anne Gunter, mentioned above. The daughter of a prosperous gentleman, Anne began to fall victim to fits and hysteria in 1604, when she was around twenty years old. Her symptoms included foaming at the mouth, temporary blindness and deafness, and the production of pins from various parts of her body. According to Benedict Allen, a gentleman of Calne, Wiltshire, these were 'wrung out of her breast, some with the head and some with the points forward'.[17] These ailments Anne blamed upon the sorcery of three local women – Elizabeth Gregory, one of the most unpopular individuals in the parish, Agnes Pepwell, who was already thought of as a witch, and Agnes's illegitimate daughter Mary Pepwell. The allegations caused a considerable stir and in March 1605 Elizabeth Gregory and Mary Pepwell were sent for trial at Abingdon (Agnes having run away before she could be detained). The case was thrown out and Anne was suspected of fraud. Her father, Brian Gunter, would not let the case rest, however, and through his contacts at Oxford arranged to have Anne brought before James I himself. The king examined the young woman on three occasions, at Oxford, Windsor and Whitehall, but doubted the veracity of her story and had her committed to the care of the chaplain to the Archbishop of Canterbury, Samuel Harsnett, and Doctor Edward Jorden, an expert in hysterical conditions. Jorden soon confirmed the king's doubts about Anne Gunter's honesty. In fact, he had already published on the subject in citing an account of a woman who, believing she was bewitched, 'was cured by conveying of nayles, needles, feathers, and such like things into her close stoole when she tooke physicke, making her believe that they came out of her bodie'. Thus was her disease, defined here as *melancholia Hyppochondriaca,* revealed by Jorden as a psychosomatic disorder.[18]

The king assured the young woman that she would not be punished if she told the truth; she subsequently admitted that the entire story had been a fabrication and that, following her father's orders, she had exaggerated her symptoms and feigned the vomiting of pins, and passing of pins in her urine, by sleight of hand.[19] Her father, she explained, wished to have revenge upon the Gregory family in the course of a feud that had arisen after he had fatally injured two Gregorys during a brawl at a village football match in 1598.

Both Anne Gunter and her father were charged with conspiracy and brought before the Star Chamber early in 1606. The verdict is unknown. Local tradition says that Brian Gunter, by all accounts a difficult man who had a tempestuous relationship with his neighbours, died at an advanced age in Oxford in 1628. According to his daughter he helped induce her bouts of sickness by giving her 'sack and sallet oil with some other mixtures of the same' which caused her to vomit 'and to tumble and to toss up and down'. In her drugged state her senses were disordered and 'she knew not what she said'. Sometimes, she claimed, her father gave her an even more powerful concoction that she described as 'green water'. She also described how, while drugged, her abusive father and the wife of one of his co-conspirators had stuck pins into her breasts, no doubt designed to be discovered thereafter as proof of enchantment; two handkerchiefs were needed to wipe away the girl's blood after their grisly work was concluded. She 'could not well bring her arms together or lift them up without much pain' when she returned to full consciousness.[20]

It is highly likely that the Gunter affair was just one among several turn-of-the-century pin-vomiting cases, even though the surviving evidence for such is slight. The influential physician and demonologist John Cotta observed in *The Tryall of Witch-Craft* (1616):

In the time of their paroxysms or fits, some diseased persons have been seen to vomit crooked iron, coals, brimstone, nails, needles, pins, lumps of lead, wax, hair, straw, and the like, in such quantity, figure, fashion and proportion, as could never possibly pass down, or arise up through the narrowness of the throat, or be contained in the unproportionable small capacity, natural susceptibility and position of the stomach. These things at any time happening, are palpable and not obscure to any eye without difficulty, offering themselves to plain and open view.[21]

The phenomenon is found in the records of a case at Chatton in Northumberland in the later 1640s when three Northumberland women, a widow called Dorothy Swinow, and two sisters, Margaret and Jane White, were suspected of witchcraft and infanticide. Their tale was told in a pamphlet published in 1650 which, unique among the pamphlets written about English witch-hunts by named authors, was written by a woman, Mary Moore.[22] According to her mother's account, when her daughter, Margaret, got home after the judges had accused her of feigning her bewitchment, the distraught girl vomited 'stones, coals, brick, lead, straw, quills full of pins' and the wire strings for a virginal.[23] In her lengthy statement in her mother's account, Margaret gave a full account of how Dorothy Swinow had caused another sibling to fall ill with a similar condition, her sister Betty. In 1656 Mary Wade was accused of bewitching a fourteen-year-old girl, Elizabeth Mallory, daughter of Lady Mallory of Studley Hall in Yorkshire, who, it was claimed, had been induced by the witch to vomit pins and feathers. Julian Cox, as detailed above, was accused of having tormented her victim, a maid, by forcing her to swallow pins.
[24] A trial of witchcraft at Bury St Edmunds in 1665 concerned two widows, Rose Cullender and Amy Duny of Lowestoft, who were charged with numerous acts of witchcraft, including the bewitching of seven children, one of whom died. The evidence of the children, who complained that the women had caused them to experience paralysis and to vomit pins and nails, was particularly damaging. The pamphlet of the trial detailed their sufferings:

Their fits were various. Sometimes they would be lame on one side of their bodies, sometimes on the other. Sometimes a soreness over their whole bodies, so as they could endure none to touch them. At other times they would be restored to the perfect use of their limbs and deprived of their hearing. At other times of their sight; at other times of their speech, sometimes by the space of one day, sometimes for two, and once they were wholly deprived of their speech for eight days together and then restored to their speech again. At other times they would fall into swoonings, and upon the recovery to their speech they would cough extremely and bring up much phlegm, and with the same crooked pins, and one time a two-penny nail with a very broad head. Which pins, amounting to forty or more, together with the two-penny nail, were produced in court, with the affirmation of the said deponent that he was present when the said nail was vomited up, and also most of the pins.[25]

A pamphlet, entitled *The Hartford-shire Wonder, or Strange News from Ware*, printed in 1669, told the story of recent remarkable events at Ware. The troubles began when a wheelwright, Thomas Stretton of Ware, crossed a local wizard. Subsequently the wizard's wife visited Stretton's house where she met his twenty-year-old daughter and asked for a drink. Unaware of her father's quarrel, the daughter gave the wizard's wife what she required. Soon after, she fell sick with fits. A week later the wizard's wife returned, this time asking for a pin, which Stretton's daughter gave her. After this her fits grew worse, her body swelling 'like a bladder puft up with wind ready to burst'. For the next six months she stopped eating, she vomited eleven pins, flames issued from her mouth, and hair or flax sometimes appeared on her tongue. Apparently the witch was discovered after foam from her victim's mouth was burned, magically forcing the wizard's wife to betray herself. The pamphlet concluded that many former sceptics were converted to belief in witchcraft when they saw the afflicted girl. The story though is not substantiated by other, more reliable records.

The troubles of John Tonken, similar to those of Thomas Stretton's daughter, were reported in a six-page pamphlet entitled *A True Account of a Strange and Wonderful Relation of one John Tonken of Pensans in*

Cornwall (1686). John was fifteen or sixteen years old when, in the spring of 1686, he was 'strangely taken with sudden fits' during which he saw an old woman 'in a blue jerkin and red petticoat, with yellow and green patches' who told him that he would not be well again until he had vomited a quantity of nutshells, pins and nails. No one else present either saw the apparition or heard her speak. Sure enough, shortly afterwards, in the midst of further fits, he began to throw up small numbers of walnut shells and pins, some of which were crooked. The mysterious woman reappeared, sometimes as before and sometimes in the form of a cat. He was heard shouting at his invisible foe and crying out that she intended to choke or poison him. Furthermore, he was observed springing from his sickbed 'three or four foot-high, from between two men who usually sat on the bed by him'. In addition to the walnut shells and pins he also coughed up 'great quantities of straws and rushes, some of them being a yard long'. In total he threw up sixteen or seventeen pins 'and as many straws and rushes as would fill the pole of a man's hat', a piece of bramble and 'several pieces of flat sticks'. On one occasion, while lying in bed, he suddenly cried out that 'he was pricked in the heel' and, sure enough, a nail was found embedded in his foot. Finally, after further persecution, the old woman and two other witches appeared before him, and she 'bad him farewell, and said she would trouble him no more'. A couple of days later he was well enough to move about with the aid of crutches. Meanwhile two old women, Jane Noal and Elizabeth Seeze, were arrested and incarcerated in Launceston Gaol. The pamphleteers – namely the Mayor of Penzance, Peter Jenken, and a JP, John Geose – concluded their account hoping 'they will be found out at the next assizes, and so receive a reward due to their merits'.

Thus, it can be presumed, the justices presented with the charges against Elizabeth Carrier in 1689 would have been familiar with the claim that bewitchment could, even *would*, entail the vomiting of pins and other bizarre objects. It is likely also, particularly if they were familiar with Bernard's *Guide*, that they would recognise the possibility that such evidence was unreliable. Bernard mentioned the case of thirteen-year-old William Perry, of Bilston ('Bilson' in Bernard) near Stafford, who became infamous as 'The Boy of Bilson' after he levelled accusations of witchcraft against an elderly woman in 1620. The resulting trial at the Staffordshire assizes acquired notoriety as one of most widely reported hoaxes of the early seventeenth century. It transpired that a Roman Catholic priest, who had planned to pull off the impression of a successful exorcism to enhance his own reputation, had taught Perry to 'throw up his food, vomit pins, rags, straw, wrench and turn his head backward, grate his teeth, gape hideously with his mouth, cling and draw in his belly and guts; groan and mourn piteously'.[26]

No evidence of charges of counterfeit from the Beckington trial survives but this may well have been the private, if not the public, conclusion drawn by Judge Holt in 1690. He might perhaps have rejected the claims, and the physical evidence that was presented with it, as a fabrication, so much 'community propaganda'[27] invented by those who despised or feared the accused. However, despite the possibility of trickery in such cases, Richard Bernard, like many others, believed that the vomiting of 'crooked pins, iron, coals, brimstone, nails, needles, lead, wax, hair, straw, or suchlike'[28] *was* a genuine characteristic of demonic possession.

To this day we speak of metaphorical 'pins and needles' when describing an unpleasant tingling sensation in the skin – the numbing of a 'dead' limb. The seventeenth-century association of intestinal pains – cramps, stoppages and the like – with pins, needles and other non-food items, could well have evolved from a similar metaphorical base.

In some parts of the world the vomiting-as-bewitchment assumption is not an outmoded concept confined to the annals of seventeenth-century demonological texts. A Ghanaian newspaper, the *Daily Graphic*, reported on 20 March 2014 a shocking account of a nineteen-year-old girl, Rebecca Ankobea, who, after disappearing from her family home for a week, 'returned and began vomiting money, broken bottles, nails, an egg and pins'. Placed in the care of the church at Lapaz in Accra, she proceeded to vomit considerable amounts of coins and banknotes. The video recordings made by the church 'to prove that the story was not a fabrication' were posted on-line and, at the time of writing, are indeed freely available. The report goes on to describe their disturbing content: 'In one video, she vomited nails; in another she threw up broken bottles [....] In several of the videos, she could be seen wincing in pain and agony, crawling on the floor, suffering a coughing fit before vomiting some of the items'. Her family 'pointed accusing fingers at unknown kidnappers or *sakawa* ritualists who, they believed, had kidnapped her at Kasoa in the Central Region and attempted to use her for rituals but failed'. In the same report the Head Pastor of the church, Simon Narh, claimed to have been divinely inspired to induce the girl's vomiting by giving her anointing oil to drink.

Tales of bewitchment and strange-vomiting in both early-modern and contemporary settings are difficult, impossible perhaps, to interpret with conviction. Some, one suspects, were entirely fraudulent, others, as they were sometimes perceived at the time, were the invention of tricksters and gullible observers. Reductive medical explanations for the behaviours of 'witches' and the 'bewitched' and the retrospective application of the modern physician's and psychiatrist's diagnostic labels to the afflicted – stroke, epilepsy, psychosis, trance disorder, and so on – are treated with suspicion by historians of the subject.[29] Instead modern historians are more inclined to speak of the *theatre* of bewitchment, the witches and the bewitched, together with their inquisitors, playing, unconsciously, their parts in culture-specific dramas that defy retroactive explanation.[30] If they are prepared to accept, broadly, the veracity of the accounts they read, they are likely to agree with Owen Davies who concluded, 'As in cases of satanic possession, the pin-voider was performing for an audience' and interpreted such antics as 'obviously fraudulent'.[31] The show they put on, doubtless, was a learned behaviour informed by the witchcraft paradigm of the times, fashioned in part by the writings of educated and influential men. However, there is another less 'rational', but plausible, explanation.

Some experts, including Davies,[32] despite his verdict on pin-voiding, and Edward Bever who, in 2008, posed the question 'What basis did early modern beliefs about witchcraft and magic have in reality?',[33] continue to apply psychological theory in attempting to unravel and explain the detail. More recently Kirsten Uszkalo, who briefly touched upon the Mary Hill case, has made a strong case for the principle that 'an awareness of current diagnostic categories can provide a necessary immediacy to the understanding of symptoms described in bewitchments',[34] and the deliberate swallowing of pins and other non-food items, perhaps as an intentional act of self-harm, has long been recognised as a psychological disorder by psychiatrists.[35] Doctor W. Turnbull recorded one such instance in the *Gentleman's Magazine* in December 1783:

> A maidservant to the Hon. Mr Baillie, of Millerstain, in Scotland, went to bed with twenty-four pins in her mouth. The consequence of which was, that in the night the family were alarmed with her cries. Mr Baillie ordered her an emetic and the whites of eggs [...] and the whole number of pins came up, and are now preserved in the family as a curiosity.[36]

The Lancet in 1854 reported the case of a girl at Vienna who had swallowed at least 242 pins, some two inches long, in an attempt to take her life.[37] The contemporary case of a twelve-year-old pin swallower was reported at a meeting of the Buffalo Medical Association in which the girl in question 'had been in the habit of swallowing them for about three months, in order to get sick so that she might not be obliged to leave home and work out'. In this instance the girl manifested symptoms familiar to readers of witchcraft cases from earlier times: 'the girl suffered occasional colicky pain, and had much swelling and tenderness'.[38]

For centuries medical experts have recognised distinct forms of eating disorder: anorexia, bulimia, and pica (or *allotriophagy*). In 1798 Philippe Pinel, a pioneer of the science of psychiatry, classified these as the three 'neuroses of digestion'.[39] Pica, the term for the obsessive impulse to ingest non-nutritive substances, is derived from the Latin word for magpie. The earliest surviving English account of the syndrome dates back to 1398 in John Tevisa's translation of *De Proprietatibus Rerum*, a thirteenth-century Latin text by Bartholomeus de Glanville.[40] An Elizabethan treatise dated 1563 speaks of 'that sickennesse which is called Pica' in relation to, among other things, children eating coal,[41] as does an article in *Psychiatric Annals* published in 2012:

> Individuals with pica may consume an eclectic variety of substances, including mud, pottery, clay, and laundry starch. Pica eating of numerous other substances, such as paper, tissues, wood, plastic straws, soap, cloth, carpet, hair, string, wool, paint, gum, metal, pebbles, chalk, charcoal, coal, and ash, has also been reported.[42]

According to the Diagnostic and Statistical Manual of Mental Disorders, to be diagnosed with pica a person will display 'persistent eating of non-nutritive substances for a period of at least one month' so long as:

> The eating of non-nutritive substances is inappropriate to the developmental level of the individual.
> The eating behaviour is not part of a culturally supported or socially normative practice.
> If occurring in the presence of another mental disorder (e.g. autistic spectrum disorder), or during a medical condition (e.g. pregnancy), it is severe enough to warrant independent clinical attention.[43]

It is widely assumed that stress factors such as bereavement, poverty, maternal deprivation and a disordered family structure – all of which define Mary Hill's condition in 1689 – can trigger pica. Then, as now, it was considered especially prevalent among women and children. James Guillimeau in 1612, remarked upon the 'depraved or immoderate appetite' of pregnant women, and those suffering with the supposed maladies of adult virginity, for 'raw or burnt flesh [...] ashes, coals, old shoes, chalk, wax, nutshells, mortar, and lime'.[44] Nicholas Fontanus in *The Womans Doctour* (1652) declared:

> Women are sometimes so extravagant and preposterous in their appetite, that they refuse wholesome meat, and long after coals, chalk, a piece of an old wall, starch, earth, and the like trash, which they devour as ravenously as a hungry ploughman will wind down a good bag pudding.

As is the case with other self-injurious behaviours,[45] those with learning difficulties and nutritional deficiencies are most at risk of developing pica.[46] In particular it is associated with brain-damaged individuals, autism and schizophrenia, parasitic invasion caused, for example, by ingestion of dog faeces, substance abuse and attention-seeking.[47] Scientific studies have indicated that pica in the modern world occasionally causes the death of people with developmental disabilities,[48] just as some in early-modern contexts who had a fatal pica habit, revealed by dissection, were found to be 'silly Men, Women, and

Maids'.[49]

Not only is the intentional ingestion of indigestible sharp objects recognised as an eating disorder by medical practitioners the world over, it even has its own scientific term: *acuphagia*.[50] In one extreme modern instance of the syndrome, widely reported in August 2016, a 42-year-old former policeman in the northern Indian city of Amritsar was found by surgeons to have forty folding knives, some open, in his stomach. His swallowing of these had been going on for about three months – a practice, hitherto, he had kept secret from his family and doctors. When questioned on the matter he claimed his behaviour had been prompted by 'spiritual powers' and that he developed a taste for metal and 'loved the way blades tasted'. Such sensational accounts in the popular press are substantiated by reports in academic literature. The *British Medical Journal* for example in June 2017 published the case of a 61-year-old man 'with a clinical history of cognitive impairment and pica' who, following a cardiorespiratory arrest, presented at a hospital in Portugal and on whom 'A rectal touch was performed with extraction of abundant faeces and foreign bodies (bones and screws)'.[51] Early modern autopsies, allegedly, produced similar evidence.[52]

A recent study conducted by gastroenterologists at Rhode Island Hospital, USA, identified thirty-three adult patients who, collectively, accounted for 305 medical interventions due to swallowing of indigestible objects such as razor blades, knives, batteries and pens.[53] A team from the Department of Surgery at Services Institute of Medical Sciences, Lahore, recently detailed the extraordinary case of a 25-year-old female patient with an acuphagia diagnosis from whom 40 razor blades and 508 sewing machine needles were recovered following a laparotomy procedure.[54] The case report, published in the *Journal of the College of Physicians and Surgeons Pakistan* in 2014, noted that

> She had been married for 8 years and had 3 children [...] She managed a stitching school. Her husband was an intravenous drug abuser and that made her the lone bread earner of the family. On inquiring, she admitted to having conflicts with her husband with a recent exacerbation.

She admitted that after each fight with her husband 'she would ingest needles from her sewing machine or any blade she could get her hands on'. The surgery was successful and she was able to returned to her customary sewing work. The report noted that 'Eighty percent of ingested foreign bodies', including sharp metal objects, 'that reach the stomach will pass uneventfully through the gastrointestinal tract'. As in other well-attested cases, graphic evidence of the ingested materials *in situ* was included with the report.

Further instances of acute acuphagia include that of a mentally ill 40-year-old Ethiopian man reported in *The Telegraph* in 2001. An emergency operation, following bouts of uncontrollable vomiting, allegedly, revealed he had ingested 222 metallic objects such as door keys, watch batteries, hairpins, and nails. A BBC news item from 2001 reported the bizarre eating habits of a mentally ill forty-year-old Ethiopian male. When surgeons at Addis Ababa operated on Gazehegn Debebe, after constant vomiting led to his hospitalization, they found his stomach contained 222 metallic objects. Like seventeenth-century witnesses in such cases, they declared it was 'incredible' that he could have swallowed and retained this material. It included nails 15 cm long, door keys, hairpins, coins and watch batteries. One doctor commented, 'He had over 750 grams of metal inside his stomach. He must have been eating these objects for at least two years, as the wall of his stomach had thickened to accommodate these inedible objects'.[55] *The Telegraph* reported in 2006 on the inquest into the death of a life-long psychiatric patient in Wales, Dewi Evans, aged sixty-one, 'who was unable to stop himself eating any non-food items he could lay his hands on'. His living area in hospital was modified 'with the water pipes boxed in and the curtain hooks and poles removed to stop him from swallowing them'.[56]

Such evidence points to the possibility that the seemingly fantastical vomiting described in the Beckington literature might have been exaggerated but was not entirely invented: what now appears, at first, *incredible*, and to the seventeenth-century observer *supernatural*, becomes, conceivably, *real*. The reported swelling of Mary Hill's belly is in accord with one of the symptoms of pica. When she was denied beer she was less likely to vomit, as Squire Player observed: 'because beer was not given her when she wanted it, she lay in a very deplorable condition, till past two in the afternoon, when, with much difficulty, she brought up a piece of brass, which the said gentleman [Player] took away with him'. Nevertheless, Player was already convinced that this very sick girl was the victim of witchcraft, telling Rector Hill 'he was satisfied of the truth of the thing, because it was impossible for any mortal to counterfeit her miserable condition'.[57] The rector, who wrote the account, was very particular in recalling in great detail his own, unglamorous, personal experience of the affair. It is striking that on the one occasion he witnessed the young woman's strange vomiting, after she fell sick and was given beer to drink, she threw up just one board nail and, sometime later, a single piece of brass, 'followed with much blood', as much as could be held in the hollow of the hand of a woman in attendance – just as one might expect of the compulsive swallower of sharp and indigestible objects. The frequent reference to pins and other items being bent, as in Mary Hill's case, and, in that of Elizabeth Mallory in 1656, a fourteen-year-old from Yorkshire who vomited pins wrapped in blotting paper, might indicate attempts to make indigestible sharp objects easier to swallow.[58]

One case of acuphagia in a community at any point in time must be considered an extremely rare circumstance and two cases, as in Beckington in 1689, that much more unlikely. However, in principle, modern psychological studies offer an explanation for this too. Jennifer Hecht[59] has explored the phenomenon of social contagion in relation to suicide. Suicide, she concluded, engenders suicide and the development of 'suicidal clusters'. In 1974 a sociologist, David Phillips, coined the phrase 'Werther Effect', after the famously suicidal young man in Goethe's *The Sorrows of Young Werther* (1774), to describe the 12 per cent increase in American suicides after that of Marilyn Monroe. In a similar episode in early 2008 it was reported that in little over a year seventeen people aged between fifteen and twenty-seven committed suicide, all but one by hanging, in the socially and economically deprived Welsh town of Bridgend. Commentators at the time spoke of the 'Werther Syndrome', 'contagion', and 'copycat' behaviour.[60] The *Great News* broadsheet implies William Spicer's illness in, or shortly before 1689, predated Mary Hill's. The author of the account – Rector Hill presumably – appears not to have been a witness to the young man's suffering. The detail is sparse and it would be considered by many readers, then and now, as probably yet another case of a boy playing tricks on his gullible neighbours. Even so, convincing fakes can influence the behaviour of others, and sometimes with devastating effect, and there is little doubt that these two 18-year-olds knew each other well.

* * *

IN A DIATRIBE against the practices of unqualified healers, quacks, witches and other 'barbarous medicine-mongers', Dr Cotta wrote an intriguing account regarding the cures provided by female healers in dealing with 'the greene sicknesse' and other 'stoppages' in young women.[61] This condition was named for the greenish-yellow discoloration of the skin caused by acute iron deficiency anaemia, sometimes identified by the term *chlorosis*. The earliest reference in English to green sickness has been traced back to 1547 and it was primarily associated with girls and women in their teens and twenties, it was also known as the 'disease of virgins' and linked to various symptoms including menstrual disturbance and eating disorders, most notably pica.[62] The 'eating of things contrary to Nature', such as ash, coal, nutshells, tobacco pipes, and old shoes, was considered a cause.[63] Almost invariably in cases of strange vomiting in early modern England the twin symptom is the suffering of convulsions. Fitting was widely regarded as an external manifestation of the internal complaints such as, but not exclusively, the 'disease of the Mother'. Both natural and supernatural causes were found by those who wrote about these 'fits of the Mother'.[64] Invariably, strange-vomiting was regarded as proof of the latter. Significantly, pica syndrome also is recognised by modern European medical experts as a pathological disorder associated with iron deficiency.[65]

According to Cotta the attempts of healers to remove the 'obstruction' in the patient included 'piercing medicines', 'as strong as steele or iron' which were conveyed 'into the stopped parts' and often caused 'incorrigible hurt and mischiefs never after able to be reformed, or by the most learned counsel to be redressed'. It seems unlikely that Cotta was alluding here to the prescribed swallowing of a sharp ('piercing') metal object to effect a cure, even if his comments could be read that way, but certainly filings and powdered metals appear in early modern medical recipe books for the cure of green sickness. Along with rhubarb and marigolds, Blagrave prescribed 'Powder of Steel' for the condition.[66]

Of the 136 illnesses and their cures he listed, this is the only one for which powdered steel was prescribed among many hundreds of herbal and other ingredients. Webster also spoke of the healing properties of metal.[67] Another contemporary text recommended purging with 'prepared Steel and other ingredients' as a remedy for green sickness, but advised that 'sharp things' in the patient's diet 'be by all means avoided'.[68] With all this knowledge a sick young girl in the seventeenth century might have turned to the desperate and potentially catastrophic measure of swallowing a steel pin to effect a remedy.

One suspects that the convulsions of a teenaged girl in Beckington in 1689 would have been interpreted as a symptom of 'the Mother' by her neighbours, some of whom might have subscribed to the popular notion that this, in turn, was caused by witchcraft and supernatural pins, nails and other indigestible materials preventing the natural working of her body. In such situations both local healers and physicians were likely to prescribe purgatives; Baxter related the story of a young man's parents 'going to a Conjuror, to give him a Vomit, which brought up Pins, Nails, Points of Knives, and many other pieces of Iron'.[69] In the account he delivered to Baxter, May Hill commented on how the afflicted girl, after 'falling one day into a Violent Fit', was given some beer and threw up 'several Pieces of Bread and Butter, besmeared with a Poysonous matter, which I judged to be Mercury'.[70] Paracelsus, the hugely influential sixteenth-century Swiss alchemist-physician who consulted with cunning folk in developing his treatments, famously included mercury in his concoctions for the treatment of syphilis.

Anthropological studies have linked pica and healing ritual in modern contexts.[71] If anyone in early modern England ever prescribed the swallowing of a bent pin to cure the agonies caused by the pricking of magic pins in the stomach of a witch's victim (I have found no evidence they ever did) they would be following to the letter the doctrine of Paracelsus, who developed the idea that, in small measures, what makes a person ill also cures him. It was widely believed pins were instrumental in the doing of magic, thus they were also regarded as having had the potential to undo magic. The logic of 'sympathetic' magic certainly sometimes necessitated drastic measures and the destruction of the property, if not the person, of the bewitched; for example a cunning man, one Dr Bourn, in 1682 advised the parents of Mary Farmer, a bewitched girl, to burn the girl's clothes, assuring them 'that then the witch which had done her the hurt, would come in'.[72] Bernard wrote of the practice of burning alive one among a herd or flock of bewitched animals 'to save the rest'.[73] 'Punish the thing bewitched' was the guidance of one Restoration-era expert in un-witching.[74]

In 1671 Joseph Blagrave, a friend of the famous antiquary, astrologer and alchemist Elias Ashmole,[75] published *Astrological Practice of Physick* in which he recounted a case from Basingstoke, Hampshire, where, for a year, the daughter of 'Goodman Alexander, a Turner by Trade', was 'perplexed with very strong Fits', each lasting twelve hours, starting at nine o'clock each evening, 'during which time with many shrieks and cries [...] she was brought so low, both in Body and Spirit, that she could not move or wag any part of her Body or Limbs from the middle downward'. On being consulted by Alexander, Blagrave concluded she was either possessed or bewitched, and set about treating her 'according to the rules of Astrology', and conducted an exorcism. At length 'the Devil came forth but invisible, with a great cry and hideous noise, raising a sudden gust of Wind, and so vanished'. Blagrave noted that 'constantly in the time of her fits, there was always brought unto her three pins'. Each time one came up 'she seemed to rejoice and smile, saying, *a*'. She would then pop the pin back into her mouth – much to the consternation of her parents who would have to act swiftly to recover it before she swallowed it. They showed Blagrave a box, nearly full, of the pins the girl had produced, one at a time, during the last twelve months. Three women were identified as witches suspected of causing her troubles, one of whom Blagrave later learned died in prison at Winchester; 'what became of the other two', he concluded, 'I know not, for I never inquired more after them'.[76] This seemingly unequivocal but unprovable account of what now would be diagnosed as a case of pica illuminates the need for further investigation of eating disorder as one among a legion of possible factors in the identification of demonic bewitchment in past and present settings. A Surrey woman in the same period, named Joan Drake, was said to have swallowed 'many great pins, so to have dispatch't her selfe' in her suicidal state of religious torment.[77] She was, in the opinion of one historian, violently ripping herself apart, 'inside out, piece by piece', turning her amplified emotions, her 'rage possession', inward.[78]

In stories of witchcraft such as the Beckington case in which many elements can be verified by other sources, researchers are bound to consider the possibility of other literal truths in these accounts. Modern sensitivities regarding the cultural contexts in which these were written and the language in which they are conveyed should not blind the reader to the reality that disturbing things *happened* and these sometimes triggered accusations. Amidst all the supposed acting out of unwritten religious and demonological scripts there is no reason to doubt that the playing of roles could engender extreme behaviours that combined the physical with the imagined. Equally there is no good reason to dispute the facts that an assemblage of nails and pins, allegedly vomited by Mary Hill, *were* presented before the judge at Taunton in 1690 or that Richard Baxter received the same of Rector May Hill in 1691. Unlike those who examined Anne Gunter in 1604 Mary Hill's careful inquisitors found no evidence of counterfeit. Deceived they might well have been and yet it is certain that on rare occasions in the seventeenth-century people intentionally swallowed pins, just as some do in the twenty-first.[79] That pin-voiding and related phenomena were such a commonplace in reports of English witchcraft cases in the seventeenth century could well be linked to a developed, largely apocryphal, tradition rooted in genuine experience – as Davies remarked in his interesting examination of the relationship between sleep-paralysis and bewitchment, this could be another case of 'experience shaping witchcraft fantasies, and fantasies being shaped by witchcraft experience'.[80]

Those imagined pins and nails and their symbolic counterparts in the witch's poppet, the cunning man's witch-bottle, and in the hands of the disturbed victims of supposed witchcraft, lay at the heart of the matter, as many contemporary writers recognised. They deserve more than a peripheral mention as mere narrative devices and archaeological curios in modern histories of the subject.

One very noticeable feature in the early-modern strange-vomiting record is the prevalence of young, usually female, subjects. In the case of the Hertfordshire girl Jane Stretton, who vomited eleven pins in or around 1669, pica-like symptoms are combined with those of *anorexia nervosa* for, during her bewitchment, she starved herself 'for nine months, save only some few liquid meats, impossible in human reason to have preserved life'.[81] It has been noted that the eating of inedible substances could be indicative of an anorexic's compulsion to suppress the appetite.[82] Students familiar with the historiography of witchcraft accusation are rightly wary of mono-causal explanations and an over-reliance on medical explanations such as hallucination-inducing ergot poisoning. Nevertheless, if at least some of these episodes could be proved genuine – which from this distance they cannot – pica, together with other self-harming syndromes, would have to be recognised as a significant factor in explanations for English witchcraft accusation.

Table 5 *Examples of English witchcraft cases featuring voiding of strange objects and other related phenomena.*[83]

Year	County	Victim details
1604	Oxfordshire	Anne Gunter of North Moreton, aged about twenty, declared a fraud.
1620	Staffordshire	William Perry, 'The Boy of Bilson', declared a fraud.
1646	Northumberland	Margaret Muschamp, a young girl who vomited stones, coals, brick, lead, straw, quills full of pins, and virginal wire.
1652	Worcestershire	Mary Ellins of Evesham, aged about ten, found to have been bewitched by Catherine Huxley (condemned and executed at Worcester); Mary voided eighty or so small pebbles via her 'urinary passages' (Baxter, *Spirits*, II: IX).
1656	Yorkshire	Elizabeth Mallory, a fourteen-year-old girl who vomited pins and feathers wrapped in blotting paper.
1657/8	Yorkshire	Two young women who vomited wool, crooked pins, and hafts of knives (one made of marble).
1657	Suffolk	Jane, daughter of Diana Bocking of Lowestoft, who vomited crooked pins daily.

Year	County	Victim details
1658	Northamptonshire	The daughter of Widow Stiff who, in just three days, vomited three gallons of water, coals weighing up to a quarter of a pound, and 500 stones.
Pre-1661	Somerset	Seventeen-year-old son of an unnamed Seavington schoolmistress who vomited an abundance of pins and needles; his suicidal behaviour included attempts to cut his own throat with knives and razors.
1663	Somerset	A servant girl forced by the witchcraft of Julian Cox to swallow pins; Cox was executed.
1664	Suffolk	Seven children in Bury St Edmunds afflicted in various ways including paralysis and the vomiting of pins and nails.
1665	Devon	Witchcraft suspected in the mysterious deep embedding of a crooked pin in the thigh of Elizabeth Brooker, servant to Mrs. Hieron of Honiton. Previously Brooker had refused to sell a pin to 'a certain Woman of Honyton Town' who was enraged and made 'many threatning Speeches'. (Baxter, *Spirits*, II: XXIII).
1665	Somerset	Stoke Trister case involving the appearance of thorns in the flesh of thirteen-year-old Elizabeth Hill.
c.1669	Hertfordshire	The seventeen-year-old daughter of Thomas Stretton of Ware who stopped eating for six months during which time she vomited eleven pins, flames issued from her mouth, and hair and flax sometimes appeared on her tongue.
1671 or earlier	Hampshire	The daughter of Goodman Alexander of Basingstoke, who vomited three pins each night for a year.

Year	County	Victim details
c.1676	Somerset	Mr Merideth of Bristol's children – a son and three daughters, aged eight to fourteen – who suffered convulsive fits, and one of whom vomited pins.
1679	Leicestershire	Alice, the young daughter of John Burt, who vomited stones and stubble (considered a 'fanciful account' by Ewen).[84]
1680	Somerset	A thirteen-year-old girl found by the trial judge at the Taunton assizes, Lord North, to have falsified her condition by plucking pins with her mouth from the edging of her stomacher.
1682	Surrey	A female child from Ewell who sickened and died under mysterious circumstances including extensive poltergeist activity and discovery of pins in her arms and other parts of her body.
1686	Cornwall	Fifteen-year-old John Tonken of Penzance who vomited sixteen or seventeen pins, several pieces of walnut shell, straws and rushes up to a yard in length, a piece of bramble, and bits of flat sticks.
1687	Dorset	Eighteen-year-old Nicholas Storch of Lyme Regis, supposedly bewitched by a woman called Deanes Grammerton, who suffered fits and was found to have a nail and several pins embedded in his skin; the same woman was accused of tormenting another local eighteen-year-old, Elizabeth Tillman, in much the same way. Case dismissed as fraudulent by Lord North.

Year	County	Victim details
1689	Somerset	Eighteen-year-olds William Spicer and Mary Hill of Beckington, the latter of whom vomited prodigious amounts of metal material; the accused were found not guilty by Lord Chief Justice Holt.
1695	Lancashire	Richard Dugdale of Whalley, a boy who vomited stones up to one and a half inches in diameter.
1695	Cornwall	Philadelphia Row of Launceston vomited pins, straws and feathers; the accused, Mary Guy, was found not guilty by Lord Chief Justice Holt following her trial at Launceston.
1696	Devon	The daughters of Thomas Bovett – Mary, aged ten, and Sarah – who vomited pins and stones; the woman accused of their bewitchment, Bett Horner, was found not guilty by Lord Chief Justice Holt at the Exeter assizes.
1701	Surrey	Richard Hathaway, a young labourer in Southwark, was declared a fraud having feigned conditions that included the apparent vomiting of pins. Sarah Moordike of Southwark was found not guilty of witchcraft by Lord Chief Justice Holt.
1712	Hertfordshire	A sixteen-year-old girl, servant to a clergyman at Walkern, suffered fits and hallucinations and vomited pins.
1717	Leicestershire	Young women of Great Wigston recorded as vomiting gravel, dirt, thatch and large stones.

If Mary Hill did *not* suffer with pica some other explanation for her condition needs to be found. For those relating her story the explanation was witchcraft; for the sceptic it was, and remains, fraud. The extraordinary ability of the skilful stage-magician and the crafty medium to conjure up objects, 'apports', is well-known. The possibility of counterfeit was the focus of Squire Player's investigation: 'So curious was he to anticipate any cheat, that he searched her mouth himself, gave her the beer, held her up in his hand, and likewise the basin into which she vomited, and continued with her all this time, without eating and drinking, which was about eight hours, that he might be an eye-witness of the truth of it'. He concluded there were 'sufficient testimonies that they were incapable of making a cheat of it'.[85] May Hill, in readiness for the court hearing, had taken similar precautions to verify Mary's illness: 'To prevent the supposition of a cheat, I had caused her to be brought to a window, and, having looked into her mouth, I searched it with my finger, as I did the beer before she drank it'.[86] Two further witnesses, Mr Francis Jesse and Mr Christopher Brewer, churchwarden and overseer of the poor respectively, declared that they had seen Mary Hill throw up, on several occasions, crooked pins, nails, and pieces of brass, which they presented at the hearing. They insisted they could not have been deceived since they had searched her mouth with their fingers before she vomited.

Crooked pins and nails which had been hooked out of Mary Hill's navel were produced in the courtroom at Taunton and examined by the judge and jury. This claim that Mary had evacuated pins through her skin could, conceivably, indicate another self-harming mode of behaviour. Self-embedding is a recognised syndrome and it is especially common among teenage girls. Data compiled in recent studies in the UK[87] reveal that it is likely that at least 13 per cent of young people aged between eleven and sixteen try to hurt themselves on one or more occasions, girls more than boys. Those who self-harm in this particular way are likely to embed a variety of sharp objects under their skin; this activity is also frequently found in association with other forms of self-injuring behaviour.

In a period when judges became increasingly wary as to what might constitute sufficient proof to condemn a witch,[88] those who sought her destruction because they genuinely believed in her malevolence and feared her magic might well have been prepared to fake evidence in the interest of defeating a greater evil. Certainly Richard Baxter was all the more convinced of the certainty of it all when 'Mr John Humphreys brought Mr May Hill to me, with a bag of irons, nails and brass, vomited by the girl'. He added, 'I keep some of them to show: nails about three or four inches long, double crooked at the end, and pieces of old brass doubled, about an inch broad, and two or three inches long, with crooked edges'.[89]

May Hill, reflecting upon Mary's plight, provided further fascinating details of her sickness. Wondering 'how it was possible for all that stuff to get into her body, which at intervals she threw up', he made a close study of the afflicted girl. He concluded 'that those things that she brought up in the morning were conveyed into her body by some diabolical power when she was in bed at night'. He noted that 'it was only in the morning that she vomited up nails etc. and scarce did anything in the afternoon'. He was informed 'that she always slept with her mouth open, and could not help it, and when asleep, she could not be awakened either by calling, jogging or pulling her for some considerable time; however, at the same time, she made such deep and painful groans as if she were awake and sensible of her sad condition'. At his own expense he paid for someone to watch her at night with the instruction to ensure her mouth was kept closed while she slept. Sure enough, 'For thirteen nights successively, while this was done, the vomiting of nails ceased, but when it was neglected she would be sure to bring up nails or some such stuff'. He then arranged for her to be 'lodged at a neighbour's house to see whether her vomiting of nails would totally cease, but it did not', for, when Mary came one day to the rectory 'to refresh herself, she had not been there two hours before she became ill'. He continued, 'We immediately gave her some beer and she vomited up a great board nail' – witnessed, it would seem, by the rector himself. Sometime later 'she threw up a great piece of brass which I saw was followed with a considerable amount of blood'. On this occasion the rector instructed a woman to open her mouth; on doing so, she 'took out as much blood as she could hold in the hollow of her hand'.[90]

* * *

M ARY HILL'S EXTRAORDINARY condition, needless to say, aroused a good deal of interest and concern. The *Great News* pamphlet relates how Mary's strange behaviour, as frequently happened in such cases, became a public spectacle. More than a hundred people gathered

THE BEWITCHING OF MARY HILL

outside Mary's home and she was brought out of the house. Unbeknown to Mary, Elizabeth Carrier had also been brought along by members of the assembled crowd, and the moment Mary stepped outside she fell into such strong fits that two or three men were scarcely able to hold her. Next she was taken up to the hill on which St George's stands and placed in a chair close to the church. As soon as the old woman was brought near her, Mary rose up over their heads into the air even though four men tried to hold her down in the chair. Only after the men, and others standing by, had caught hold of her legs was she pulled back down again. This remarkable act of levitation, reminiscent of the bewitchment of Richard Jones of Shepton Mallet some years before, was the third crucial piece of evidence in Carrier's accusation.

Great News from the West of England also detailed another public revelation of witchcraft in the village when Carrier was taken down to the River Frome on the western side of the village to be forced to undertake a 'swimming' test.[91] Doubtless only a few of the cases of the swimming of supposed witches, so important in the Selwood Forest witchcraft episodes, have survived in written records, since these were not considered part of the due process of English law. This 'ordeal by water' was the traditional test carried out by the witch's neighbours to demonstrate her guilt by observing whether or not a body of water, a pure substance, rejects the individual thrown into it. To prevent the accused from treading water or swimming, according to some sources, it was customary to bind her with rope, her right hand tied to her left foot, and her left hand to her right foot. To prevent her floating away or drowning, and also, conveniently, keeping her on the surface, she was secured by men on the banks of the pond or river who held the ends of a rope tied around her waist.

James I, before he became King of England, had advocated swimming tests in his *Daemonologie* back in 1597, but the first known case in England was the swimming, in 1612, of Arthur Bill of Raunds in Northamptonshire, who was accused of using witchcraft to murder Martha Aspine. A 1613 pamphlet reported the recent swimming of Mary Sutton, accused of witchcraft, of Milton Mills in Bedfordshire. Having been beaten with a cudgel 'till she was scarce able to stir', the woman sank for a moment when thrown into a body of water then floated as if on a plank. After another swimming and a bout of interrogation (and, probably, further cudgelling) Mary Sutton eventually 'confessed all; and acknowledged the Devil had now left her to that shame that is reward to such as follow him'. Mary and her mother, also accused of witchcraft, were convicted at Bedford on Monday 30 March 1613, and executed on the Tuesday.[92]

Another Bedford 'swimming' story dates to around 1637 and is told in *Daimonomageia* by W. Drage, printed in 1665. Having begged a maid for some 'Pease' (presumably for her Pease pudding – the regular fare of labouring folk in the past) and been refused, 'Goodwife' Rose was accused of bewitching it and making it 'worm-eaten'. She was also suspected of making a man ill. Both she and the maid were subjected to the swimming test. Goodwife Rose would not sink but the maid did with such certainty that she nearly drowned and had to be resuscitated by the onlookers. Doubtless this would have confirmed Goodwife Rose's guilt but the outcome of the case, if real, is not known.

Several swimmings occurred in the mid-1640s in the east of England in association with the 'Witchfinder General', Matthew Hopkins. The Selwood Forest cases of 1689–94 fall between a case in Kidderminster, Worcestershire, in 1660, and the swimming of Widow Coman of Coggeshall in Essex in 1699. Like Elizabeth Carrier of Beckington in 1689, she was subjected to three swimmings, each carried out on a different day, and the ordeal resulted in her death.

With her legs tied, Elizabeth Carrier was thrown into the River Frome, and, despite struggling to get herself under water, she could not, and floated on her back, bobbing about 'like a piece of cork'. At least twenty people witnessed this first swimming but, to convince the rest of the community and other interested parties, a second swimming test was organised, this time in front of more than 200 spectators. Once again she floated on the surface. Many of those gathered, however, were still not convinced and so, to prove the point, 'a lusty young woman' was put into the water who sank immediately, and would have drowned, had it not been for the help that was at hand. To satisfy the onlookers, and to leave no room for doubt, the old woman was put into the water a third time and she still bobbed about as before. At this third swimming a huge crowd included people from both Beckington and the surrounding country, many of them 'persons of quality'. Almost everyone, the author of *Great News* asserted, was now convinced of the truth of the matter.

Presumably these three swimmings took place over a period, perhaps several days, as news spread and those interested in witnessing the spectacle thronged to Beckington and the banks of the Frome. That an octogenarian survived such an ordeal is in itself remarkable.

With this fourth piece of evidence in place a warrant from a JP was again requested, this time for the arrest of Elizabeth Carrier. The local JP in the area around Beckington in 1689 was George Horner whose father, Sir George Horner, had investigated the Beckington conventicle in 1670.[93] His son served as a magistrate from 1675 until his death in 1707 and many of the cases in which he was involved concerned people in such east Somerset parishes as Rode and Beckington. He was also an MP from 1685, High Sheriff of the county between 1680 and 1681, and Deputy Lieutenant from 1680 until 1687. He was removed from his official positions for a short time in 1688 for refusing to support the repeal of the Test Act before being reinstated as a JP in 1689 and re-elected to Parliament in the same year.

There is no way of knowing whether the magistracy was at all convinced by the witchcraft allegations in Beckington in 1689. So long as witchcraft was recognised in law even the most sceptical of judges had a professional obligation to accept it as a possibility. Whatever their private views were on the matter, a measure of public judicial ambivalence was to be expected at all levels, if only for the avoidance of 'antagonizing local opinion',[94] especially in situations such as this where so many had already expressed their interest by gathering in considerable numbers on several occasions.

The old woman was apprehended by a warrant from a justice of the peace and committed to the county gaol at Ilchester. It seems Mary Hill ceased to suffer from seizures and supernatural vomiting for a full two weeks thereafter. Even though there was, seemingly, little chance of a successful prosecution, the evidence of other cases indicates a popular belief that the mere act of bringing a witch before a judge could be enough to alleviate or even undo her *maleficium*. Sharpe has provided several examples.[95]

It was at some point around this time that the village was visited, incognito it seems, by Squire Player of Castle Cary, who turned up one Saturday at the rectory. Player's role in the Beckington case might well have been instrumental in its escalation to the point of the opening of trial proceedings and the publication of testimonies. There is little doubt that the man in question was William Player, a wealthy landowner who had bought the manor in Castle Cary in conjunction with a lawyer, William Ettricke, who was probably also his brother-in-law.[96] Between 1687 and when he visited Beckington in 1689 he built Hadspen House, subsequently developed into a mansion, between Bruton and Castle Cary.[97] The Players kept the property until 1785 when it was acquired by the Hobhouses, a Bristol merchant family. A record from 1714, concerning the sale of the Bruton manor and the relinquishing of the previous owner's electoral rights, named several men involved in the proceedings; these included both Player and John Hunt, the son of Joseph Glanvill's informant, Robert Hunt, and a fellow JP. Hunt was active in the Michaelmas sessions of 1689[98] but it is not known if he was involved in the hearings of the Beckington case at Bruton. Incidentally, Player, like Glanvill before him, was a man of science as well as one clearly interested in preternatural occurences – Elmer notes he was 'an amateur natural historian who forwarded fossil specimens from his estate at Castle Cary to the eminent geologist and natural philosopher John Woodward'.[99]

The question arises as to who took the initiative to start the court proceedings against the old woman. Typically, in cases where the bewitched was a young person, the legal accusation would be made by a parent. Thus Henry Jones of Shepton Mallet seems to have made the case against Jane Brooks for the enchantment of his son Richard, aged twelve, in 1657. Likewise, Richard Hill, a yeoman from Stoke Trister, close to Wincanton, opened the proceedings in the trial against Elizabeth Style in January 1665 for the bewitching of his thirteen-year-old daughter. That he could afford to do so is indicated by his yeoman status in Glanvill's record of the case. In the Beckington affair Mary Hill did not have a parent, let alone the means, to resort to the courts to have her revenge on Elizabeth Carrier. However, unlike William Spicer, who seems to have shared a similarly impoverished family background, as a girl 'kept at the charge of the parish', she had someone acting, in effect, *in loco parentis* – the rector, May Hill. With the rector and his churchwardens supporting her claims, the case could be opened. But for this, it is doubtful that her bewitchment, let alone that of William Spicer, would have left any historical trace whatsoever – a salutary reminder that the great bulk of witchcraft accusations in early-modern England doubtless evaded the court records. The childless Rector Hill might have developed a paternal interest in the plight of Mary; this is further indicated by the fact that, deeply moved by her deplorable condition, he resolved to take the disturbed girl into his own house, where, in a short time, her vomiting ceased, even though, for a while, her fits continued. Perhaps he felt a sense of remote kinship with the orphaned child who, by coincidence, shared his own surname. He was glad to be able to report to Richard Baxter at the start of April that: 'blessed be God, she is now, and has been for a considerable time in very good health and fit for a position in service'.

The course of a witchcraft accusation involved a number of stages, at any of which someone in authority could dismiss the case and bring it, in legal terms at least, to an end. In the first instance a complainant needed to raise the matter with the local magistrate, by reporting it in person at the JP's residence or, more likely, through the representation of a constable or some other local official. The parish constables were expected to attend the sessions where the cases from their parishes were being heard, and this is certainly what happened in the hearing of the Beckington witchcraft case.

Carrier was searched by 'a jury of women'. This search was ordered by an unnamed JP and probably supervised by one of the constables – William Minterne or William Cowherd. In addition to 'purple spots' on her body that were insensitive to being pricked, they found other marks that heightened their suspicions. The author of *Great News* does not go into further detail but the likelihood is that they found one or more supposed supernumerary nipples by which she suckled her imps. By this point in the seventeenth century it is most probable that these were found in her pudenda. The earliest record of such a search in England dates back to 1579 – a court leet record from Southampton.[100] That a JP should be co-ordinating such an investigation as late as 1689 is notable but certainly not out of the ordinary. James Sharpe has related the interesting account of how, in 1686, an Oxfordshire gentlewoman, Joan Walker of Bicester, called for a jury of twenty-four 'sober and judicious matrons' to search her to prove to all that she did not bear the Devil's marks.

Even as late as 1689, the combination of popular belief in witchcraft

Fig. 7-2 *A search for the Devil's mark in a mid-nineteenth-century depiction of the Salem witchcraft examinations a couple of years after similar events in Beckington.* (Examination of a Witch *by T.H. Matteson)*

and a credulous judge was a potentially fatal one for Carrier. Following her arrest by warrant of an unnamed magistrate, who received the damning oaths of 'two Persons', she was committed to the notoriously unhealthy County Gaol in Ilchester, thirty miles or so south-west of Beckington, to await her trial at the next assizes, to be held at the start of 1690 at Taunton.

Meanwhile, Mary Hill's condition seems to have improved. However, within a fortnight she was vomiting nails, pieces of nails, pieces of brass and handles of spoons, and would continue to do so for the next six months or more. In her fits, she said there appeared before her an old woman named Margery Coombes and also one Ann More. A warrant for their arrest was issued by two JPs, and these two women were apprehended and brought before the bench at the Bruton sessions.

Sessions had been held in the town since at least 1540, but the Royalist stance of the town probably explains their discontinuance in the Commonwealth era. Following the Restoration, sessions were held here at least once every year up until 1786.[101] In 1684 a market house was built, by subscription, on the site of an earlier structure dating back to 1642 on the north side of the town's main thoroughfare, High Street. The first floor was used for quarter sessions until about 1790, when the sessions were moved to nearby Wincanton.[102] Since 1932 the mainly nineteenth-century building that now occupies the site has been used as a Masonic Hall by the Royal Clarence Lodge of Freemasons.[103] It was here that Coombes and More were presented, presumably at the Epiphany sessions at the very start of 1690.[104]

After their Bruton hearing Carrier's alleged accomplices were also sent to Ilchester to await trial at Taunton. Within a short time of her arrival at this prison Margery Coombes was dead.

The identification of a further two suspected witches in Beckington in association with Elizabeth Carrier is not unusual. Multiple indictments of witches from the same parish were recorded in many cases – a group of three or so being typical in the early modern period. Although groups of suspect women were sometimes revealed as, essentially, 'covens' in the literature, in many episodes, as at Beckington, there is no clear statement regarding the nature of the relationship between the accused. However, it remains likely that an unwritten subtext of maleficent conspiracy underpinned that published in the two Beckington accounts.

Margery Coombes was almost certainly the woman who was married to Richard 'Combs' at St George's on 1 January 1640. Her maiden name was Compton and she had been born in Beckington, the daughter of John Compton, at the start of 1613. Her sister Elizabeth married Robert Davys at St George's parish church in 1638, but of her brother John, born in 1618, there is no further trace. Her father and the woman who was almost certainly her mother, Anne Coombes, 'widow', died in 1660 and 1662 respectively. Two people by the name of Richard Coombs appear in the Beckington burial records – one in 1693 and one in 1706. Thus it is very likely that her husband, who was born in around 1619, died three years after Margery's own death in the County Gaol at Ilchester. Margery Coombes, as expected, cannot be found in the Beckington burial records – those executed usually were buried in the churchyard nearest to the place of their punishment,[105] and it is reasonable to suppose that this was typical of those who died in prison while awaiting trial.

Back in August 1686 Carrier had confirmed that Seymour ('Semur') Coombs, son of John and Sarah, had been buried in wool.[106] Margery Coombs herself swore an affidavit on 20 June in the same year. There is no record of Margery having had children but her marriage and the years of her greatest fertility were in the 1640s, when the parish records were scarcely maintained. Unlike some of the other families involved in the case, the Coombs family was a small one with a single branch. It is likely that John was her son, named after her own father, and that Seymour therefore was her grandson. John Coombs buried his daughter, Sarah, on 28 January 1686. At the time of her arrest Margery Coombes was about 76 years old.

Fig. 7-3 *Late seventeenth-century bellarmine stoneware 'witch bottles' in Andover Museum found buried in the foundations of what was once a house in Abbotts Ann in Hampshire.*

Ann More is a more elusive figure in the surviving records than both Elizabeth Carrier and Margery Coombes. Indeed, the surname More very rarely crops up in the registers for St George's for the seventeenth century – the baptism of a Margery More ('Mor'), daughter of Richard, in 1606, is the single More baptismal entry between 1590 and 1670. There is just one burial record for a More for the hundred years between 1630 and 1730, but it is a tantalising one: Ann More, the wife of Philip, was buried on 5 June 1703. The affidavit that she was buried in wool was made by Mary Hillman. This could well be the Ann More that the Reverend May Hill spoke of in the account he gave to Richard Baxter. The absence of other Mores in the Beckington records suggests that she had migrated to the village from elsewhere – probably from a neighbouring parish such as Rode or Frome, in both of which the record for Mores is comparatively abundant. In July 1687[107] she is recorded as providing the affidavit for Alice Lyde in Beckington's buried in wool register.

The two Beckington women who, 'upon their oaths deposited, that they hooked out of the navel of the said Mary Hill, as she lay in a dead fit, crooked pins, small nails, and small pieces of brass', were named Susannah Belton and Ann Holland. Belton was born in the village at the start of 1665 and she was a young woman of about twenty-four when summoned to give evidence before the court at Taunton. She came from a large family – one of at least eleven siblings, many of whom survived the hazards of infancy. Her father, Robert Belton, had lost his first wife, Elizabeth, in November 1653; she was buried just three days before their infant son, Thomas, who was barely a month old when he died. Remarkably, just over a month later, on 7 January 1654, he married again – this time to a local girl called Anne Cox. The record of the marriage in the parish register reveals that one of the two witnesses to their marriage was John Hill, and Mary Hill, his wife, the mother of the Mary Hill in the 1689 witchcraft episode, was one of three additional witnesses to their banns. The Belton–Hill family alliance seems to have extended to relations between their children – in giving evidence before the judge, Susannah Belton was acting in the interests of the daughter of a couple who may well have been her parents' closest friends. There is also an earlier connection between the Beltons and Elizabeth Carrier: in 1686, a couple of years after the death of Robert Belton, Elizabeth Carrier made affidavits that Jane and John Belton, both of whom were probably the children of Robert and Anne (and Susannah's brother and sister), were buried in wool.[108] Soon after Elizabeth Carrier's trial Susannah Belton married John Morse at St George's in April 1694. John Morse was a member of the same Beckington family as that of the churchwarden, recorded as 'Pollidore Mosse', who attested to the truth of the account of the Beckington case in the 1689 *Great News* tract.

Ann Holland can also be identified, tentatively, in the Beckington register. The Hollands were a prolific family in the community. She may have been the Ann Holland who married Richard Street in 1699, ten years after the witchcraft allegations. Alternatively, and much more likely, she was Anne, wife of Walter Holland, who buried two of their four children in 1685 and 1691. Since the first of these, Elizabeth in 1685, was a near-natal infant death, and the second, Ruth in 1691, that of a two-year-old, it can be presumed, despite the absence of a marriage record, that this Ann Holland was of a similar age to Susannah

(1)

Great News from the
West of England.

Being a True Account of Two Young Persons lately *Bewitch'd* in the Town of *Beckenton* in *Somerset-shire*: Shewing the sad Condition they are in, by Vomiting, or Throwing out of their Bodies, the Abundance of *Pins*, *Nails*, *Pewter*, *Brass*, *Lead*, *Iron*, and *Tin*, to the Admiration of all Beholders.

And of the old *Witch* being carryed several Times to a great River; into which, her Legs being tied, she was Thrice thrown in; but each Time, she Swam like a *Cork*.

AFTERWARDS,

By Order from a *Justice of Peace*, she was Search'd by a Jury of Women, and such Signs and Marks being found about her, positive Oath was given in against her; so that she is Committed to Jayl, until the next Assizes.

Licensed and Entred according to Order.

I Know there be Persons in the World, who will not believe there are *Witches*; that is, such Persons, who, by a League and Confederacy with the Devil, do get him to enter, possess, and torment the Bodies of Children, and others: But whosoever, shall read this ensuing Narrative, if he be not an Atheist in his Heart, as well as in his Practice, may be easily Convinc'd; and see the Necessity of keeping close to GOD, in a constant Performance of his Duty; that GOD may keep close to him in his dayly Preservation and Safety.

IN the Town of *Beckenton*, about Two Miles from *Froom*, and Seven from *Bath*, in *Somerset-shire*, liveth one *William Spicer*, a young Man about eighteen Years of Age; as he was wont to pass by the *Alms-house* (where lived an Old Woman, about Fourscore) he would call her *Witch*, and tell her of her *Buns*; which did so enrage the Old Woman, that she threatened him with a *Warrant*; and accordingly did fetch one from a Neighbouring *Justice of the Peace*; at which he was so frightened, that he humbled himself to her, and promised never to call her so again. Within a few days after this Young Man fell into the strangest Fits that ever Mortal beheld with Eyes, and these, by turns, held him about a Fortnight: When the Fits were upon him, he would often say, That he did see this Old Woman against the Wall in the same Room of the House where he was, and that sometimes she did knock her Fist at him, sometimes grin her Teeth, and sometimes laugh at him in his Fits. He was so strong, that three or four Men could scarce hold him; and when he did call for *Small Beer* to drink, he would be sure to bring up some *Crooked Pins*; first and last, to the Number of Thirty, and upwards.

In the same Town liveth one *Mary Hill*, about the same Age of this Young Man; who meeting with this Old Woman, demanded the Ring she borrowed of her; and through her Importunity, she prevailed to get the Ring (with this Threatning) from the Old Woman, *That she had been better to have let her kept it longer*. About a Week before the said *Mary* was taken with Fits, she met this Old Woman in the Street; who taking her by the hand, desired her to goe with her to *Froom*, to look after some *Spinning Work*; for none in the Town would suffer her to have any: The said *Mary* being afraid, refused to go with her: About four days after she met the Old Woman again, who would have begg'd an *Apple* of her, having newly bought some, which she refused to give her.

The *Sunday* following, she complained of a pricking in her Stomack; but on *Monday*, as she was Eating her Dinner, something arose in her Throat, which was like to have Choaked her; and at the same time fell into Violent Fits, which held her till Nine or Ten a Clock at Night; the Fits were so strong and violent, that Four or Five Persons were scarce able to hold her, and in the midst of them, she would tell how she saw this old Woman against the Wall, grinning at her, and being struck at, would step

A aside

Fig. 7-4, 7-5 Great News from the West of England *tract (1689).*

aside to avoid the blows. The day after, she was taken with the like Fits, and would tell how she did see her as afore, and that she was the Person that had bewitcht her.

The *Wednesday* following, she began to throw up *Crooked Pins*, and so continued for the space of a Fortnight: After this, she began to throw up *Nails* and *Pins*; and then she ceased for the space of Eight Days: And then she began to throw up *Nails* again, and *Handles* of *Spoons*, both of *Pewter* and *Brass*; several pieces of *Iron*, *Lead*, and *Tin*, with several clusters of *Crooked Pins*; some tied with Yarn, and some with Thread, with abundance of Blood between while; and so she continued to do for some considerable time: She threw up in all, above Two Hundred *Crooked Pins*, besides several clusters of *Crooked Pins*, Sixteen or Seventeen in a cluster, Seven Pieces of *Pewter*, Four Pieces of *Brass*, being *Handles* of *Spoons*, Six Pieces of *Lead*; some whereof were *Handles* of *Spoons*, and some, the *Lead* of a *Window*, besides one solid Piece of *Lead*, which weighed full two Ounces; Six long Pieces of *Latten*, with *Wire* belonging to them; Five Pieces of *Iron*, one whereof was round, but hollow, and very big; and Two and Twenty *Nails*, some whereof were *Board-Nails*, above three Inches and a Quarter long.

The People of the Town seeing the sad and deplorable Condition of the said *Mary*, and being much concerned for her, did cause this old Woman to be brought near the House where the said *Mary* Lived, unknown to her; and being gathered together above an Hundred People, the said *Mary* was brought forth into the open Air, who immediately fell into such strong Fits, that two or three men were scarce able to hold her: And being brought upon the Hill by the Church; and the old Woman brought near her (notwithstanding there were four men to hold the said *Mary* in a Chair) she mounted up over their Heads into the Air; but the men, and others standing by, caught hold of her Legs, and pulled her down again.

This Woman was ordered by a *Justice* of the *Peace*, to be searcht by a *Jury* of Women, who found about her several purple Spots, which they prickt with a sharp Needle, but she felt no pain: She had about her other Marks and Tokens of a *Witch*, of which the Women upon Oath, gave an Account to the *Justice*; and some Swearing positively against her, she was sent to the County *Jayle*, where she is remaining to be Tryed the next *Assizes*.

This old Woman was had to a great River near the Town, to see whether she could sink under Water; her Legs being tied, she was put in, and tho' she did endeavour to the uttermost (by her Hands) to get her self under, yet she could not, but would lie upon her Back, and did Swim like a piece of Cork: There were present above Twenty Persons to Attest the Truth of this, yet could not gain Credit in the minds of People: Therefore, she was had to the Water a second time, and being put in, she swam as at first; and tho' there were present above Two Hundred People to see this Sight, yet it could not be believed by many. At the same time, also, there was put into the Water, a Lusty young Woman, who sunk immediately, and had been drown'd, had it not been for the help that was at hand. To satisfy the World, and to leave no Room for doubting, the old Woman was had down to the Water the third time, and being put in as before, she did still Swim. At this Swimming of her, were present, such a Company of People of the Town and Country, and many of them, Persons of Quality, as could not well be Numbred; so that now, there is scarce one Person that doubts of the Truth of this thing.

It is full Ten Weeks ago (from the *Twenty Eight* of *October* last past) that this young Woman was first seized with these Terrible Fits: And tho' she had been Visited by the Minister of the Place, who for sometime Prayed with her Twice a Day; and by a *Non-co*...... that Lives in the same Parish, that Twice performed the like Office, yet she continues to be often seized with terrible Fits, and to bring up both *Nails* and *Handles of Spoons*, and is still remaining an Object of great Pity, and to be remembred at the Throne of Grace daily.

The Truth of this is be Attested by Us,

May *Hill*, Rector of *Beckenton*,

Francis *Jesse*, } Church-Wardens.
Pollidore *Mosse*, }

October, 26th. 1689.

Christo. *Brewer*, } Over-Seers of the Poor.
Francis *Francke*, }

Will. *Minterne*, } Constables.
Will. *Cowherd*, }

LONDON, Printed by *T. M.* in *Jewen-street*, 1689.

Belton. It is possible that she was Anne, Susannah's older sister, born in 1654, ten years before her sibling. That there was some kind of Belton–Holland connection is evident from the fact that Anne Belton, most probably Susannah's mother, is recorded as swearing the affidavit for the burial in wool of John Holland in June 1679. This, in turn, suggests a family connection with another of the people signing off the *Great News* document – the overseer of the poor, Christopher Brewer. In 1681 Thomas Brewer and Ruth Holland were married at Beckington, and in 1682 Anne Belton swore the affidavit at the time of a 'Mr' Christopher Brewer's burial.[109] This man, most probably, was our Christopher Brewer's father, who also became father to a Christopher, baptised at St George's on 23 July 1689, just as the witchcraft panic was about to erupt in the village.

Two of the men listed as testifying to the truth of the *Great News* pamphlet – one of the two churchwardens, Francis Jesse, and Christopher Brewer – were also examined by Judge Holt, and they both declared they had seen Mary Hill on several occasions vomit crooked pins, nails and pieces of brass, which they too 'produced in open court'. They further stated that, to be certain 'it was no imposture', they had searched her mouth with their fingers shortly before she vomited.

Having heard these statements Rector Hill was summoned. He told Richard Baxter, 'The court thought fit to call for me, who am Minister of the Parish, to testify the knowledge of the matter, which I did to this effect, that I had seen her at several times, after having given her a little small beer, vomit up crooked pins, nails, and pieces of brass'. He, too, 'to prevent the supposition of a cheat', had placed her near a window and looked into her mouth and searched it with his finger before giving her the beer that would make her throw up. Nevertheless, both women, no doubt to the deep dismay of those who had sent them there, were acquitted.

A careful reading of the two surviving accounts of the Beckington case, in conjunction with the parish records, permits the approximate reconstruction of events as a fairly detailed timeline, *Great News from the West of England* providing most of the information for the story up to the end of October 1689, and the Baxter version providing its denouement:

c. **Monday 12 August 1689:** Mary Hill refuses to accompany Elizabeth Carrier to Frome to look for work.

c. **Friday 16 August 1689:** Mary Hill refuses to give Elizabeth Carrier an apple.

Sunday 18 August 1689: Mary Hill experiences a pricking sensation in her stomach.

Monday 19 August 1689: start of Mary Hill's illness – she suffers fits from dinner-time until 9 or 10 pm.

Tuesday 20 August 1689: Mary Hill identifies Elizabeth Carrier while suffering a fit.

Wednesday 21 August 1689: Mary Hill throws up crooked pins and continues to do so for a fortnight (200 crooked pins in total).

Second week in September 1689: Mary Hill starts to vomit nails and pins.

Third week in September 1689: Mary Hill in recovery (for the space of eight days).

Fourth week in September 1689: Mary Hill starts to vomit a wide variety of metal items.

c. **September 1689:** Elizabeth Carrier is subjected to three swimming tests; a Justice of the Peace orders her to be searched by a jury of women who, upon oath, report 'marks and tokens of a witch' on her body and she is sent to the County Gaol at Ilchester to await trial at the next assizes.

Saturday 26 October 1689: the statement regarding the case that will be printed before the end of the year as *Great News from the West of England*, is produced by the Rector of Beckington, two churchwardens, two overseers of the poor and two constables.

November 1689–April 1690: Mary Hill continues to vomit metal objects and suffer fits during which she has visions of her tormentors, Ann More and Margery Coombes; two Justices of the Peace issue warrants for the arrest

c. **January 1690:** Margery Coombes and Ann More appear at the Epiphany sessions in Bruton and are committed to the County Gaol where Margery Coombes dies on arrival.

Tuesday 1 April 1690: Gaol Delivery at Taunton of Ann More and Elizabeth Carrier; those giving evidence at the assizes include

Susannah Belton and Ann Holland, Francis Jesse and Christopher Brewer, Mary Hill and May Hill; Lord Chief Justice Holt acquits Carrier and More for lack of evidence; Mary Hill eventually recovers at the home of May Hill.

March 1691: May Hill is introduced, by John Humfrey, to Richard Baxter in London.

4 April 1691: May Hill provides his testimony for Richard Baxter.

1   John Cotta, *The Tryall of Witch-Craft, shewing the true and right Methode of the Discovery with a Confutation of Erroneous Wayes* (London: 1616).
2   Anon., *Great News*.
3   Richard Baxter, *The Certainty of the Worlds of Spirits* (1691), 74.
4   1688 in the list of affidavits.
5   Baxter, *Worlds of Spirits*, 77.
6   16 February 1679 (i.e. 1680).
7   Richard Hill and Katherine Evans, married in 1639, had two children – one, a boy, died in infancy unbaptised, the other was a girl, baptised Mary in 1642, who is likely to be the woman of the same name who married William Cook at St George's in 1663. Richard was probably the brother of the children's grandfather, John Hill, who had married Margaret Phillips in 1629 and probably died in the period around 1650 when the parish records ceased to be maintained.
8   Mary, the daughter of Roger and Christian Carrier, was baptised at St George's, Beckington, on 17 May 1650. A baptismal entry for 10 February 1654 (i.e. 1655) records another Mary Carrier, this one the daughter of John and Margaret Carrier. A third Mary Carrier was born to William and Ann Carrier in the village in 1661. One certain conclusion that can be drawn is that Mary was a typical Carrier family name for children born in the period.
9   Anon., *Great News*.
10 *Ibid.*
11 This apparent psychosomatic fact is central in Edward Bever's attempt to unravel cases of bewitchment in the early modern period. (Bever, 'Witchcraft Fears', 2000, 583.)
12 The 1689 pamphlet testimony is dated 26 October 1689, but in the text it states 'It is a full ten weeks ago (from the twenty-eighth of October last past) that this young woman was first seized with these terrible fits'.
13 Collinson, *History*, Vol. II, 198.
14 Bernard, *Guide*, 226–8.
15 Sharpe, *Instruments*, 156.

16 Pearson, 'Pamphlets of the supernatural', 64–5.
17 James Sharpe, *The Bewitching of Anne Gunter* (London: Profile Books, 2000), 45.
18 Edward Jorden, *A Briefe Discourse of a Disease Called the Suffocation of the Mother* (1603).
19 Sharpe, *Anne Gunter*, 171–72.
20 *Ibid.*, 1–11.
21 Cotta, *Witch-Craft*, 98–99.
22 Mary Moore, *Wonderfull News from the North, or, a true Relation of the sad and grievous torments Inflicted upon the Bodies of three Children of Mr George Muschamp, late of the County of Northumberland, by Witch-craft* (1650).
23 Where most witch-hunts focused on the lives of people from pretty humble backgrounds, this is an unusual case in that the chief protagonists seem to have had fairly well-to-do, respectable backgrounds. Dorothy Swinow was the wife and widow of a colonel; the family that accused her presumably had at least one highly literate member (Mary Moore, the author of the 1650 account), possessed a virginal, and was wealthy enough to consult a range of physicians.
24 Ewen, *Witchcraft and Demonianism*, 398; Surtees Society, vol. 40, 85–88.
25 'Taken by a Person then Attending the Court', *A Tryal of Witches at the Assizes held at Bury St Edmonds for the County of Suffolk; on the Tenth day of March, 1664* (1680).
26 Bernard, *Guide*, 31.
27 Bever, 'Witchcraft Fears', 582.
28 Bernard, *Guide*, 173.
29 Peter Elmer, 'Medicine and Witchcraft' in Brian P. Levack, *The Oxford Handbook of Witchcraft in Early Modern Europe and Colonial America* (Oxford: Oxford University Press, 2013), 567.
30 See, for example, Brian P. Levack, *The Devil Within: Possession and Exorcism in the Christian West* (London: Yale University Press, 2013).
31 Owen Davies, *Witchcraft, Magic and Culture, 1736-1951* (Manchester: Manchester University Press, 1999), 198; Davies found no cases of witchcraft-induced strange vomiting in Britain later than the mid-eighteenth century.
32 'behind the descriptions provided by those suffering from supposed witchcraft in early modern and later trial records, a number of modern categories of physical ailment and psychological or neuropsychological condition are recognisable'; Owen Davies, 'The Nightmare Experience, Sleep Paralysis, and Witchcraft Accusations', *Folklore* 114 (2003): 181.
33 Edward Bever, *The Realities of Witchcraft and Popular Magic in Early Modern Europe: Culture, Cognition, and Everyday Life* (Basingstoke: Palgrave Macmillan, 2008), xiv-xvi; drawing on 'new studies of cognition and perception' and 'fringe phenomena' Bever has considered psychosomatic

theory in the projection of hostility and its capacity for causing or contributing to a variety of ailments.
34 Kirsten C. Uszkalo, *Bewitched and Bedeviled: A Cognitive Approach to Embodiment in Early English Possession* (New York: Palgrave Macmillan, 2015), 48.
35 See, for example, Armando Favazza, *Bodies Under Siege: Self-mutilation, Non-suicidal Self-injury, and Body Modification in Culture and Psychiatry* (Baltimore: Johns Hopkins University Press, 2011).
36 J. Walker (ed.), *A Selection of Curious Articles from the Gentleman's Magazine* (London: Longman, Hurst, Rees, and Orme, 1809), 449.
37 Paul F. Eve, *A Collection of Remarkable Cases in Surgery* (Philadelphia: J.B. Lippincott and Co., 1857), 235.
38 W.W. Morland and Francis Minot, *The Boston Medical and Surgical Journal*, Volume 61 (Boston: David Clapp, 1860), 227.
39 Philippe Pinel, *Nosographie Philosophique* (1798), in Walter Vandereycken and Ron van Deth, *From Fasting Saints to Anorexic Girls: The history of self-starvation* (London: Athlone Press, 1994), 116.
40 B. Parry-Jones, W.L. Parry-Jones, 'Pica: Symptom or eating disorder? A historical assessment', *The British Journal of Psychiatry*, Volume 160, March 1992, 341.
41 *Ibid.*
42 Andrea S. Hartmann, Anne E. Becker, Claire Hampton, Rachel Bryant-Waugh, 'Pica and Rumination Disorder in DSM-5', *Psychiatric Annals*, 42:11 (2012), 427.
43 Diagnostic and Statistical Manual of Mental Disorders (DSM-5; November 2015).
44 Anne Laurence, *Women in England 1500–1760: A Social History* (London: Phoenix Press, 1994), 101.
45 Christopher Gillberg, Henrik Soderstrom, 'Learning Disability', *Lancet*, Vol 362, September 2003, 811-21.
46 Challenging Behaviour Foundation, Information Sheet, 'Pica (Eating Inedible Objects)', Registered charity no. 1060714 (England and Wales). Registered office: The Old Courthouse, New Road Avenue, Chatham, ME4 6BE. www.challengingbehaviour.org.uk, last updated July 2008, accessed 4 November 2017.
47 I am grateful to Dr Anna Scarna, lecturer in Psychology at Oxford University, for her guidance in this respect.
48 Don E. Williams, David McAdam, 'Assessment, behavioural treatment, and prevention of pica: Clinical guidelines and recommendations for practitioners', *Research in Developmental Disabilities*, Volume 33, Issue 6, November-December 2012, 2050-2057.
49 William Drage, *Daimonomageia: A Small Treatise of Sickness and Diseases from Witchcraft* (1665), 5-6.

50 Ben McNaughten, Thomas Bourke and Andrew Thompson, 'Fifteen-minute consultation: the child with pica' Arch Dis Child Educ Pract Ed 2017; 102: 226–229.
51 Mourato Nunes I, Pedroso AI, Irimia M, *et al.*, *British Medical Journal*, published online 8 June 2017.
52 See William Drage, *Daimonomageia*, 5, for a citation of the work of Johann Weyer and others concerning such matters.
53 BBC News, NDTV, CNN, ABC News, etc.
54 Samiullah Bhatti, Awais Amjad Malik, Mudessar Rafaqat, Usman Ishaque and Mahmood Ayyaz, 'Acuphagia as a Cause of Gastric Bezoar Causing Gastric Outlet Obstruction', *Journal of the College of Physicians and Surgeons*, Pakistan 2014, Vol. 24 (Special Supplement 3): 190-92.
55 http://news.bbc.co.uk/1/hi/world/africa/1402616.stm accessed 17/02/16.
56 Robert Colvile, 'Man died after eating coins and a magnet', *The Telegraph*, 28/09/2006.
57 Baxter, *Worlds of Spirits*, 77
58 Northern Circuit Assize record in Ewen, *Witchcraft and Demonianism*, 398.
59 Jennifer Hecht, *Stay: A History of Suicide and the Philosophies Against It* (Yale: Yale University Press, 2013).
60 Gordon Rayner and Richard Savill, 'Bridgend suicides: a town tainted by death', *The Telegraph*, 23 February 2008.
61 John Cotta, *A True Discovery of the Empericke with the Fugitive Physition and Quacksalver* (1617), 21.
62 Helen King, *The Disease of Virgins: Green Sickness, Chlorosis and the Problems of Puberty* (London: Routledge, 2004), 18.
63 William Salmun, *Aristotle's Master-piece Compleated* (1702), 57.
64 Jorden, *Of the Suffocation of the Mother*, 25.
65 See Anthony Lopez, Patrice Cacoub, Iain C. Macdougall, Laurent Peyrin-Biroulet, 'Iron Deficiency Anaemia', *Lancet*, 2016; 387: 907-16.
66 Blagrave, *Astrological Practice*, 67.
67 Webster, *The Displaying of Supposed Witchcraft*, 161.
68 Salmun, *Aristotle's Master-piece*, 57-58.
69 Baxter, *Certainty of the Worlds of Spirits*, 98.
70 *Ibid.*, 79.
71 E.A. Rose, J.H. Porcerelli, A.V. Neale, 'Pica: Common but commonly missed', *Journal of the American Board of Family Medicine, 13*(5), 2000, 353-58.
72 Owen Davies, *Popular Magic: Cunning-folk in English History* (London: Hambledon Continuum, 2003), 109.
73 Bernard, *Guide*, 213.
74 Drage, *Daimonomageia*, 21.
75 DNB, 'Blagrave, Joseph'.
76 Blagrave, *Astrological Practice*, 168–73.

77 John Hart, *The Firebrand Taken out of the Fire* (London: 1654), 30.
78 Uszkalo, *Bewitched and Bedeviled*, 15.
79 It could be on the increase: Ranit Mishori, professor of family medicine at Georgetown University School of Medicine in Washington, D.C., has observed, 'A recent study by the Agency for Healthcare Research and Quality found that hospitalizations for pica in a 10-year span jumped 93 percent, from 964 in 1999-2000 to 1,862 in 2008-2009'. The Washington Post. https://www.washingtonpost.com/national/health-science/pica-the-compulsion-to-eat-dirt-and-other-oddities-is-found-in-many-cultures/2012/05/14. Accessed 11 November 2017.
80 Davies, 'The Nightmare Experience', 182.
81 M.J., *The Hartford-shire Wonder or Strange News from Ware* (1669).
82 Vandereycken and Deth, *Fasting Saints*, 141.
83 This information has been gleaned form multiple sources; it is a partial record and only includes cases where details including dates and locations are available in the historical record.
84 Ewen, *Witchcraft and Demonianism*, 459.
85 Baxter, *Worlds of Spirits*, 77.
86 *Ibid.*, 76.
87 The National Institute for Health and Care Excellence (NICE), 2014.
88 Gaskill has noted that after 1680 this was the case 'for all crimes', not just witchcraft; Gaskill, *Crime and Mentalities*, 92.
89 Baxter, *Worlds of Spirits*, 74.
90 *Ibid.*, 77-9.
91 This disreputable practice, repudiated for example by Richard Bernard, is not mentioned in the version of May Hill's account published by Richard Baxter.
92 Ewen, *Witchcraft and Demonianism*, 453.
93 Sir George was head of the family that held Mells Manor at the time of the dissolution of the monasteries, thought to be commemorated in the nursery rhyme 'Little Jack Horner'. Iona and Peter Opie, *The Oxford Dictionary of Nursery Rhymes* (Oxford: Oxford University Press, 1951), 236. Whether or not the Horners actually stole the manor, Mells historian Frank Cleverdon remarked: 'One has a suspicion that the rhyme, so long associated with the family, was applied to them at this time'. *The History of Mells* (Frome: Frome Society for Local Study, 2014), 43.
94 Gaskill, *Crime and Mentalities*, 91.
95 Sharpe, *Instruments*, 155.
96 I am grateful to Maureen Wincott, a direct descendant of Richard Bernard, for this information.
97 VCH, 'Pitcombe', Somerset, Vol. 7.
98 On 16 September he heard evidence given by Edward Brook of Queen Camel, concerning horses found by 'Mr Middlemay's boy' that were put

in the pound belonging to Peter Higdon, also of Queen Camel. Brook was charged with recovering them without paying the obligatory fine. On 24 September a cordwinder from North Barrow presented his complaint before the judge concerning the activities of one of his workers, a man named Isaac Hutchins of West Lydford. Hutchins had been in trouble before – he was tried at Taunton for marching with Monmouth to Sedgemoor in 1686. SRO Q/SR/177/12–13; SRO Q/SR/177/14–15.
99 Elmer, *Witchcraft*, 213, fn. 124.
100 Sharpe, *Instruments*, 179.
101 Randell, *Crime*, 197.
102 VCH, 'Bruton', Somerset, Vol. 7; Phyllis Couzens, *Bruton in Selwood* (Sherborne: Abbey Press, 1968), 65.
103 English Heritage, British Listed Buildings, number 261565.
104 Bruton Epiphany sessions 1689 (1690) parchment cover, SRO Q/SR/178/27.
105 Gittings, *Death*, 67.
106 Recorded as 1688 in the erroneous burials in wool register.
107 Incorrectly recorded as 1689 in the surviving 1696 compilation of the original, now lost, records.
108 The buried in wool register erroneously records these burials for the year 1688.
109 Erroneously recorded as 1684 in the buried in wool register; it is interesting to note that Anne Belton also swore the affidavit for William Spicer's supposed mother, Margaret, in 1687.

8

CREDIBLE MINISTERS

Fig. 8-1 *The Devil seemingly conjured by gentlemen-wizards who appear to be standing within a magic circle. (Contemporary woodcut)*[1]

[In] other cases, when wicked or mistaken people charge us with crimes of which we are not guilty, we clear ourselves by showing that at that time we were at home, or in some other place, about our honest business; but in prosecutions for witchcraft, that most natural and just defence is a mere jest, for if any cracked-brain girl imagines (or any lying spirit makes her believe) that she sees any old woman, or other person pursuing her in her visions, the defenders of the vulgar witchcraft […] hang the accused parties for things they were doing when they were, perhaps, asleep on their beds or saying their prayers

– Francis Hutchinson, An Historical Essay Concerning Witchcraft (1718), vi-vii.

CREDIBLE MINISTERS

THE GAOL DELIVERY of Ann More and Elizabeth Carrier at Taunton on the charge of bewitching Mary Hill, spinster, is recorded for 1 April 1690.[1a] By then Elizabeth Carrier had survived five months in custody at Ilchester. At Taunton they would be tried by Lord Chief Justice Holt, the judge for the Western Circuit assizes. Just as the outlook of the JPs was crucial in the advancing of a witch accusation, that of the assize court judges was critical.

Sir John Holt was raised in a lawyer household. His father, Sir Thomas, was a barrister of Gray's Inn and also recorder of Abingdon, close to the family home in Oxfordshire. During the 1660s he served as MP for the town. After studying at Oriel College he was called to the bar, without graduating, in 1664. With over twenty years in a career as a successful barrister, he was knighted by James II in 1686 and made Recorder of London. He relinquished this position following the execution of a soldier for desertion. Holt had contested this punishment, since the country at the time was not at war – the only one of nine judges hearing the case to do so. On 17 April 1689 he became Lord Chief Justice of the King's Bench and the most influential assize court judge of his generation. He is remembered not as a judge 'with a peculiar sensitivity for the accused'[2] but as one with a strong sense of justice through scrupulous application of the law. It was fortunate for the Beckington women that such a man as Holt had been so recently raised to the King's Bench and that he happened to be hearing cases for the Western Circuit at the start of 1690. Holt has been seen as a central character in the story of the decline of witchcraft persecution in England and

Fig. 8-2 *Lord Chief Justice Sir John Holt, 1642-1710.*

it is fair to conclude that, but for him, and other equally sceptical judges, the execution of Alice Molland at Exeter in 1685 might not have been the last. Francis Hutchinson, using Holt's trial notes with the judge's special dispensation as the major source for his *Historical Essay concerning Witchcraft* (1718), concluded that Holt had heard the cases of at least eleven 'witches', all of whom were released without charge.[3] However, the much greater incidence of acquittal than punishment in the surviving assize records for the whole of the seventeenth century indicates that most of those presiding over witchcraft cases should not be remembered as 'hanging judges'. Holt's leniency in the Beckington case was very reminiscent of a case heard at Taunton a full ten years before by another judge celebrated for his careful and fair-minded consideration of every case brought before him: Lord North.

Roger North (1651–1734) wrote a biography[4] of his illustrious brother, the Right Honourable Francis North (1637–85), Baron of Guilford and Lord Keeper of the Great Seal under two kings – Charles II and James II. He served on occasion as a judge on the Western Circuit and came to dread 'the trying of a witch', for, as his biographer explained: 'It is seldom that a poor old wretch is brought to trial upon that account, but there is, at the heels of her, a popular rage that does little less than demand her to be put to death, and, if a judge is so clear and open as to declare against that impious vulgar opinion, that the devil himself has power to torment and kill innocent children, or that he is pleased to divert himself with the good people's cheese, butter, pigs, and geese, and the like errors of the ignorant and foolish rabble, the countrymen (the triers) cry this judge hath no religion, for he doth not believe witches; and so, to show they have some, hang the poor wretches'. Thus it was an anxious Lord North who finally came to preside over a witchcraft trial when 'he was forced to try an old man for a wizard' at Taunton in about 1680. His brother also attended the trial out of 'curiosity of observing the state of a male witch, or wizard' and he managed to find a seat 'near where the poor man stood'. North's account contains interesting parallels with the Beckington case and sheds light on the form of trial that Elizabeth Carrier and Ann More experienced a few years later in the same court.

The evidence against him was, the having bewitched a girl of about thirteen years old: for she had strange and unaccountable fits, and used to cry out upon him, and spit out of her mouth straight pins; and, whenever the man was brought near her, she fell in her fits, and spit forth straight pins. His Lordship wondered at the straight pins, which could not be so well couched in the mouth as crooked ones; for such only used to be spit out by people bewitched. He examined the witness very tenderly and carefully, and so as none could collect what his opinion was; for he was fearful of the Jurymen's precipitancy, if he gave them offence. When the poor man was told he must answer for himself, he entered upon a defence as orderly and well expressed as I ever heard spoke by any man, counsel, or other; and if the Attorney General had been his advocate, I am sure he would not have done it more sensibly. The sum of it was malice, threatening, and circumstances of imposture in the girl; to which matters he called his witnesses, and they were heard. After this was done, the Judge was not satisfied to direct the Jury before the imposture was fully cleared, but studied, and beat the bush a while, asking sometimes one, and then another, questions as he thought proper. At length he turned to the Justice of the Peace that committed the man, and took the first examinations, and 'Sir', said he, 'pray will you ingenuously declare your thoughts, if you have any, touching these straight pins which the girl spit; for you saw her in her fit?' Then, 'My Lord', said he, 'I did not know that I might concern myself with this evidence, having taken the examination, and committed the man. But, since your lordship demands it, I must needs say I think the girl, doubling herself in her fit, as being convulsed, bent her head down close to her stomacher, and, with her mouth, took pins out of the edge of that, and then, righting herself a little, spit them into some bystander's hands'. This cast a universal satisfaction upon the minds of the whole audience, and the man was acquitted. As the judge went downstairs, out of the Court, a hideous old woman cried, 'God bless your Lordship'. 'What's the matter, good woman?' said the Judge. 'My Lord', said she, 'forty years ago they would have hanged me for a witch, and they could not; and, now, they would have hanged my poor son'.[5]

* * *

Fig. 8-3 *Richard Baxter (1615-91), theologian and demonologist.*

By the time the Civil War broke out Richard Baxter, based at Kidderminster, had begun to make a name for himself as an inspirational preacher who 'never administered the Lord's supper, never baptised a child with the sign of the cross, never wore a surplice'.[6] He sided with Parliament in the conflict – a dangerous position to adopt in a county, Worcestershire, which was, broadly speaking, Royalist. He was preaching at Alcester on the Worcestershire–Warwickshire border while the battle of Edgehill was fought less than twenty miles to the east. Obliged to retreat further into Warwickshire, he joined a number of fellow fugitive ministers at Coventry. He visited the battlefield at Naseby and served as a chaplain in Colonel Whalley's regiment. Despite his parliamentarian leanings, as a monarchist, he was compelled, at great risk to himself, to speak out against the regicides who had taken Charles I's life. When the monarchy was restored he became one of the new king's chaplains and was even offered the bishopric of Hereford, which he turned down. Unwilling to consent to the conditions of the Act of Uniformity in 1662, he left the Church of England and retired to Acton in Middlesex. He was imprisoned for six months as a practising nonconformist. When James II acceded, his position was further imperilled and, following a trial before Judge Jeffreys in 1685, he was fined 500 marks for sedition and imprisoned until it was paid. He spent a year and a half in gaol. He continued to preach after his release, drawing vast crowds to hear his sermons. Baxter was instrumental in forming the coalition of dissenters and Church of England clergy against the papism of James II. When William and Mary were instated in the revolution of 1688 he accepted the terms of the Toleration Act which permitted, by licence, the preaching of nonconformist ministers who had taken an oath of allegiance. His publication of the Beckington witchcraft case in *Certainty of the Worlds of Spirits* would be one of his last. He died, well into his seventies, in December 1691 at his home in Charterhouse Yard in Finsbury, less than a year after his meeting there with May Hill.

Fig. 8-4 *Statue of Richard Baxter at Kidderminster erected in 1875 in recognition of 'his Christian learning and his pastoral fidelity'.*

Baxter was a most prodigious and influential writer. One biographer claimed, 'He was the creator of our popular Christian literature. Regarded intrinsically and as literature, his books need fear no comparison with contemporaries'.[7] More recently N.H. Keeble remarked: 'Puritanism had always utilized the press, but there had never been a literary career like this, either in scale or in success: Baxter was the first author of a string of best-sellers in British literary history'.[8] In his lifetime he put out well over a hundred books on theology and many other matters. Hence, although he is remembered in this context as the writer of a demonology, to regard him merely as a 'demonologist', it must be admitted, would be somewhat misleading. Indeed, this aspect of his work was ignored entirely by his hagiographers in the past. Like James I in *Daemonologie,* in the previous century, he attempted in *Certainty of the Worlds of Spirits* to steer a course between excessive credulity and unacceptable incredulity.[9] He was part of the late seventeenth-century wave of what Clark has defined as 'eschatologically' inspired collecting of supernatural accounts – relations that would advance the theological science pertinent to death, judgement, Heaven and Hell.[10] 'There are in this great city of London', he wrote on 20 July 1691, 'many persons that profess their great unbelief, or doubt of the life to come, the immortality of the soul, and therefore much more of the truth of the Gospel, and Christian faith, and supernatural revelations'. Such people, Baxter declared, claimed that if they could be 'certain of spirits, apparitions, witchcraft and miracles, it would do more to convince them than the assertions of the scriptures'. 'For the sake of such', he continued, 'I have elicited many credible instances in this book'.[11]

The Beckington witchcraft case is the main subject of the third chapter in *Certainty of the Worlds of Spirits.* Since Baxter made no reference to the two-page *Great News* broadsheet, printed five months before the case was concluded, and there is no comment at all on the bewitchment of William Spicer, which appears only in that account, it is likely that he had not seen it. Most probably he first heard of this 'strange story' from a fellow nonconformist with whom he frequently corresponded and knew well: John Humfrey, Glanvill's predecessor as vicar of St John's, Frome, and the man who introduced Baxter to Hill.

Living to the age of ninety-eight, after Nathan Denton, who lived until the following year, Humfrey is thought to have been the last of

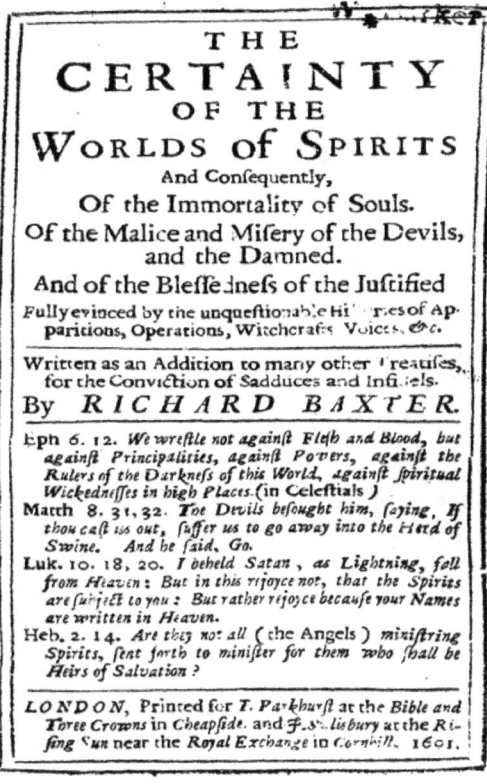

Fig. 8-5 *Richard Baxter,* The Certainty of the Worlds of Spirits *(1691).*

these surviving when he died in 1719, having become 'a Congregational man in London'.[12] During the intervening years he further established his reputation as a prolific writer of sermons, letters, pamphlets on books on political, theological, and other matters, including witchcraft. Humfrey's whereabouts in the later 1660s are unknown but he is likely to have remained in Somerset for a while before moving to London. In 1672 he received special dispensation to preach in his home at Kingsbury.[13] However, the following year his publication, *Comprehension Promoted*, earned him a short term in the Gatehouse prison in Westminster. In 1708, he was instrumental in establishing an Independent meeting house in Duke's Lane. In August 1682 a fine of £100 was imposed upon him at the Middlesex sessions for preaching without authorisation. His will, drawn up on 12 February 1715, identifies his two married daughters, Elizabeth and Hannah, as his heirs. He is recorded in its preamble as the Clerk of St Giles in the Fields, Middlesex. His wife and son William are not mentioned; it is very likely that they had pre-deceased him.[14]

Humfrey must have known Beckington well. The fact that Humfrey brought May Hill to London to visit Baxter suggests that he had maintained his contacts with Frome many years after leaving Somerset and that he was acquainted with Beckington's rector.

When he became involved in the Beckington affair of 1689 it was not the first time John Humfrey had participated in an investigation into a case in which a girl suffered convulsions thought to have been caused by supernatural forces. In a fifty-page pamphlet he published in London in 1708 entitled *An Account of the French Prophets and their Inspirations*, he recalled events from 'about forty years ago'. Living at that time in an unnamed place, he heard 'talk of a maid possessed with the Devil' about twelve miles away from his home. Her alarming condition had aroused a good deal of local interest and 'some sober, godly men' told him how they had themselves conversed with the Devil through the young woman he had entered. He rode the twelve miles to see her in the company of a 'religious gentleman' and two or three others. When he arrived he first spoke to her parents, both of whom confirmed the truth of the matter. He then observed the girl, whose name was Mary, who 'After a little time we were in the house [...] fell into a fit, not of shaking, but of convulsions'. She then began to speak in a 'strained, squeaking voice' and asked Humfrey, 'Will he pray?' More fits and a conversation of sorts followed until Humfrey contrived to interrogate her in Latin and Greek, at which point Mary became quiet and her 'possession' ended. Humfrey returned home and, when pressed for his considered opinion on the matter, concluded that, just as all those who flocked to see her were convinced she was possessed, she had convinced *herself* and 'out of that imagination did not only frame a voice', but answered as well and appropriately as she could 'all that came to her to talk with the Devil'. In a subsequent publication that year he referred to the episode again, this time declaring he considered the girl's fits 'Histerical ones' even though the girl's father, who he met again in London some years later still maintained she had been bewitched.[15] However Humfrey was also witness to a similar case in Tewkesbury where a girl inflicted by 'such a Variety of Fits, a whole Night together, and one of them a Maniacal Fit, and so Raving' convinced him this was indeed the Devil's work. Such evidence he no doubt hoped might 'serve to convince the Atheist and this Unbelieving Age of the Being of Invisible Things, and the Reasonableness of Religion'.[16] Outliving Glanvill, More, Baxter and Hill by many years, he was the last of their generation to champion their common cause from the discovery of the Selwood witches at the start of the 1660s until his death in 1719.

Someone who had connections with the world of the London press brought about the printing of *Great News from the West of England*. While there is no certain record of May Hill ever having published independently, Humfrey, like his associate Baxter, and those from Selwood – Alleine and Glanvill - was a prolific writer and the published author of numerous tracts of a religious and polemical character. He put out around sixty-five publications, some just a couple of sheets long, others books of hundreds of pages. This output was spread across more than half a century, the first dating to the early 1650s, and he used at least seventeen different printer-publishers. He relied on the services of some, such as Thomas Parkhurst of Cheapside, much more frequently than others. All of his works, bar one from Oxford, were printed in London. Most significantly, in the present discussion, on at least two occasions he probably used the same printer as the one to whom *Great News* is attributed. This two-sided sheet was 'Printed by T.M. in Jewen-Street, 1689'. It was followed soon after by T.M.'s printing of a two-sided single-page account of recent 'dreadful apparitions' in the West Country entitled *Strange and Wonderful News from Exeter* (1690). In 1678 Humfrey's *The Healing Paper, or, a Catholic Receipt for Union* was printed by 'B.T. and T.M.' in London, and, in 1700, 'T.M.' of London also printed the author's *A Paper to William Penn at the departure of that Gentleman to his territory, for his perusal, in Pennsylvania*. In 1682 the printing of Baxter's *Pneumatou diakonis* was done by 'T.M.' on behalf of Thomas Pankhurst. The 'T.M.' who printed *Great News*, conceivably, was the London printer Thomas Malthus who, in 1684, had made available Richard Bovet's *Pandaemonium*. However, after a very busy couple of years in 1683-4, Malthus produced two further publications in 1685 and, seemingly, no more thereafter.[17] It is far more likely that the 'T.M.' who printed *Great News* in 1689 was a man called Thomas Milbourne.

Milbourne lived for forty years in the same house in Jewen Street and was remembered as being 'a tender husband' to each of his four wives. He died in his seventy-fourth year. Although he was recorded as being 'a nice conformist', he had a spell in the 'gatehouse',[18] discharged in July 1667, for printing unlicensed books.[19] In 1686, shortly before he published *Great News*, he was again forbidden to print by order of the Company of Stationers.[20]

The 1666 will of Alexander Huish,[21] the previous rector of Beckington and May Hill's father-in-law, reveals that one of his three daughters, Margaret, baptised in Beckington at the start of 1634, was one of Milbourne's four wives: the man who printed *Great News* was Hill's brother-in-law. Jewen Street no longer exists but it once ran east from Aldersgate in the City of London and adjoined Red Cross Street close to St Giles Cripplegate. Here, in 1662, one of Milbourne's sons, Alexander,[22] no doubt named after his grandfather, was baptised. A near neighbour, who lived at the east end of Jewen Street between 1661 and 1663, was John Milton, who wrote most of *Paradise Lost* while living there.[23] Alexander followed in his father's footsteps and is listed as a printer in London between 1684 and 1693, issued on one occasion with a warrant for his arrest when his house was searched for treasonable and seditious libels in print or manuscript.[24] Another of Milbourne's sons, James, was baptised in Beckington in 1666. It is unlikely to be a coincidence that their maternal grandfather's patron when he (Huish) was appointed to the Somerset parish of Hornblotton, which he held (from February 1639/40) in tandem with Beckington, was one John Milborne, possibly John Milbourne of Milborne Port, who died in about 1664.

St Giles Cripplegate was the parish in which John Humfrey and his wife lived by the turn of the century – the Humfreys and Milbournes were near neighbours and they shared close connections with Selwood Forest in Somerset. When May Hill and Anne Huish were married at Chobham, Surrey, in 1675, she was registered as a spinster of St Giles Cripplegate; presumably she was living at her sister and brother-in-law's home before her relocation to Beckington as the wife of its new rector.[25] Incidentally, in 1682 Richard Baxter delivered a sermon on 'The Cure of Melancholy and Overmuch-Sorrows by Faith and Physick' at St Giles Cripplegate.[26] In 1682 'T.M.' printed Baxter's *Pneumatou Diakonia* for Thomas Parkhurst who also made available several of Humfrey's works.

It is quite possible that May Hill was not only related to Milbourne but also to Humfrey: Hill's widow, Anne, in her will drawn up in 1713,[27] bequeathed ten shillings to her 'cousin' Sarah Humphry, one of nine relations granted a portion of her estate. If they were related this could certainly help explain why Hill was persuaded by Humfrey to travel to London for his meeting with Richard Baxter in 1691. In addition, it would further explain the coincidence of Hill and Humfrey seeming to share the same London printer.

This raises the question: is there any further evidence for a possible link between Humfrey and Beckington? A trawl through the parish registers for the whole of the seventeenth century produces just one entry for Humfrey (or its variant spellings): on 20 April 1653 Elizabeth Humfrie was baptised at St George's. Most unusually, the register also recorded the date of her birth – 31 March. The total absence of other Humfreys in the register suggests that she was born to parents who were not natives of the village. This singular entry, recording a birth for a time when very few other entries made it to the parish register, is intriguing and it might denote a family of some local importance. Could she have been the daughter, Elizabeth, mentioned in John Humfrey's will? If so, she was born just over a year before he took up the living of Frome Selwood. Unfortunately, the names of the child's parents were not included in her baptismal record.

Richard Baxter, who died almost twenty years before Humfrey, had been a close associate, a friend even, although they did not always see eye-to-eye in all matters of theology. They certainly met on occasion, exchanged manuscripts,[28] and maintained a lively correspondence over several decades. The earliest surviving letters between Baxter and Humfrey date from 1654. On 11 May and 7 December of that year, Humfrey addressed letters to Baxter from Frome, the first a few weeks before he became vicar of St John's. He wrote to him a further three times between the autumn of 1657 and the spring of 1658, and once in 1662. In 1669 they exchanged further letters concerning Humfrey's quandary over whether he should take the Oxford Oath.[29] Thereafter Baxter was in regular correspondence with Humfrey, that 'Credible Minister',[30] through the 1670s and 1680s.

A letter from Humfrey to Baxter, thought to date from March or, at the earliest, late February 1691, refers to a visit he made to Baxter at his London home in Charterhouse Yard on the previous day. Humfrey wrote that he had visited 'yesterday on purpose to be informed in a point that seemed dark to me in your book to Mr Beverley',[31] and he went on to ask Baxter to reconsider – 'to think on it again' – his discussion of Christ's millennial kingdom before the book, already 'in the press', was released. Humfrey continued: 'Let me again beg you leave out the title all and put in only this for a title *Of National Churches in order to a Comprehension* [...] This will make the book sell, and all look into it [....] If God put it into your heart to own comprehension the very word will stir up'. Baxter, however, did not take this advice and the book was published under the title *Of National Churches: The Description, Institution, Use, Preservation, Danger, Maladies and Cure: Partly Applied to England*.[32] It is quite plausible that at the same time they discussed the Beckington witchcraft case. Certainly, it must have been around this time that Humfrey, who clearly had maintained his Selwood Forest connections, brought Hill to meet Baxter at his London home.

Humfrey sent two more letters to Baxter over the next few weeks in which the focus of the discussion was upon their different views regarding Church unity and Baxter's conception of a 'national' (or what today might be termed an ecumenical) Church. Humfrey told Baxter, 'It were madness to think of uniting the separatists and conformists for worship'.[33] The last known correspondence between them is Baxter's lengthy riposte, written in the summer of 1691, to Humfrey's criticisms of his *Of National Churches*. Although he found the writing of his sixteen-page letter 'unpleasant work', not responding, he declared, would be 'treachery to Christ and his Church'.[34] Whether or not their theological differences ended their acquaintance is uncertain, but no further letters between Baxter and Humfrey are known for the remaining few months of Baxter's life.

* * *

Great News from the West of England ends:

> It is a full ten weeks (from the twenty-eighth of October) since this young woman was first seized with these terrible fits. Although she has been visited by the minister of the place, who for some time prayed with her twice a day; and by a nonconformist minister that lives in the same parish, who twice performed a similar office, she continues to be often seized with terrible fits, and to bring up both nails and handles of spoons, and remains an object of great pity, and to be remembered at the Throne of Grace daily.

Who was this unnamed nonconformist minister who was living in Beckington in 1689? The former rector of Beckington, John Aster, who was ejected at the time of the Restoration, was probably living in London by this time.[35] It is much more likely that this enigmatic figure praying at Mary Hill's side was Humphrey Philips, formerly minister at Sherborne until his ejection in 1662. Philips was born in Somerton in around 1633 and graduated from Wadham College, Oxford, the new college of which May Hill's predecessor and father-in-law, Alexander Huish, had been made a fellow some seventy-five years before. Following a severe bout of sickness, he was permitted to retire to the country for a year to recover his health. He spent a few months at Poltimore, near Exeter, as a chaplain and tutor to the influential Bampfield family. On his return to Oxford he was chosen as a fellow of Magdalen College. He first arrived in Sherborne in 1658, briefly serving as an assistant or curate to a close acquaintance of Baxter's, Francis Bampfield, who was also a graduate of Wadham and became well known largely because he published an autobiography[36] detailing his persecution during the Restoration era. Bampfield had taken the living in 1657 on the death of his predecessor, William Lyford. For a couple of years Philips was back in Oxford as a Fellow of Magdalen College before 'Being turned out [in 1660] by the [University] Visitors after the Restoration',[37] on which he returned to work with Bampfield at Sherborne. For the time being Bampfield's position was secure for, although many were ousted from their livings after September 1660 as previously ejected ministers were reinstated, Lyford had died in office. However, the Act of Uniformity, requiring full submission to episcopal authority, proved disastrous for Bampfield and his equally principled colleague, Humphrey Philips, both of whom were dismissed on 24 August 1662 for refusing to submit to re-ordination. As was the case with John Humfrey, Philips had been ordained according to Presbyterian principles. On 19 September Bampfield and ten or so of his congregation were arrested at worship in his home. The minister and around twenty of his supporters, including Philips, were confined, at their own expense, in the New Inn at Sherborne. On their release, while awaiting hearings at the next quarter sessions, they refused to be bound by an instruction not to preach, and departed for Bampfield's brother's residence at Dunkerton, near Bath, where they preached 'first to a small number' that 'increased gradually'.[38] Bampfield was rearrested in Shaftesbury on 23 July 1663 and spent nine years in 'close and hard imprisonment'[39] in Dorchester Gaol for refusing to pay the fine imposed upon him for his defiance.[40] Of this he later wrote he was 'honoured with an imprisonment for Christ's sake, for the Gospel's sake, for Righteousness' sake, for the Elect's sake'.[41] Meanwhile his brother, Thomas, and his assistant, Philips, were both incarcerated at Ilchester Gaol. Thomas Bampfield was released after a month but Philips was held for just under a year. Calamy provided a grim account of Philips's experiences:

> Mr Philips, after eleven months confinement, was brought from prison in the depth of winter, and a snowy time, to the Assizes at Wells, where he met with hard usage, being put into a chamber like Noah's Ark, full of all sorts of creatures, and put into a bed with the Bridewell-keeper, where the sheets were wet, and clung to his flesh. The Justice who committed him, gave him hard language: but the Judge discharged him; he having satisfied the law.[42]

Following his excommunication by the Bishop of Bath and Wells, he took a trip to Holland with 'a son of Colonel Strode, a Member of Parliament', before returning to Dunkerton 'where he continued to preach with good success'. He continued to face 'various trials' including 'many removals from place to place, and diverse bodily infirmities'; he was frequently fined for his activities and 'had much trouble from the Bishop's court, which drove him from his home to Bristol, London, and other places'. These trials appear to have ended when, in 1672, he secured a licence to preach, as a Presbyterian, under the terms of the Declaration of Indulgence. He left his congregation at Bath and returned to Sherborne for a year until his licence expired and he was 'forced away'. 'After several removes' he ended up 'at his own estate at Beckington' from where he preached 'far and near to diverse congregations, and particularly that at Frome'.[43] He died on 27 March 1707, his name, spelt 'Phillips', appearing in the register for St George's, Beckington, with a burial date of 3 April 1707.[44]

The funeral sermon, delivered by his son-in-law, John England, was published in 1713 as an annexe in a pamphlet containing England's funeral sermon for John Derbie, former Receiver-General for Somerset.

CREDIBLE MINISTERS

Philips's funeral, according to the frontispiece, was conducted at Frome on 3 April – it is unclear if this should be presumed to indicate Beckington or if the burial at St George's on the same day followed a ceremony three miles away at St John's in the neighbouring town. In his oratory England commemorated Philips's four years of service to Bampfield at Sherborne, 'whose joint labours God had given remarkable success, both as to the reformation of the town in general, and the conversion of many souls'. He spoke too of a life 'full of trouble and danger' in the years that followed. To Philips he attributed 'the planting of churches' in the Selwood area, 'setting them up, and keeping them up'. One interesting detail is reminiscent of the activities of the brief appearance of the unnamed nonconformist minister in the account of the bewitching of Mary Hill:

> He did not confine his labours to the pulpit, but imitated St Paul in this, in teaching privately, and from house to house. His visits usually were but short, but seldom or never without some pious instruction or counsel, or some discourse of the things of God.[45]

Whether or not the minister at Mary's bedside was Philips, it is reasonable to suppose a local preacher, receptive to providential signs of these troubled times, could have helped whip up the enthusiasm that propagated the trial.

If Philips, now in his mid-fifties, did indeed get involved in the 1689 affair it was certainly not the first time he had been a witness to witchcraft allegations. Exactly thirty years before, at the time when he was assisting Francis Bampfield in Sherborne, a shocking discovery of witches was made. This was recorded the following year by Richard Blome, a London publisher, in his *Fanatick History*:

> In September 1659 there was a discovery of diverse witches in and near Sherborne in Dorsetshire, there being near two hundred of them at one meeting, most of them Quakers and Anabaptists. Three men and two women, formerly Quakers, committed to Dorsetshire Gaol, who have confessed on examination, and since their commitment, to sundry [men] of quality:
> 1. That when the Devil first appeared to them and tempted them to

Fig. 8-6 *The Quaker and prophetess Anna Trapnel who was imprisoned after being accused of witchcraft in Cornwall in 1654.*

become witches he persuaded them to renounce their baptism, which they actually did, before they made a contract with him.

2. That he did often visibly appear to them in sundry forms, and persuaded them to fall down and worship him, which they did.

3. That he instigated them to torment, bewitch and destroy Mr Lyford, minister of Sherborne, who being tormented with a painful and sharp disease, died; and Mr Bamfield [*sic*.] his successor, whom

they have forced by their witchcrafts to desert the town. (You see whom the Devil is so set against.)

4. The two women confess to all that the Devil has often had actual copulation with them in sundry shapes.

5. Since their imprisonment he has frequently appeared to them all, and actually possessed them, bruising [them and] tossing them frequently up and down the prison in a strange manner, tormenting them with strange fits of convulsions, quakings, shakings in all their joints, and swellings in their whole bodies, that their skins are ready to break, which makes them cry and roar with great horror, as eyewitnesses of quality attest.[46]

A slightly longer version of Blome's text had appeared at the end of 1659 in a twelve-page pamphlet entitled *A Gagg for the Quakers*, printed anonymously in London. The text has been attributed to Thomas Smith. His interpretation of Quakerism as the consequence of the Devil's ensnarement of religious 'fanaticks' was not at all unusual in this period. Smith described Bampfield as 'a very godly laborious minister', and claimed that when the witches copulated with the Devil he was 'most commonly in the shape of Mr Lyford and Mr Bamfield, the Ministers of Sherborne, whom he and they most hated and endeavoured to destroy'.[47] The likely truth of the matter is that Lyford and Bampfield hated, and aimed to destroy, the Quakers. Their discovery in Sherborne at this particular point in time, a time of political and religious crisis, fits well with recent constructions of belief and persecution.[48] This, of course, is also true of the 1689 episode in Beckington.

On 10 September 1660 the judges on the Western Circuit at Dorchester issued the following order at the summer assizes:

> It is ordered by this court that Sir John ffitz James, knight, Esquire, and Winston Churchill Esq., five of the justices of the peace of this county, or any two of them, do take care, that the business concerning the witchcraft and consultation with the Devil and evil spirits in Sherborne in this county be with all speed examined, [and any] concerned in the said business be by them or any two of them bound to good behaviour. And to appear at the next assizes and general gaol delivery to be held for this county to answer the same. And that they

also bind over as aforesaid such persons of those as by them are to be now examined as they shall think fit. And also such persons to prosecute against them as they shall also think [fit] and certify their said examinations and information at the assizes.[49]

In the interdenominational struggles of the 1650s accusations of witchcraft by one sect against another 'became the norm'[50] and the practice continued beyond the Restoration. In building his case regarding the politicization of witchcraft Elmer has remarked 'the frenzied events of 1659-60 almost certainly exacerbated [...] underlying tensions, evidenced by the increasingly ferocious attack on sects such as the witch-like Quakers'.[51] At the height of their persecution in Somerset, between 1660 and 1661, over 200 Quakers were imprisoned in the County Gaol at Ilchester,[52] and the eminent Quaker preacher John Whiting was held prisoner there periodically from 1679–86. An illuminating near-contemporary account of conditions in Ilchester Gaol survives in a letter addressed to Giles Bale, Keeper of his Majesty's Gaol at Ilchester, concerning the deplorable conditions in which around sixty local Quakers were imprisoned in 1683. The letter records how, after they arrived there at about 8 pm, sixteen of the prisoners were 'cast into the common gaol' by Bale and his wife, where 'among felons, men, and women together', they were 'constrained to lodge on the bare ground, in a nasty stinking place, having not a seat to sit on, nor so much as straw to lie on'.[53]

Despite his tolerance of and friendship towards Richard Baxter and certain other moderate nonconformists, in Glanvill's opinion hard-line dissenters, atheists and witches all served a common diabolical purpose.[54] In 1663 Robert Hunt complained of the 'very longe and troublesome imployment' presented by a gaol full of Anabaptists, Quakers and Presbyterians, arrested for attending illegal conventicles, noting, 'I suppose I may bee complained of for houldinge to the rule of lawe, but I will not complain if I am left out of the commission'.[55] However, neither he nor Glanvill were friends to the Quakers: as rector for Street[56] Glanvill prosecuted certain Quakers in 1677 for not paying him tithes, and, in 1673, Hunt signed the warrants that suppressed a Quaker conventicle held in John Cary's barn in Bruton.[57] Conceivably, the people denounced as witches who met at night in the neighbouring

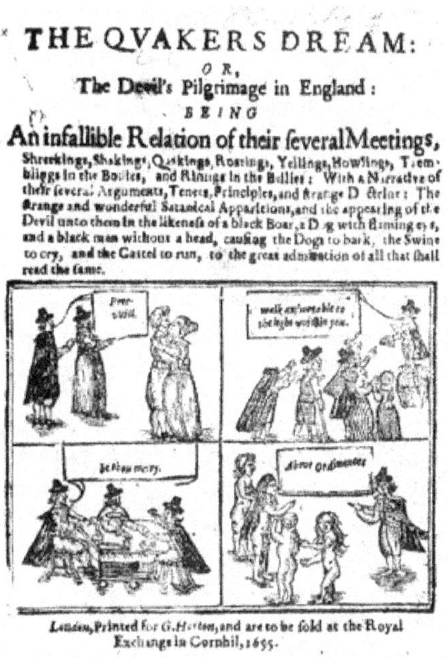
THE QVAKERS DREAM:
OR,
The Devil's Pilgrimage in England:
BEING
An infallible Relation of their ſeveral Meetings,
Shreekings, Shakings, Quakings, Roarings, Yellings, Howlings, Tremblings in the Bodies, and Risings in the Bellies: With a Narrative of their ſeveral Arguments, Tenets, Principles, and ſtrange Doctrine: The ſtrange and wonderful Satanical Apparitions, and the appearing of the Devil unto them in the likeneſs of a black Boar, a Dog with flaming eyes, and a black man without a head, cauſing the Dogs to bark, the Swine to cry, and the Cattel to run, to the great admiration of all that ſhall read the ſame.
London, Printed for G. Horton, and are to be ſold at the Royal Exchange in Cornhil, 1655.

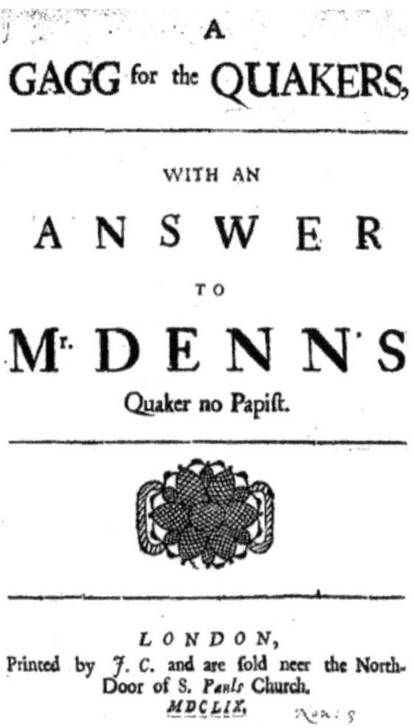
A
GAGG for the QUAKERS,
WITH AN
ANSWER
TO
Mr. DENNS
Quaker no Papiſt.
LONDON,
Printed by J. C. and are ſold neer the North-Door of S. Pauls Church.
MDCLIX.

Fig. 8-7 The Quaker's Dream *(1655) depicting Satanic interventions and a range of supposed Quaker offences.*
Fig. 8-8 *Anti-Quaker propaganda, dated 1659, concerning such matters as the recent problem with Quaker-witches in Sherborne.*

parish of Brewham, ten years earlier and in less tolerant times, were part of the same emerging local Quaker community. Hunt was also named by George Whitehead as one of those 'several Magistrates' guilty of 'Cruelty and Injustice' in *A brief account of some of the late and present sufferings of the people called Quakers* (1680) for fining several people who attended the burial of Samuel Clothier on 29 June 1670 at Alford, close to Castle Cary, on the charge of forming a conventicle even though 'nothing was spoke at the Grave' and all were 'silent and quiet'. Back in 1657 Hunt had been instrumental in the arrest at Martock, primarily on a charge of vagrancy, of an influential itinerant first generation Lancashire Quaker, Thomas Salthouse.[58]

Cotton Mather, the correspondent of both Baxter and Glanvill, a New England Congregationalist and great advocate of the Salem witch trials, was equally prejudiced. In a letter written in 1682 he revealed an outrageous plan for dealing with William Penn, the recent founder of Pennsylvania, and his Quaker supporters:

> There be now at sea a ship called *Welcome*, which has on board 100 or more of the heretics and malignants called Quakers, with W. Penn, who is the chief scamp, at the head of them. The General Court has accordingly given sacred orders to Master Malachi Huscott, of the brig *Porpoise*, to waylay the said *Welcome* slyly as near the Cape of Cod as may be, and make captive the said Penn and his ungodly crew, so that the Lord may be glorified and not mocked on the soil of this new country with the heathen worship of these people. Much spoil can be made of selling the whole lot to Barbados, where slaves fetch good prices in rum and sugar, and we shall not only do the Lord great good by punishing the wicked, but we shall make great good for His Minister and people.[59]

The Quaker movement was one among a plethora of new sects that emerged in the chaos of the English Civil War. By 1660 the movement had spread into the south and west, with important Quaker centres established at London and Bristol. To outsiders their practices seemed bizarre and frightening and the rapidity of the movement's growth convinced many, including Baxter, that so much witchcraft was the likely explanation. In a letter written back in 1654 Baxter identified the Quakers as part of a diabolical conspiracy to destroy the English Church.[60] Margaret Fell, George Fox's wife from 1669, and the leading lady of the movement until her death in 1702, recalled how her own conversion was received:

> many were in a mighty rage. And [they] went to meet my then husband, as he was coming home, and informed him, that a great disaster was befallen among his family, and that they were witches; and that they had taken us out of our religion; and that he might either set them away, or all the country would be undone.[61]

Contemporary critics spoke of Fox's use of enchanted trinkets – bracelets, bottles, ribbons and the like – to ensnare followers.[62] In 1653 a puritan minister, Francis Higginson (1617–70), published a damning account of the wicked practices of the Quakers – those 'ministers of Satan'. Most interestingly, in relation to the Selwood Forest witchcraft

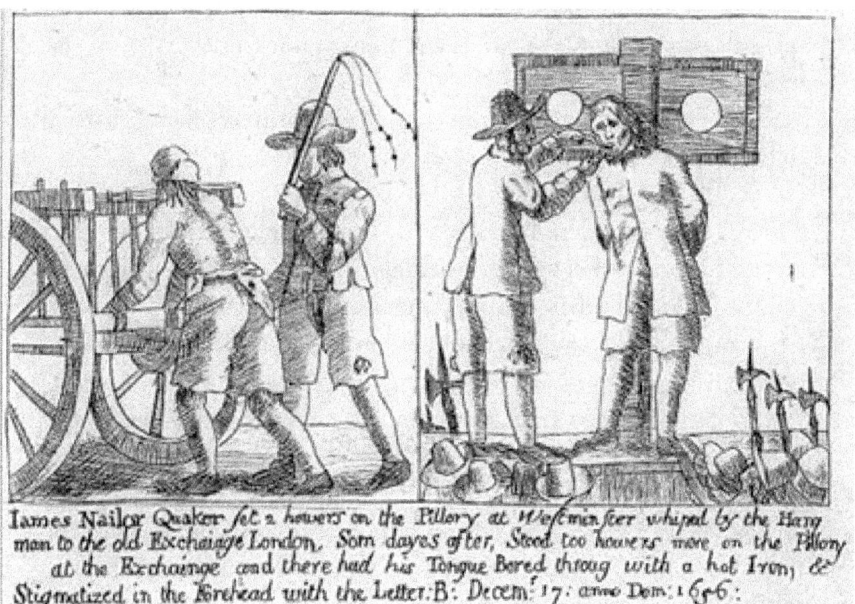

Iames Nailor Quaker set 2 howers on the Pillory at Westminster whiped by the Hangman to the old Exchainge London. Som dayes after, Stood too howers more on the Pillory at the Exchainge and there had his Tongue Bored throug with a hot Iron, & Stigmatized in the forehead with the Letter B. Decem: 17: anno Dom: 1656:

Fig. 8-9 *Contemporary illustration of the punishment received by Quaker leader, James Nailor, in London in 1656.*

cases, Higginson provided fascinating details of the 'black wicked practices' of Quakers and their meetings that opponents might have interpreted as witches' sabbats.[63] He spoke of mysterious night-time assemblies in out of the way places, often in the open air, that greatly alarmed 'the neighbouring inhabitants [...] who have professed they could scarcely sleep in their beds without fear.' His description of the speaker at such assemblies bears a resemblance to that of the low-voiced man in black who attended the meetings of the Brewham and Stoke Trister covens in Selwood Forest:

> For the manner of their speakings, their speaker for the most part uses the posture of standing, or sitting with his hat on, his countenance severe, his face downward, his eyes fixed mostly towards the earth, his hands and fingers expanded, continually striking gently on his breast. His beginning is without a text, abrupt and sudden to his hearers, his voice for the most part low, his sentences incoherent, hanging together like ropes of sand, very frequently full of impiety

and horrid errors, and sometimes full of sudden pauses, his whole speech a mixed bundle of words and heap of nonsense.[64]

The 'quaking fits' that gave these enraptured enthusiasts their nickname could easily be interpreted as possession:

> Though their speakings be a very chaos of words and errors, yet very often while they are speaking, so strange is the effect of them, in their unblest followers, that many of them, sometimes men, but more frequently women and children, fall into quaking fits. The manner of which is this: those in their assemblies who are taken with these fits fall suddenly down, as it were in a swoon, as though they were surprised with an epilepsy or apoplexy, and lie grovelling on the earth, and struggling as it were for life, and sometimes more quietly as though they were departing. While the agony of the fit is upon them their lips quiver, their flesh and joints tremble, their bellies swell as though blown up with wind, they foam at the mouth, and sometimes purge as if they had taken physic. In this fit they continue sometimes an hour or two, sometimes longer, before they come to themselves again, and when it leaves them they roar out horribly with a voice greater than the voice of a man –the noise, those say that have heard it, is a very horrid fearful noise, and greater sometimes than any bull can make.[65]

Higginson affirmed that the ringleader of the sect, George Fox, 'is vehemently suspected to be a sorcerer'. His followers, like witches, were prone to verbally abusing their unconverted neighbours and, worse, men of the cloth. 'They are also as horrible railers as ever any age brought forth', he wrote, and declared the 'Billingsgate oyster-women are not comparable to them'. According to Higginson 'It is ordinary with them in the letters they write to other men to call them fools, sots, hypocrites, vain men, beasts, blasphemers, murderers of the just' and 'to tell them they are dogs, heathen, etc.'. Regular ministers in England they considered 'liars of Jesus Christ' and accused them of upholding 'the kingdom of Antichrist' and being motivated 'for filthy lucre'.

In keeping with much contemporary iconography of witchcraft, in which its subjects were frequently depicted naked, Higginson claimed that for some Quakers 'To go naked is [...] accounted a decency becoming their imagined state of innocency better than apparel; the ablest of them plead for this obscenity'. One such, according to Higginson, 'ran stark naked to the [market] cross' at Kirkbymoorside in Yorkshire 'in the view of many, and stood in that posture [...] speaking to the people'. Another 'ran like a mad man naked, all but his shirt, through Kendal, crying, "Repent, repent, woe, woe, come out of Sodom, remember Lot's wife" with other such stuff'.

Higginson concluded that in Quakerism, like witchcraft, was the spawn of diabolical conspiracy:

> This one thing to me doth plainly evidence the way of these apostalates to be of the Devil. No sooner is anyone became a proselyte to their sect but he is possessed with a spirit of malice, and wrath, and turns enemy to all men that are not of their way. Especially those that appear against it. To such they use menacing speeches as of a day that is coming wherein they shall be avenged, and talk frothily sometimes of levying forces, choosing colonels and captains, etc.[66]

An extraordinary account of witchcraft and transformation in Cambridgeshire was published in a pamphlet, eight pages long, in 1659. It was entitled *Strange and Terrible Newes from Cambridge being a True Relation of the Quakers Bewitching of Mary Philips*. In the preamble its anonymous author spoke of sorcerers which 'in this age' were springing up 'like so many mushrooms'. In a tirade against Quakers, the tale tells of how Mary Philips lapsed for a few weeks into Quakerism by joining a group associated with Robert Dickson and Jane Cranaway before returning to the Church of England. Subsequently, she was transformed by the Quakers into a mare and made to carry them to an unnamed town four miles from Cambridge for a Quaker meeting. Of this Elmer has remarked, 'Though descriptions of sabbats are very rare in English witchcraft, we have what looks suspiciously like a Quaker sabbat'.[67] Transforming back into human form, Mary Philips had Dickson and Cranaway arrested, having shown the constables bruises on her hands and feet and her smock torn and bloodied where her riders' spurs had struck her sides. The prisoners pleaded not guilty at the Cambridge assizes and were released.

Fig. 8-10 *Image from Henry Hunt,* A Peep into a Prison; or, the Inside of Ilchester Bastile *(1821).*

Ironically, this most unadorned and egalitarian approach to Christian worship was commonly condemned by its critics as a conspiracy steered by Jesuits. By Elmer's reckoning 'Elite anxiety of this kind probably reached fever pitch' in the later 1650s.[68] In the wake of the colossal political disorder of the Civil War and the establishment of the Protectorate, anything that threatened the social and religious order of the times – be it Quakerism or witchcraft – was intolerable to those struggling to assert their moral authority and maintain control. Elmer has commented on the polarising effect of the war, and the breakdown of consensus, in conjunction with the politicisation of ideas regarding witchcraft, and the demonization of Quakers and other nonconformists. Certainly the language of witchcraft accusation, as metaphor and simile perhaps, was regularly invoked, not least by Quaker pamphleteers, in the vicious slandering of opponents in the political and religious arguments of the times. After 1660 other religious and political dissidents, those tainted by their place within the regime of the 1650s, joined the ranks of the Quakers as the subjects of magisterial persecution – 'surrogate witches' even, as Elmer has suggested. Accusations of shape-shifting and other magical practices were levelled against Quakers in this period. Like others accused of witchcraft, Quaker women were subjected to pricking and swimming tests. Elmer has noted that 'Quaker apologists routinely complained' and one, John Crook, 'claimed in 1664 that an arresting officer pricked the arms of several Quaker women 'till they were black".[69] In Reading, between 1664 and 1676, a local magistrate, Sir William Armour, it was alleged, routinely pricked his female Quaker prisoners with 'a sharp instrument somewhat like a pack needle' until he drew blood.[70] Two Quaker women visiting Oxford were taken by their abusers 'to the pump in John's College, where they pumped water upon their necks, and into their mouths, till they were almost dead; after which they tied them arm to arm, and inhumanly dragged them up and down the College, and through a pool of water'.[71] Quakers' disregard for conventional assumptions regarding authority made them especially repugnant to ministers and magistrates. By the 1660s, there were women preachers, and Quaker women were establishing their own conventicles. The intolerance of these women towards the sinful behaviour of others was bound to rouse hostility, as one French traveller in the period noted:

> You might as soon persuade a Presbyterian to preach in a surplice [...] as a she-Quaker [...] to be the least civil to anybody. The women sometimes preach in their meetings, but more rarely than the men. There is one woman in a village near London, that has a common place against topknots, and the other ornaments of women, and this is all she knows. To see her preaching, you have nothing to do, but to carry two or three ladies into the meeting; the moment Mrs Doctor spies a ribbon, the Spirit moves her, and she falls into one of her fits; up she gets upon the bottom of some tub, with her pinched up cap, and her screwed up countenance; she sighs, she groans, she snorts through the nose, and then out she bursts into such a jargon as no mortal man can make head or tail of.[72]

It is tempting to suppose that the contemporary demonization of this new sect, spreading rapidly southwards from its northern birthplace, could have had at least something to do with the enthusiasm of Selwood Forest justices, notably Robert Hunt, and clergymen, notably Joseph Glanvill, to root out nests of witches, mostly women, on their patch.

1 Francis Hutchinson, *An Historical Essay Concerning Witchcraft* (1718), vi-vii.
1a Ewen, *Witchcraft and Demonianism*, 376.
2 ODNB, 'Holt, Sir John'.
3 Hutchinson, *An Historical Essay*, 46.
4 Roger North, *The Life of the Honourable Francis North, Baron of Guilford, Lord keeper of the great Seal, under King Charles II and King James II* (London: 1742).
5 *Ibid.*, 131–32.
6 DNB, 'Baxter, Richard'.
7 DNB, 'Baxter, Richard'.
8 ODNB, 'Baxter, Richard'.
9 Clark, *Thinking with Demons*, 183.
10 *Ibid.*, 367.
11 Baxter, *Worlds of Spirits*, 80–81.
12 Joseph Foster, *Alumni Oxonienses 1500–1714* (Oxford: Oxford University Press, 1891), 748–84.
13 His ODNB biographer, E. C. Vernon, does not clarify which Kingsbury is eluded to – presumably Kingsbury, Harrow, but possibly Kingsbury Episcopi near Yeovil in Somerset.
14 DNB, 'Humfrey, John'.
15 John Humphrey, *A Farther Account of Our Late Prophets* (1708), 15.
16 Ibid., 15-16.
17 Barry, *Witchcraft and Demonology*, Chapter 4.
18 Probably the Gatehouse Prison, Westminster, where John Humfrey was imprisoned briefly in 1673.
19 Charles Henry Timperley, *A Dictionary of Printers and Printings* (London: H. Johnson, 1839), 693; Michael Treadwell, 'London Printers and Printing Houses in 1705' in *Publishing History*, 7 (1980), 31; D.F. McKenzie and Maureen Bell, *A Chronology and Calendar of Documents Relating to the London Book Trade 1641–1700*, Vol. I, 1641–1670 (Oxford: Oxford University Press, 2005), 578.
20 Henry Robert Plomer, *A Dictionary of the Printers and Booksellers who were at Work in England, Scotland and Ireland* (Oxford: Oxford University Press, 1922), 205; McKenzie and Bell, *Chronology and Calendar* Vol. III, 1686–1700, 24.
21 PROB 11/327/333 Alexander Huish.
22 Bequeathed 30 shillings in Deborah Huish's will in 1671.

23 Gordon, *Freedom*, 293.
24 McKenzie and Bell, *Chronology and Calendar* Vol. III, 1686–1700, 149.
25 Armitage, *Publications*, 149.
26 John F. Sena, 'Melancholic Madness and the Puritans', *The Harvard Theological Review*, 66:3 (1973), 302.
27 PROB 11/533/130 Anne Hill.
28 In 1684, for example, Humfrey sent Baxter a presentation copy of his latest work, 'The Axe Laid at the Root of Separation' (Nuttall and Keeble, *Richard Baxter*, Vol. 2, letter 1147).
29 Nuttall and Keeble, *Richard Baxter*, Vol. 1.
30 Nuttall and Keeble, *Richard Baxter*, Vol. 2, letter 1036.
31 Thomas Beverley, independent minister and author of theological tracts.
32 Nuttall and Keeble, *Richard Baxter*, Vol. 2, letter 1222.
33 *Ibid.*, letter 1204.
34 *Ibid.*, letter 1241.
35 Calamy, *Memorial*, Vol. I, 79.
36 Francis Bampfield, *A Name, an After-one* (1681).
37 Calamy, *Account*, 259–61.
38 *Ibid.*
39 Bampfield, *A Name*, 21.
40 David S. Katz, *Sabbath and Sectarianism in Seventeenth Century England* (Leiden: Brill, 1988), 96.
41 Bampfield, *A Name*, 7.
42 Calamy, *Account*, 259–61.
43 *Ibid.*
44 The affidavit that he was buried in wool was sworn by Alice Coock. He was predeceased by his wife Anna, who was buried at St George's on 25 September 1701.
45 John England, *A Funeral Sermon for John Derbie, Esq.* (1713).
46 Richard Blome, *The Fanatick History* (1660), 117–18.
47 Thomas Smith [?], *A Gagg for the Quakers* (1659).
48 See, for example, Elmer, *Witchcraft*, 183-84, 189, 191.
49 Order of the judges on the western circuit at the Dorset Summer Assizes in Dorchester, 10 September 1660, to investigate witchcraft at Sherborne.
50 Elmer, *Witchcraft*, 154; in 1655, for example, George Hopkins, minister of Evesham in Worcestershire and a close friend of Baxter, 'preached on the subject of diabolism and witchcraft and then proceeded to lead the whole congregation in a full-scale attack upon a local Quaker meeting' (Elmer, 'Saints or Sorcerers', 152.)
51 Elmer, *Witchcraft*, 174.
52 VCH, 'Ilchester', Somerset, Vol. 3.
53 Joseph Besse, *A Collection of the Sufferings of the People Called Quakers*, Volume I (1753), 629.

54 Davies, *Science in an Enchanted World*, Chapter 7.
55 In Barry, *Witchcraft and Demonology*.
56 Street, adjacent to Glastonbury, later became famous as the place where the Clark family, philanthropic Quakers, established their well-known shoemaking business.
57 Barry, *Witchcraft and Demonology*, 29.
58 Charlotte Fell Smith, 'Salthouse, Thomas', DNB; Barry, *Witchcraft and Demonology*.
59 Cotton Mather to John Higginson (1682) in Frank Kermode and Anita Kermode, *The Oxford Book of Letters* (Oxford: Oxford University Press, 1995), 49–50.
60 Peter Elmer in Barry *et al.*, *Witchcraft in Early Modern Europe*, 148.
61 Margaret Fell, *A Journal or Historical Account of the Life, Travels, Sufferings, Christian Experiences and Labour of Love in the Work of the Ministry of That Ancient, Eminent and Faithful Servant of Jesus Christ, George Fox* (1694).
62 Peter Elmer in Barry *et al.*, *Witchcraft in Early Modern Europe*, 147.
63 Francis Higginson, *A Brief Relation of the Irreligion of the Northern Quakers, Wherein Their Horrid Principles and Practices, Doctrines and Manners, as Far as Their Mystery of Iniquity Hath Yet Discovered Itself, Are Plainly Exposed to the View of Every Intelligent Reader* (1653).
64 Ibid.
65 Ibid.
66 Ibid.
67 Elmer, 'Saints or Sorcerers', 150.
68 Ibid., 161.
69 Ibid., 152; John Crook, *A True Information to the Nation, from the People Called Quakers* (London: 1664).
70 Elmer, 'Saints or Sorcerers', 153; Anon., *Persecution Appearing with Its Open Face, in William Armour* (London: 1667).
71 Contemporary account cited by Elmer, 'Saints or Sorcerers', 154.
72 John Ozell (trans. from the French), *M. Misson's Memoirs and Observations in his Travels over England.* 1719, 228–29.

9

CREDULITY AND INCREDULITY

Fig. 9-1 *A group of (Quaker?) witches dance in a circle around a central figure. (Contemporary woodcut)*

Spectre and apparition make a great noise in the world [...] between our ancestors laying too much stress upon them, and the present age endeavouring wholly to explode and despise them, the world seems hardly ever to have come to a right understanding about them.
– Daniel Defoe, 1738[1]

BY THE TIME Lord Chief Justice Holt heard the Beckington case in 1690 he was a member of the Privy Council and, in 1700, he was offered the Lord Chancellorship but turned it down, preferring instead to continue riding the assize circuits. He died in March 1710 and was buried at Redgrave in Suffolk.

Holt went on to try several more witches, ten at least, having heard the evidence against Elizabeth Carrier and Ann More at the start of his judicial career. The details of at least some of these trials he made available to Francis Hutchinson via the notes of Sir James Montague 'which he took of the depositions that were made at the time'.[2] All those brought before him on witchcraft charges were acquitted. In 1694 he heard the case of Mother Munnings of Hartis in Suffolk at Bury St Edmunds who stood accused of harm to property and people – 'a dangerous woman' who 'could touch the line of life' with the assistance of an imp in the form of a polecat. The jury however 'were so well directed, that they brought her in, 'Not Guilty''.[3] At Ipswich in the same year he acquitted Margaret Elnore whose grandmother and aunt, allegedly, had both been hanged as witches. In 1695 he was in Cornwall where at Launceston he presided over a case in which Mary Guy was accused of bewitching Philadelphia Row who 'vomited pins, straws, and feathers'.[4]

The following year Holt tried Elizabeth ('Bett') Horner at Exeter. According to an account of the trial preserved in a letter written by Archdeacon Blackburne, who witnessed the proceedings, Bett Horner was accused of persecuting the daughters of Thomas and Elizabeth Bovet. Thomas Bovet testified that the youngest, Alice, had died suddenly and mysteriously at about four years of age. The physicians could find no natural cause for her death. Alice's older sister Mary, about ten years old, suffered from a curious condition that crippled her for a period of about seven weeks. During her illness her distorted, twisted legs would lead her, eyes closed in a trance, towards the open fire. On such occasions she declared that Bett Horner made her do it. Meanwhile another daughter, Sarah, when she was in bed, was scratched by a cat that she knew to be the shape-shifting witch. When questioned she was able to describe perfectly the witch's present costume, despite not having set eyes on her for half a year. Consequently Bett Horner was arrested and imprisoned. During this time the two surviving daughters were assailed by some invisible foe that left bruises and bite marks on their arms and faces. Equally incredible, they vomited quantities of stones and pins. Sarah passed two crooked pins in her urine and another emerged from her body through the skin of her middle finger. Her mother, Elizabeth Bovet, testified to having seen her daughter, bewitched by Horner, walk up and down, in parallel fashion, the nine-feet-high wall of her room. In her distress Sarah denounced Horner as the murderer of Alice. Ten-year-old Mary testified before the court that she had seen the witch suckle

CREDULITY AND INCREDULITY 221

a toad through a teat on her left shoulder. However, when Horner was requested to expose her shoulder before the court, all that was found was one innocuous mole.

Four more witnesses made allegations against Bett Horner. John Fursey claimed he had seen the witch at night, on three occasions, materialise out of the ground before him. Alice Osborne reported the mysterious disappearance of the contents of a barrel of her recently brewed beer after she had had a row with Horner. Margaret Armiger declared she bumped into the witch twenty miles away from the prison in which she was being held. However, although Horner faltered a little over 'Forgive us our trespasses' when commanded to recite the Lord's Prayer, the judge and jury found no evidence sufficient to convict her and she was released.[5]

In 1701 Holt tried a further case which ended in the acquittal of the accused and the committal of her accuser, Richard Hathaway, 'a cheat and imposter'.[6] Hathaway, a blacksmith's apprentice in Southwark, claimed he had first become bewitched in September 1690, about a year after the opening of the proceedings against the Beckington women. He seemed to have become deaf and blind, did not appear to eat for a full ten weeks, 'vomited great numbers of pins', and he secured the witness statements of one of his watchers in his sickness that he had passed 'by stool' 'a lump of hair, loose pins, a stump of a nail, half a nutshell, and two or three pieces of stone'. In his fits he foamed at the mouth, barked like a dog, and 'burnt like a flame of fire'. He claimed he was the victim of Sarah Moordike who was horribly treated: 'assaulted in her own house, and grievously abused; her hair and face torn; she was kicked, thrown to the ground, stamped on, and threatened to be put in the horse-pond, to be tried by swimming, and very hardly escaped with her life'. She was arrested in the Easter of 1701, stripped and searched for suspicious marks. Even worse, Hathaway was permitted to scratch her until he drew blood, an ancient custom thought to have the power of lifting the witch's curse. After Holt steered the jury to the unpopular acquittal of Moordike and in the subsequent trial of Hathaway his fraudulence was discovered:

> To prove that his vomiting pins was by a trick it was deposed that immediately after he had vomited great numbers, in appearance, upon the ground, and was going to vomit more, care should being taken that he should vomit into a chamber-pot, and his hands being

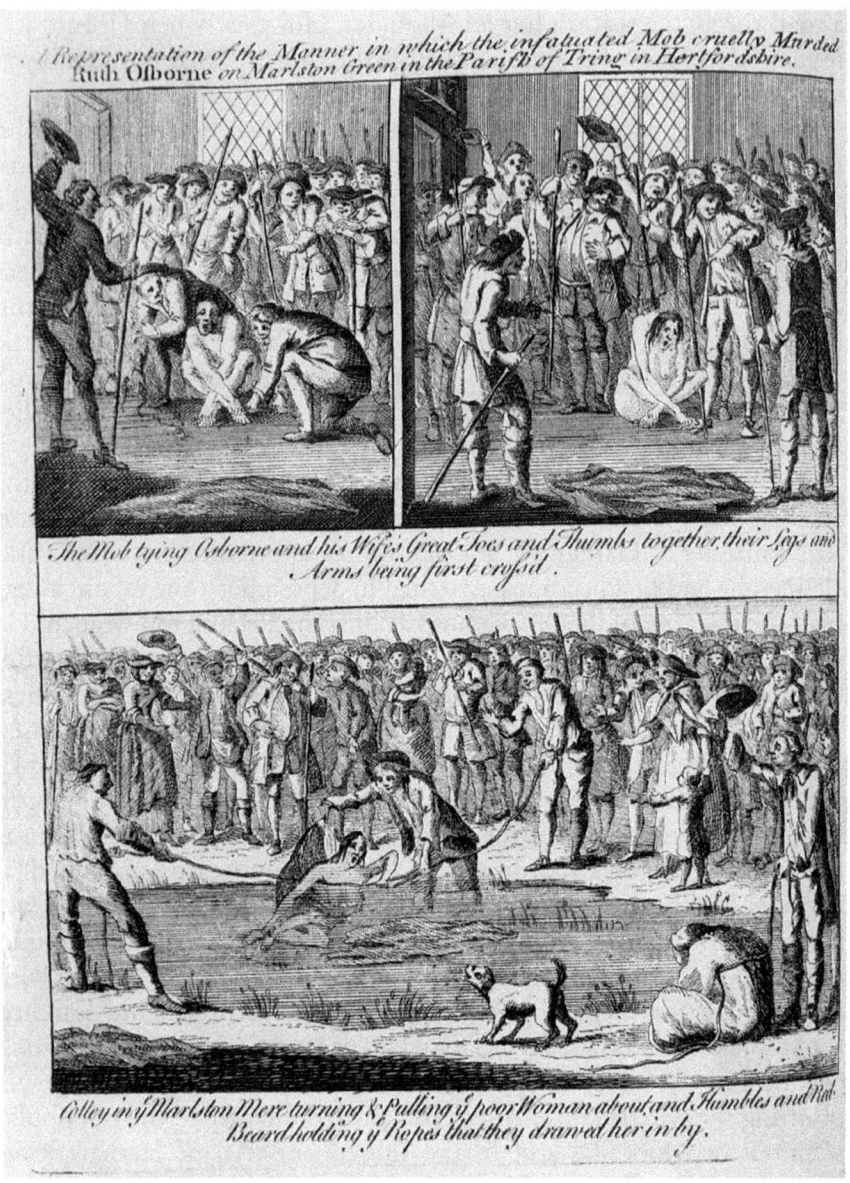

Fig. 9-2 *Graphic contemporary account of the swimming for witchcraft of Ruth Osborne (1680-1751) and her husband at Tring in Hertfordshire in 1751.*

kept down below it, there was not a pin in the pot, but a great many crooked ones in his pockets, in readiness to have played his tricks with.[7]

For a time Hathaway seems to have become something of a local celebrity and this, in part at least, seems to have motivated his actions, for 'By what he got by gifts and collections [to help fund his legal expenses among other things], it was proved that he had tried to make a gain by printing a narrative of his own case'.[8] Hathaway was found guilty, imprisoned for a year, and obliged to stand in the pillory on three occasions.

* * *

Mary Hill and her sister Margaret probably remained spinsters for the rest of their lives. A Mary Hill was buried at St George's, Beckington, on 4 December 1724, and her affidavit that she was buried in wool was sworn by one Margaret Hill. This, almost certainly, was the eighteen-year-old in the 1689 case; if so, she died aged fifty-three. Margaret, assuming it is she, died eighteen years later in 1742.[9] Their younger sisters seem to have married – an Elizabeth Hill married John Harfoot at St George's in 1700 and a Jane Hill, who may be the same person as the 'Jone' Hill recorded as the fourth of the sisters, married Samuel Loaden in the parish in 1715.

While May Hill and his wife died childless at the turn of the new century,[10] three generations of their Hill relations served as the rectors of nearby Hemington, fulfilling the role for the span of 108 years. Mary, wife of May Hill's brother Stephen, gave birth to at least nine children, most of whom survived into adulthood. A baby born just two years before his Beckington uncle's death was given the same unusual name, for a boy at least, of 'May' and the name was passed on to a subsequent generation of Hemington Hills in the following century.

The Beckington witchcraft case was by no means the last recorded for the Selwood Forest region. The swimming of Elizabeth Carrier in 1689 would be the fate of Margaret Waddom and others in the adjoining Somerset parish of Rode just five years later.[11] Very likely the 1689 Selwood episode was a catalyst for that of 1694. This was, after all, as Baxter had lately declared in *Certainty of the Worlds of Spirits* (1691), a time in which 'Satan's prevalency [...] is most clear in the marvellous number of witches abounding in all places'. Where once witchcraft was the occupation of a few foolish old women 'now we have known those of both sexes, who professed much knowledge, holiness and devotion drawn into this damnable practice'. In Suffolk and Essex they were numbered in hundreds.

While the three swimmings of Carrier were, apparently, ordered by a local JP, that of Margaret Waddom was enacted without authority and three men were prosecuted for swimming her in the Avon 'until such time as she was near dead'.[12] The witness statements have survived – all testimonies of those afflicted, not by the alleged witches, but by the members of the lynch mob formed to persecute them.

The first victim was the elderly mother of Thomas Haberfield or Habberfield of Rode. Haberfield declared that on 4 July 1694 she was attacked at her home in Rode by a 'rabble' of men including, among others unidentified, Daniel Keepen, broadweaver, William Moore, tailor, Thomas Caninge, chandler, and William Carter, pedlar, all residents of the neighbouring Wiltshire parish of North Bradley, and also William Palmer of nearby Coleford in Somerset. Claiming they were officers with the authority to take custody of Haberfield's mother, they broke into her house, even though she had locked the doors, 'and

Fig. 9-3 *The swimming in a millpond of Mary Sutton at Bedford in 1613.*

entered the same and let in the rest of the rabble, part of which went upstairs and fetched the mother of this informant down while Moore held him with the help of Keepen part of the time'. She was then forced to endure the swimming test, ostensibly to prove she was a witch:

> After this they pulled her out of her house, and while they were so doing, part of the company had provided a hand barrow in order to carry her to the river, but this informant, entreating very much did at last prevail with them not to do so, but let her go to the river without it, which they did, and there put her into the same water and continued her for quarter of an hour until such time she was nearly dead.

Haberfield's wife corroborated his account. This woman, 'Mathew Haberfield' as she appears in the records of the quarter sessions, was almost certainly Martha Haberfield, the wife of Thomas Haberfield of Rode, who died in 1700 and was probably born in the parish in 1668, the son of Thomas and Anne Haberfield. Martha's testimony added detail to the drama of the struggle in the house as the men from the neighbouring villages endeavoured to capture her mother-in-law:

> When Daniel Keepen and the other persons went up the stairs to fetch his mother down, she, this informant, and his mother endeavoured to defend themselves by keeping the said persons down the stairs with a crutch that the old woman went by. Notwithstanding which the said Keepen forced himself up the stairs with a great chair before him and, with the help of the other persons, seized the said old woman in her chamber and had her from thence by force to a river and put her in and continued her in the water for a quarter of an hour.

An Anne Haberfield, widow, was buried in Rode on Christmas Day 1706 – probably the same old woman who was almost drowned twelve years before.

On the same day as the assault on Anne Haberfield the same mob attacked two of their North Bradley neighbours, Anthony Waddom and his mother, when they were milking their cows on Rode Common. Moore, Caninge and Palmer are all mentioned in Anthony Waddom's statement together with one Anthony Stock. These men 'threw down the milk of two cows and forcibly had away his mother, Margaret Waddom, to a river about two furlongs from the common and there put her into the water to see if she could swim, and kept her in until she was nearly dead'. When her son attempted to intervene 'William Palmer fell on him and beat him and tore a good coat from his back'. Rode Common is to the east of the village and the Avon is on its western side; almost certainly the swimming was carried out in the vicinity of Rode Bridge, two furlongs or thereabouts along the road from the common to the river, and a place where Rode Mill would have provided still waters well-suited to their purpose.

Once again, as in Shakespeare's *Macbeth*, the Beckington case and many other early modern cases, a group of three witches was hunted down in Rode on 4 July 1694. This might have been pure coincidence but, equally, it might reflect a popular assumption linked to the three Fates of antiquity. The three Fates, from which the English word 'fairy' derives, were mystical women associated, at least by the time of the Renaissance, with the three stages of life – birth, marriage and death. Their control over human destiny was represented by the thread they spun on a distaff and cut with shears. In the same tradition, the three Norns, in Wagner's *Götterdämmerung*, the fourth part of the *Ring* cycle, spin the rope of destiny, which breaks, precipitating the end of the gods. Early modern depictions of the Fates, notably Hans Baldung Grien's *The Three Fates* (1513), had much in common with contemporary witchcraft iconography.[13] The omnipresent magical distaff in this tradition could well explain the witch's broomstick in the other.

The third 'witch' punished in Rode in 1694 was the mother of Elizabeth Kneall of North Bradley. On the same day, Wednesday 4 July, William Moore and company came to the old woman's home and commanded her daughter, who was visiting, to open the door so that they could take away 'the old witch'. Once more, when asked on whose authority they made this demand, they claimed to be officers of the law. Moore, who seems to have been the ringleader, instructed Palmer to break down the door and the mob entered the house. Next, preventing her daughter and son 'with a great deal of violence' from intervening, they 'seized their mother and pulled her out of the house and had her away to a river in Rode and there put her into the water'. Her son managed to free himself and save her from drowning but, after he got

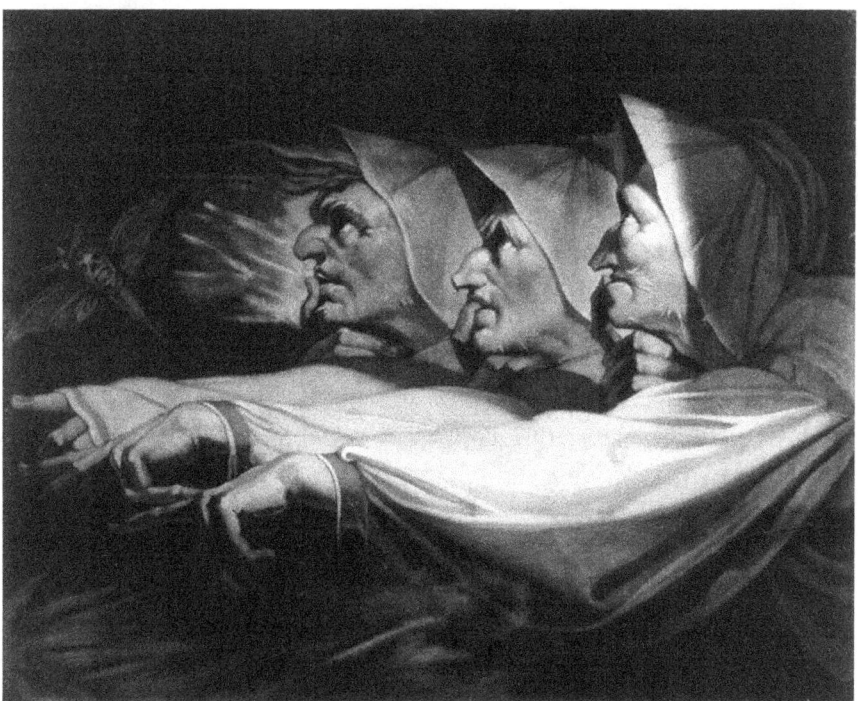

Fig. 9-4 *By the time Royal Academian Henry Fuseli painted* The Weird Sisters or the Three Witches *(1783) the English witchcraze was long passed.*

her safely on the bank, the old woman's assailants threw her back in again and kept her there 'until she was almost dead'. Elizabeth Kneall also complained in her testimony that William Moore had stolen a knife she kept 'in her bosom', perhaps for self-protection from such as he.

In addition to the three women hunted as witches in Rode on 4 July 1694, one man, Oswald Browne, was accused of being a wizard and threatened with a swimming:

> Daniel Keepen [...] together with several other persons, came to his house in Rode [...] and commanded this person to come forth, and told him they suspected him to be a wizard [...] and also told him before they went away they would try whether he was one or not by swimming him in the river in Rode as they had done three old women before, and also threatened him that if he did not come forth then they would have him and his wife out the next day or else they would fire his house about his ears.

When he met him in the street on the same day William Moore had behaved in the same way as Daniel Keepen 'and called him 'wizard' several times and abused him very much and told him he would have him out in the afternoon and swim him in the river'. The fact that Browne was named as a 'wizard' is interesting: the gendering of witchcraft over many decades seems to have finally evolved, by the end of the seventeenth century, into the modern stereotype whereby the word 'witch' denotes a female and, typically, an elderly woman. Until now the Rode swimmings have received less attention than they deserve.[13a] They were an extremely rare early incidence of what has been described as a 'reverse witch trial'. When they are considered in relation to the 1689 swimmings of Elizabeth Carrier in neighbouring Beckington, the argument that the years immediately before and after 1690 mark a turning point in the history of the decline of witchcraft prosecution becomes even more compelling.

* * *

Long after courts ceased persecuting witches, the lynch mob continued the work of the witch-finder. In 1718 Francis Hutchinson railed against 'our country-people', still as fond of swimming witches 'as they are of baiting a bear or bull'.[14] In 1751, seventy-year-old Ruth Osborne and her husband, long suspected by locals at the village of Long Marston in the parish of Tring, Hertfordshire, of being witches, were taken to a pond by an angry mob of several thousand people. One witness described how the old woman, clad only in a sheet, was bound at the wrists and feet and dragged through the water, which was five feet deep, to the opposite bank by means of rope tied round her. Others recalled her being forced to the middle of the pond by two men; one of them, who used a stick to push her repeatedly under the surface, was identified as a chimney-sweep called Thomas Colley. Ruth Osborne drowned and Coley, the ringleader of the mob, was hanged for her murder. A very similar episode occurred in Frome in 1730, three or four miles away from Beckington where, forty-one years before, Elizabeth Carrier had been subjected to the same ordeal. The case, first reported in the *Daily Journal*, appeared four months later in the first edition of the long-running *Gentleman's Magazine*, in January 1731. It appeared in the *Gentleman's Magazine* under the title 'The Melancholy Effects of Credulity in Witchcraft':

> From Burlington in Pennsylvania we have an account that the owners of several cattle, believing them to be bewitched, caused some suspected men and women to be taken up, and trials to be made for detecting them. Above 300 people assembled near the governor's house, and a pair of scales being erected, the suspected persons were each weighed against a large Bible; but all of them vastly outweighing it, the accused were then to be tied head and feet together, and put into a river, on supposition that if they swam they must be guilty. This trial they offered to undergo, in case as many of their accusers should be served in the like manner; which being done, they all swam very buoyant, to the no small diversion of the spectators, and clearing of the accused. This has revived a like tradition in Somersetshire in September last, and another in France.
>
> The first is from Frome published in the *Daily Journal*, January 15, relating that a child of one Wheeler, being seized with strange unaccountable fits, the mother goes to a cunning man who advised her to hang a bottle of the child's water, mixed with some of its hair, close stopped over the fire, that the witch would thereupon come and break it. Does not mention the success, but a poor old woman in the neighbourhood was taken up, and the old trial by water ordeal revived. They dragged her, shivering with an ague, out of her home, sat her astride on the pommel of a saddle, and carried her about two miles to a mill-pond, stripped off her upper clothes, tied her legs, and with a rope about her middle, threw her in, 200 huzzaing and abetting the riot. They affirm she swam like a cork, though forced several times under water; and no wonder, for when they strained the line, the ends whereof were held on each side of the pond, she must of necessity rise; but by hauling her from one bank to the other, and often plunging, she drank water enough, and when almost spent, they poured in brandy to revive her, they drew her to a stable, threw her on some form of litter, in her wet clothes, where in about an hour after she expired. The coroner upon his inquest of the ring-leaders, although above forty persons assisted in the fact, yet none of them

could be persuaded to accuse his neighbour, so that they were able to charge only three of them with manslaughter.

The exact location of these events is uncertain although Kinglsey Palmer, citing the account of the case in the *Somerset Year Book* for 1922, claimed 'The story concerns a village called Woodlands'.[15] The adjoining hamlets of East and West Woodlands, part of the Longleat estate in the eighteenth century, lie directly to the south of Frome.

Several more swimmings in the eighteenth century are recorded for the eastern counties including Leicestershire (1717, 1736, 1760, 1776), Norfolk (1748), Cambridgeshire (1769), Suffolk (1752, 1795), and Kent (1735).[16] In some instances those swum volunteered themselves in order to prove their innocence.[17] Although swimming the witch was a long established tradition, the long history of these extra-judicial swimmings, continuing throughout the eighteenth century, could be regarded as evidence in support of Gaskill's contention that 'When the facility to seek formal redress against witches waned in the later seventeenth century, the incidence of informal violence against suspects [...] increased'.[18]

Table 6 *Ordeal by water ('swimming') episodes.*[19]

Year	Location
1612	Raunds, Northamptonshire
1613	Milton Mills, Bedfordshire
c.1637	Bedford, Bedfordshire
c.1642	Baldock, Hertfordshire
c.1644	Northamptonshire
1645	Bedfordshire
1645	Kent
1645	Framlingham Castle, Suffolk
1645	Rye, Sussex
1660	Kidderminster, Worcestershire
1667	Bedfordshire
1689	Beckington, Somerset
1694	Rode, Somerset
1699	Great Coggeshall, Essex

CREDULITY AND INCREDULITY

1701	Southwark, Surrey
1704	Rosemary Lane, Middlesex
1709	Horninghold, Leicestershire
1716	Fladbury, Worcestershire
1717	Great Wigston, Leicestershire
1730	Frome, Somerset
1735	Cambridgeshire
1735	Kent
1736	Leicestershire
1737	Oakley, Hertfordshire
1748	Norfolk
1751	Long Marston, Hertfordshire
1752	Suffolk
1795	Suffolk

The continuing concern with witchcraft in Somerset is evident in a brief article that appeared in *The Western Gazette* on Friday 29 June 1866:[20]

> A girl here [Castle Cary] is popularly supposed to have been bewitched. For some weeks, she has occasionally suffered from what appear to be fits, but it is mentioned as a somewhat suspicious circumstance that she appears to have a 'fit' at any time she pleases. During these attacks, she has named several persons who, she says, have bewitched her, and refers to one in particular as having appeared to her and tempted her to drown herself. Her friends have raised a subscription, and spent the proceeds in a journey to Somerton, to consult a 'witch' residing there. The verdict of this 'witch' was, that the girl was *not* bewitched, but that somebody had 'wished her a very bad wish'; and this valuable information was all the poor foolish people got for their money. And yet we are apt to talk as if all the heathen lived in distant countries!

The folklorist Ruth Tongue found evidence for the survival into the twentieth century of another local tradition, and one that was so central in Glanvill's accounts of the Brewham and Stoke Trister sabbat meetings. The following remarks were made by a woman in the Frome area some time between 1960 and 1963:

> There was an old woman in our village who everyone was afraid of if she 'looked at you'. If you made her angry, she used to say, 'I'll turn 'ee into a tom-tit.' She could do cures, but if she wasn't spoken to right, you got worse. My mother said she has a mommick [mommet] to stick thorns into.[21]

* * *

IAN BOSTRIDGE HAS spoken of 'widespread educated credulity' concerning witchcraft around 1670.[22] The involvement of members of the local elite in the Beckington case, together with the apparent participation of numerous unnamed locals witnessing the swimming of Elizabeth Carrier and the torments of Mary Hill, suggest that, in fact, witchcraft belief in Selwood Forest, across all social divides, was strong at the end of the seventeenth century. For May Hill, Humphrey Phillips, Squire Player, John Humfrey and Richard Baxter, witchcraft, as the century arrived at its last decade, remained a most serious matter. Their concerns were founded, not least, on the discoveries of their illustrious Selwood associates, Robert Hunt and Joseph Glanvill.

Darren Oldridge has written, 'If the tumultuous years between 1642 and 1660 were the zenith of Satan's political career, the period after the Restoration marked the beginning of his slow retirement from one area of public life'.[23] The preoccupation with the Devil in the work of Glanvill, Bovet, Baxter, Beaumont and company has much to do with what David Berman has identified as 'an explosion of atheism'[24] among the upper classes in Restoration England. This was largely inspired by the writings of Thomas Hobbes (1588–1679). The threat of this emergent atheism was the single most compelling reason for the demonological output of the second half of the seventeenth century. Fear of atheism is the common thread that binds together the post-1660 works discussed in this book. The Selwood Forest and other Somerset witchcraft cases are found at the centre of their discourse. Baxter's interest in Hill's account of the Beckington witchcraft case lay in his conviction that it was further proof of the supernatural – how these events might be explained in theological terms was not the main issue: that they were miraculous was what mattered. Alongside

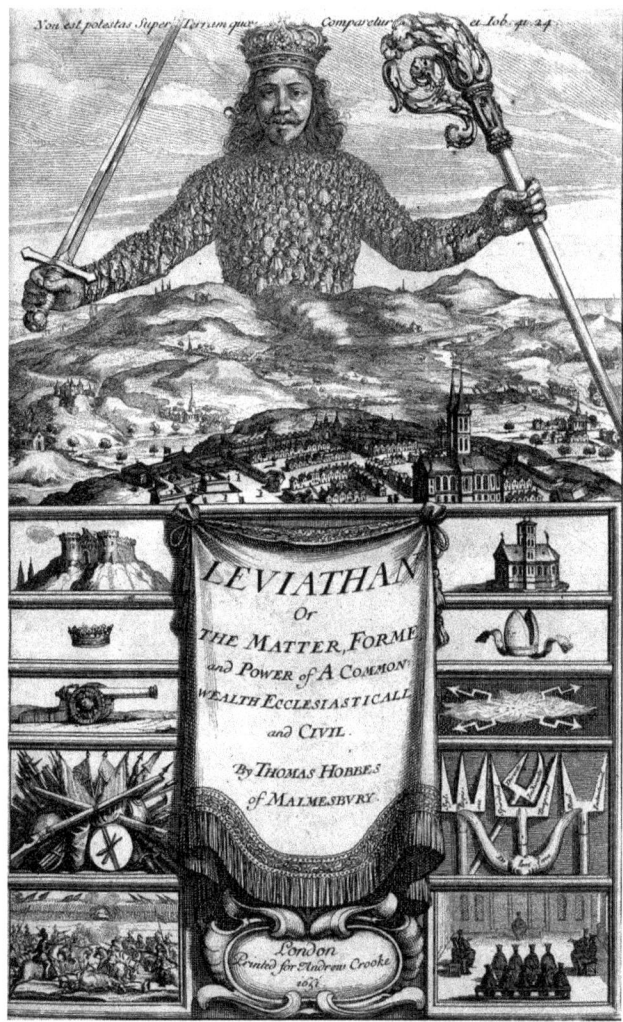

Fig. 9-5 *Thomas Hobbes*, Leviathan, *1651*.

stories of possession and bewitchment he included other miracles, such as that of the flowering of the Glastonbury Thorn on Christmas Day. The appetite of revered figures such as Baxter, More and Glanvill for instances of bewitchment might even help account for why some came to light, or worse, came to court, in the first place. Certainly the particular interest and concern of the rector in the Beckington affair were instrumental in its development. While the case is strong for the decline of witchcraft anxiety in England in the later seventeenth century as 'an essential by-product of the growing politicization of the country [...] in the wake of the civil wars',[25] the continuing fascination with witchcraft in Selwood was driven by a religious and moral imperative shared by moderate clerics and justices on both sides of the post-1660 divide.

Atheism in Restoration England did not necessarily define complete disbelief: any position that doubted the active involvement of God, and, by extension, the Devil, in the affairs of men was considered atheist. Such lack of faith, many thought at the time, must surely incur the wrath of God, 'some signal judgement' as John Evelyn put it in 1699.[26] The writings of Thomas Hobbes were condemned by many as blasphemous – they were proscribed by the University of Oxford and burnt by the public hangman.[27]

Many years before the passing of the Blasphemy Act in 1697, more severe acts to discourage irreligion were drafted. The first of these, 'for punishing and suppressing of atheism" and 'prophaness', appeared at the start of 1667. It intended to punish 'Any person who denies or derides the essence, persons, or attributes of God the Father, Son or Holy Ghost given in the Scriptures, or the omnipotency, wisdom, justice, mercy, goodness, or providence of God in the creation' with imprisonment until a fine of up to 50 shillings was paid. The second proposal, dated January 1668, also aimed to imprison 'any person, being of the age of sixteen years or more not being visibly and apparently distracted out of his wits by sickness or natural infirmity, or not a mere natural fool, void of common sense' who was guilty of 'those crying sins of atheism and blasphemy'.[28]

The fashionable Hobbesian atheism of the day was lampooned in 1675 by an anonymous Restoration wit in a ten-page pamphlet:

> His religion (for now and then he will be prattling of that too) is pretendedly Hobbian, and he swears the Leviathan may supply all the lost leaves of Solomon, yet he never saw it in his life, and for ought he knows it may be a treatise about catching of sprats, or [...] regulating the Greenland fishing trade. However, the rattle of it at coffee-houses has taught him to laugh at spirits, and maintain that there are no angels but those in petticoats: and therefore he defies Heaven [...] imagines Hell only a hothouse to flux in for a clap and

calls the Devil the parson's bug-bear, and sometimes the civil old gentleman in black. He denies that there is any essential difference betwixt good and evil, deems conscience a thing only fit for children, and ascribes all honesty to simplicity and an unpractiseness in the ways of the town.[29]

Nevertheless, it was these 'town-gallants' more than the sceptical members of the Royal Society or even those outside it, such as John Webster, who led the way in the abandoning of belief in magical principles. For fear of ridicule by the wits of the coffee-houses and playhouses, members of the Society generally steered clear of witchcraft and related phenomena at their meetings, even though, Michael Hunter has written, they might 'dabble in alchemy or astrology, or promote miraculous cures, or compile accounts of witchcraft' when back home. This attitude, he concludes, 'helped relegate such investigations to the realm of pseudo-science, and there they have remained ever since'.[30] Even by the time of the Beckington trial in 1690 and the publication of its outcome in Baxter's *Certainty of the Worlds of Spirits* the following year, educated concern with the maleficent witch was primarily that of those die-hard latitudinarians (May Hill?) and dissenters still on the look-out for the preternatural signs of God's providence.[31] Meanwhile medical practitioners advanced neurological explanations over the diabolical for the bizarre behaviour of their disturbed patients.[32]

Although Hobbes took care to avoid incriminating himself, and his personal philosophical position is obscure, his critics, such as Archbishop Tenison in *The Creed of Mr Hobbes Examined* (1670), more clearly delineated his supposed atheism. The anti-Hobbesian writings of Tenison, Ralph Cudworth,[33] Seth Ward[34] and others fanned the fire of the alarmists, provoking horror in educated circles, while the alleged atheists themselves remained, in print at least, more or less silent. Not all were so hostile: another famous man of letters from the period, and the most highly regarded seventeenth-century antiquarian, John Aubrey (1626–1697), considered him a friend and wrote his biography, the 'Life of Mr Thomas Hobbes of Malmesbury', for inclusion in his *Brief Lives*. In this Aubrey set out to show how Hobbes had been misunderstood and that he did not share the position of his namesakes, the so-called Hobbists, as defined by such as Glanvill and More.[35]

Fig. 9-6 *"Credulity, Superstition and Fanaticism"* by William Hogarth (1762).

More had written in his commentary on Hunt's Selwood Forest cases that it was a 'special piece of providence that there are ever and anon such fresh examples of apparitions and witchcrafts as may rub up and awaken benumbed and lethargic minds into a suspicion at least, if not assurance, that there are other intelligent beings besides those that are clad in heavy earth or clay'.[36] A century later, John Wesley, the Bristol-based leader of the Methodist movement, cited the Drummer of Tedworth during a preaching tour of Sunderland in 1768 in his conviction that sceptics 'well know, (whether Christians know it, or not,) that the giving up of [belief in] witchcraft is, in effect, giving up the Bible; and they know, on the other hand, that if but one account of the intercourse of men with separate spirits be admitted, their whole castle in the air (Deism, Atheism, Materialism) falls to the ground'.[37]

The rector of Beckington, living in Glanvill's shadow, fought a rear-guard action of his own in the struggle with atheism when, in 1689, he brought attention to the shocking incidence of witchcraft in his parish. May Hill could number among his allies the local squires who helped bring the case to court, and the illustrious theologian Richard Baxter.[38] His participation in the same decades-old campaign his Selwood contemporary Glanvill had shared with Baxter suggests he was, at least, sympathetic to latitudinarian principles. Other cases in the 1680s have, rightly, been viewed through the lens of emergent Whig and Tory political identities and 'the rage of party'.[39] The personal politics of the printer of *Great News*, Thomas Milbourne, *may* have had a bearing on its publication, but the case, certainly in Baxter's handling of it, is more obviously interpreted in conjunction with that older struggle for a unitary state. Hill's willingness to co-operate with the likes of Baxter and Humfrey sheds light on both his theological and political convictions. By 1689 belief in witchcraft was a political issue, its advocacy already tainted by its association with nonconformism and other forms of dissent. The battle was not yet lost, indeed, in Hunter's reckoning, 'the orthodox consensus remained in favour of the reality of witchcraft, or at least in favour of staying neutral on the subject, well into the eighteenth century'.[40] Few, however, would now question Elmer's acknowledgement that 'More scrupulous evidentiary standards in law and new understandings of the mechanical did, without doubt, underscore a growing tendency toward scepticism with regard to witchcraft prosecutions'[41] in this period. The appearance of the Beckington women before Justice Holt at the beginning of 1690 was the last of the Selwood cases to end in a witch trial: in the courts, if not elsewhere, incredulity, it seems, had quashed belief.

1 Daniel Defoe (under the name 'Andrew Moreton'), *Secrets of the Invisible World Disclos'd* (1738), Preface.
2 Hutchinson, *An Historical Essay*, 45.
3 *Ibid.*, 43.

4 *Ibid.*, 44.
5 Ewen, *Witchcraft and Demonianism*, 377–78.
6 Hutchinson, *An Historical Essay*, 226.
7 *Ibid.*, 226.
8 *Ibid.*, 227.
9 Margaret Hill, the daughter of John and Mary, was baptised on 24 June 1669; she died at the age of seventy-three and was buried on 14 November 1742.
10 There is no indication of their having had any children in either the parish registers or their wills. PROB 11/459/353 May Hill, PROB 11/533/130 Anne Hill.
11 I am most grateful to Marek Lewcun of Norton St Philip, Somerset, who introduced me to this important case in B.H. Cunnington (ed.), *Records of the County of Wiltshire, being extracts from the Quarter Sessions Great Rolls of the Seventeenth Century* (Devizes: George Simpson, 1932), 279–82; the case is also mentioned in Gaskell, *Crime and Mentalities* (2000), 83.
12 Owen Davies, *Witchcraft, Magic and Culture 1736–1951* (Manchester: Manchester University Press, 1999), 89.
13 Deanna Petherbridge, *Witches and Wicked Bodies* (Edinburgh: National Galleries of Scotland, 2013), 84.
13a The one reference I have found in modern scholarly texts to the Rode witch-swimmings is a two-sentence summary in Malcolm Gaskill's Crime and Mentalities in Early Modern England (Cambridge: Cambridge University Press, 2000), 83.
14 Hutchinson, *An Historical Essay*, 139.
15 Kingsley Palmer, *Folklore of Somerset* (London: Batsford, 1976, 63; see also Gaskill, *Crime and Mentalities*, 82.
16 Sharpe, *Instruments*, 282; contemporary records.
17 Thomas, *Religion and the Decline of Magic*, 619.
18 Gaskill, *Crime and Mentalities*, 118.
19 Compiled from various sources including contemporary literature, Kittredge (1929), Ewen (1929, 1933), Gaskill (2005), Walker (2004) and Sharpe (2007), Elmer (2016).
20 I am grateful to Ellen Watson for bringing this case to my attention.
21 R. L. Tongue, 'Some Notes on Modern Somerset Witch-Lore', *Folklore*, 74:1 (1963), 323.
22 Ian Bostridge, 'Witchcraft Revealed', in Barry *et al.*, *Witchcraft in Early Modern Europe*, 312.
23 Oldridge, *Devil*, 195.
24 David Berman, *A History of Atheism in Britain from Hobbes to Russell* (London: Routledge, 1988), 48.
25 Elmer, *Witchcraft*, 231.
26 Evelyn in Michael Hunter, *Science and Society in Restoration England*

(Cambridge: Cambridge University Press, 1981), 164.
27 Hunter, *Science and Society*, 168.
28 In Berman, *A History of Atheism*, 48–49.
29 Anon., *The Character of a Town-Gallant exposing the extravagant fopperies of some vain self-conceited pretenders to gentility and good breeding* (1675), 9.
30 Michael Hunter, 'The Royal Society and the Decline of Magic', *Notes and Records of the Royal Society of London*, 65:2 (2011), 110.
31 See Elmer, *Witchcraft*, 231.
32 Ibid. 232.
33 Ralph Cudworth (1617–88) was a Cambridge scholar and cleric, born a short distance beyond the western boundary of Selwod Forest at Aller in Somerset. In 1650 he was presented with the living of North Cadbury, close to its southern edge, which was held by Clare Hall, the Cambridge College where Cudworth was Master and Regius Professor of Hebrew. As one of the leaders of the Cambridge Platonists he knew Henry More well. It is unlikely he spent much time in Somerset after his childhood. In 1678 Cudworth published *The True Intellectual System of the Universe: the first part, wherein all the reason and philosophy of atheism is confuted and its impossibility demonstrated*.
34 One of the original members of the Royal Society, Seth Ward (1617–89) became Bishop of Exeter in 1662 and of Salisbury in 1667. His *Vindiciae Academiarum* (1654), written with John Wilkins, challenged the views of Joseph Glanvill's great adversary in the Restoration era, John Webster.
35 Hunter, *Science and Society*, 168.
36 More in Glanvill, *Saducismus*, 26.
37 John Wesley, *The Journal of John Wesley*, 25 May 1768.
38 The close scrutiny of the Beckington case lends support to Brian Levack's conclusion that very few of the elite gave up believing in witchcraft 'until the trials were almost over'. Brian Levack, *Witch-hunting in Scotland: Law, Politics and Religion* (London: Routledge, 2007), 132.
39 See, for example, Elmer's analysis of the trial of the Bideford witches at Exeter in 1682; Elmer, *Witchraft*, 246.
40 Michael Hunter, 'The Decline of Magic: Challenge and Response in early Enlightenment England', *The Historical Journal*, 55:2 (2012), 417.
41 Elmer, *Witchcraft*, 2.

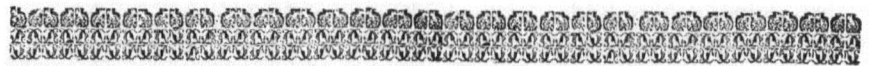

SOME CONCLUSIONS

IN SEVENTEENTH-CENTURY ENGLAND the publication of accounts of witchcraft cases, the bedrock of historical enquiries in this field, was a monopoly of the elite. The survival of the history of the Selwood 'witches' is largely due to the good fortune that the investigating JP, Robert Hunt, kept detailed memoranda on their cases and other aspects of his work.[1] While some witchcraft cases, such as these, became very well-known and were retold in many subsequent publications, the detail for most is lost and will never be recovered. No doubt hundreds are entirely unknown, and hundreds more appear in the scant records of gaol deliveries and the like. These all represent complex narratives of human dramas that remain hidden from history.

The accounts of meetings of alleged witches in out-of-the-way places in and around Selwood Forest, recorded by Hunt and Glanvill, are truly exceptional. These must be analysed with due consideration of sectarian divisions, the exclusion of nonconformist ministers, and the persecution of Quakers and other dissenters in the era of the Restoration. The history of the conventicles helps explain the mystery of the covens. The unusually well-documented Beckington case of 1689 was a traditional account of the *maleficia* of elderly women targeting the young. It bore the hallmarks of a conventional English witchcraft episode – what Sharpe has termed the 'normal' themes – 'the concern over *maleficium*, the witch stereotype of the poor elderly woman, the importance of that distinctive element in English witchcraft, the familiar spirit'.[2]

For the people of Beckington the bewitchment of the two teenagers was an exceptional event. It attracted the attention of the community at large – hundreds came to see the bewitched and to witness Elizabeth Carrier's trials by water. Certainly, in the opinion of the rector and his associates, it was something worth following up. The evidence of the swimming of a witch was unlikely to impress a judge but that of the extraordinary quantity of vomited metal objects must have seemed to her enemies sufficient for a successful prosecution. This vomiting of indigestible material is the most striking feature of the story. Richard

Baxter detailed several more shocking examples of the phenomenon in *Certainty of the Worlds of Spirits*. Whether this was a deceit on the part of the victim or those who brought the accused to trial, or whether it was the manifestation of a potentially lethal eating disorder, cannot be determined.

When Alan Macfarlane studied the assize records for witchcraft cases in early modern Essex he discovered that only 'fifty out of 460 indictments [for bewitching property or persons] placed victim and witch in different villages'. Thus, he concluded, 'accusations seem to have been limited to an area of intense relationships between individuals'. The Selwood cases are also tales of interpersonal conflict and the persecution of and by neighbours. In Essex Macfarlane discovered 'quarrels over gifts and loans of food, and to a lesser extent, money and implements, precipitated the majority of the witchcraft attacks'. In Somerset too, cases emerged from sometimes petty altercations between people who knew each other well. The refusal to help one's neighbour – for example Mary Hill's refusal to accompany Elizabeth Carrier to Frome to look for work – might have caused the final and total severing of relationships that were already strained, and hence 'the enormous emotion' generated by a seemingly minor dispute can be more easily understood.[3]

When Mary Hill fell out with Carrier it is quite logical that the girl would resort to the witch-allegation to exact her revenge. The fact that William Spicer, before her, would tease the old woman by calling her a witch and making reference to her demon-familiars implies that she was already under suspicion. Perhaps, like others before her, Mary simulated those well-known characteristics of demonic possession in order to ruin, once and for all, Carrier's already tarnished reputation. If so, the rector, who was a firm believer in the reality of witchcraft, was readily taken in, and so, it seems, was everyone else. As James Sharpe concluded in a consideration of witchcraft in Pendle Forest at the start of the century, one can conclude that the inhabitants of Selwood Forest over half a century later were living 'in an intellectual and social milieu where gossip about witchcraft, knowledge of witchcraft and worry about witchcraft were commonplace'.[4] Mary Hill in 1689 was a young woman in a very desperate condition: impoverished and orphaned, with three younger siblings to care for. Whether she contrived it or not, her bewitchment brought her the attention she craved – while the lives of three of her neighbours were in jeopardy, her fortunes were turned around when the rector took her into his home.

The claim of bewitchment in the village is not the unusual feature of the Beckington case but the fact that it was taken up by the higher authorities, especially this late in the century, is rather more remarkable. The prosecution of a witch entailed certain expenses that the prosecutor would be expected to pay. Most witchcraft cases no doubt were sorted out, if at all, at an extra-judicial level, counter-magic perhaps being applied to undo the *maleficium*. That the Beckington case, like the Hunt-Glanvill ones before it, should end up in court must surely be because of the interest taken by the rector and the other parish officials in the matter. Quite probably parish funds were made available to start the proceedings; perhaps some well-off, concerned observer of these alarming events, such as Squire Player of Castle Cary, made a contribution. The attitude of magistrates was especially important in its potential to move from the local sessions to the assize court.

* * *

WHILE THE OBVIOUS societal, collegiate and political associations of the intellectuals engaged in what has been called the 'Glanvill-Webster' debate regarding the reality of witchcraft is well known,[5] the web of relations among witch-finders in the localities set in that broader London-centric context, are easy to miss. In this instance, primarily because the various elements that form a regional history of fascination with witchcraft have not previously been considered first and foremost in geographical terms, they have been overlooked and, at best, only partially understood. As they have come to light in a succession of surprising connections, they begin to reveal their hitherto under-appreciated role in driving and reviving the witch-hunt through the second half of the seventeenth century.

The correspondence of Richard Baxter confirms the respect in which he was held by Glanvill and Humfrey, and all had at least an intellectual relationship with Richard Bernard of Batcombe. They were bound together too by their printer, Thomas Milbourne, who, in turn, helped bring the rector of Beckington, May Hill, into their orbit. Perhaps what is most remarkable in this discussion is the discovery of so many prolific writers and highly influential theologians, natural philosophers and demonologists, who had a special relationship in the seventeenth century with that very small part of the west of England still known as Selwood Forest.

Close examination of the Selwood witchcraft accusations mostly reveals them to be an unfortunate consequence of ordinary folk, living in troubled times, going about their regular business – working and worshipping, begging and providing – and sometimes falling foul of their neighbours in the process. That these might escalate to court hearings, occasionally with dire consequences, had much to do with the mind-set of local authority figures who were the gatekeepers in these disputes, especially magistrates like Robert Hunt, seem to have shared, and were perhaps educated by, the core beliefs of local writers with demonological interests such as Batcombe's influential pastors, Bernard and Alleine. This meeting of minds, the collusion of elite and popular culture, could make mountains of molehills. That the Selwood Forest cases are known at all is largely due to seventeenth-century print culture and the personal and professional compulsion of intellectuals, philosophers and scholarly clerics – Glanvill, Humfrey, Hill and Baxter - to make their unique mark upon it.

1 Hunt's fascinating 'Memorandum Book of Robert Hunt, Sheriff of Somerset 1654–1656' was transcribed and published by J. S. Cockburn in *Somerset Assize Orders 1640–1659* (Frome: Butler and Tanner, 1971), 57–81. This includes a detailed account of his activities in overseeing the trial and execution of those involved in the Penruddock rising.
2 Sharpe, *Instruments*, 148.
3 Macfarlane, *Witchcraft*, 168.
4 Sharpe, *Instruments*, 202.
5 See, for example, Sharpe, *Instruments*, 268, and Jobe, 'The Devil in Restoration Science'.

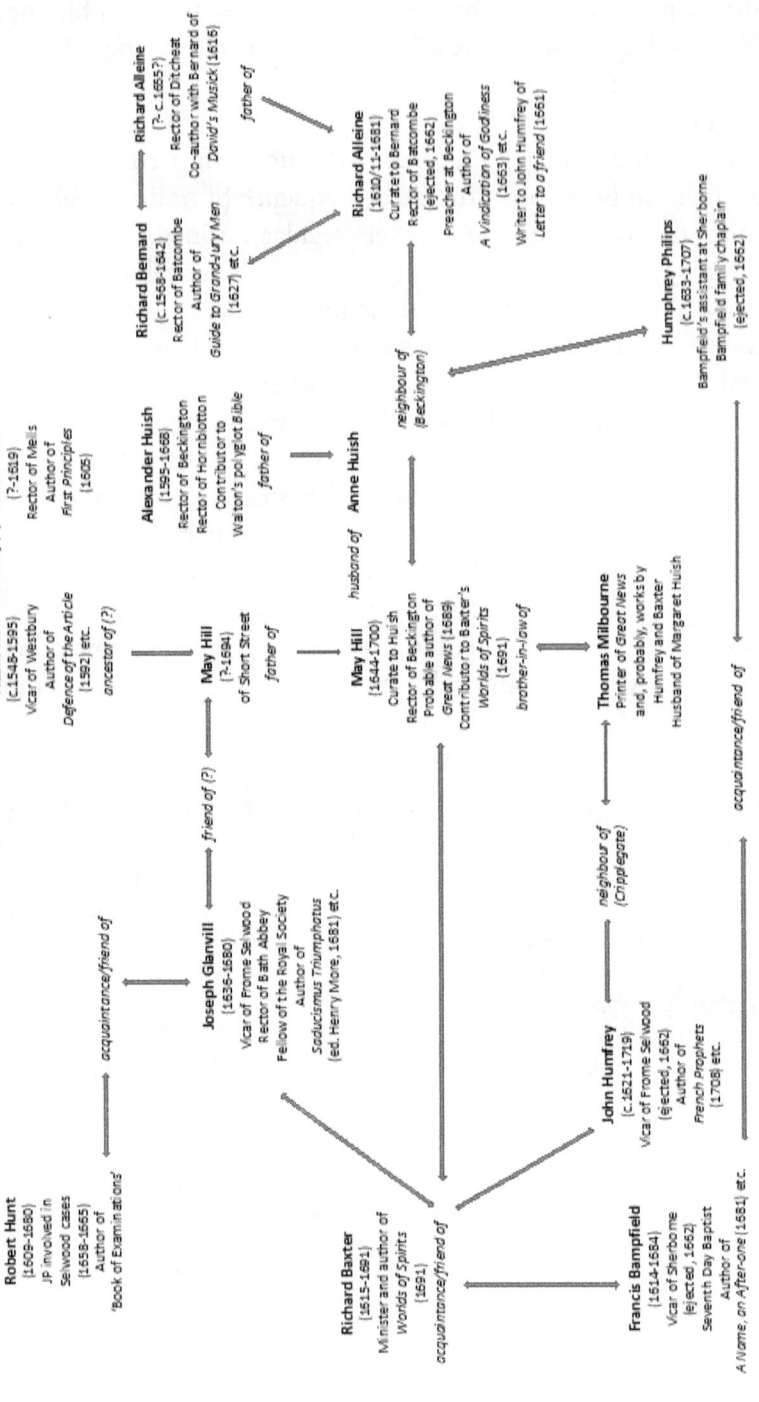

Table 7 Selwood connections.

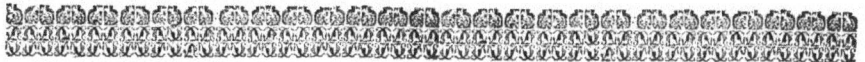

CHRONOLOGY AND LOCATIONS

1604 Witchcraft Act
1612 Trial of the Pendle witches at Lancaster
1613 Richard Bernard becomes rector of St Mary's, Batcombe
1626 Edward Bull and Joan Greedie indicted at Taunton assizes for bewitching Edward Dynham (Richard Bernard probably in attendance)
1627 Publication of Bernard's *A Guide to Grand Jurymen with respect to Witches*
1628 Alexander Huish made Rector of St George's, Beckington
1636 Beckington communion table riot
1640 Indictment in Parliament of Alexander Huish
1641 Death of Richard Bernard
1642 Start of the English Civil War
1644 Birth of May Hill, future rector of Beckington
1645 Matthew Hopkins, 'Witchfinder General', active in East Anglia
1649 Execution of Charles I
1650 Alexander Huish formally dispossessed of his Beckington living
1651 End of the English Civil War; publication of Thomas Hobbes' *Leviathan*
1658 Trial of Jane Brooks of Shepton Mallet
1659 Discovery of a mass gathering of Quaker 'witches' at Sherborne
1660 Restoration of the monarchy under Charles II; Alexander Huish reinstated as Rector of St George's, Beckington
1662 Act of Uniformity imposed the Book of Common Prayer and reasserts the principle of episcopal ordination; the Quaker Act could be invoked obliging subjects to take an oath of loyalty to the king – something contrary to Quaker principles; Joseph Glanvill (1636–1681) appointed Vicar of Frome Selwood; founding of the Royal Society
1663 (January) Joseph Glanvill and 'Mr Hill' visit Mr Mompesson's haunted house at Tidworth in Wiltshire; trial for witchcraft of Julian Cox in Taunton (summer assizes)
1664 The Conventicle Act suppresses meetings of dissenters; Joseph Glanvill becomes member of the Royal Society
1665 Trial of Elizabeth Style of Stoke Trister—Style dies in gaol before her execution can be carried out; trial of Alice Duke of Wincanton; trial of Christian Green of Brewham; trial of Margaret Agar of Brewham; Five Mile Act (also known as the 'Oxford Act', the 'Nonconformists

	Act'); May Hill appointed curate of St George's, Beckington; death, allegedly by witchcraft, of a 'young maid' at Kilmington; the Great Plague
1666	Joseph Glanvill made a rector of Bath Abbey; the Fire of London
1668	Toleration Act helps emancipate religious dissenters; publication of Glanvill's *A Blow at Modern Sadducism*; May Hill appointed rector of St George's, Beckington
1670	Anne Slade charged and acquitted in Somerset on two witchcraft charges
1671	Ann Blake, wife of Henry Blake, found not guilty at Wells on charges of bewitching an infant, Anne Wrentmore, to death, and laming Elizabeth Penney by witchcraft
1672	Joseph Glanvill exchanges Frome living for Street and Walton; Margaret/Margeria Stevens, wife of John Stevens, charged and acquitted in Somerset on charges of laming Jane Bayneham and Mary Bridge by witchcraft
1674	John and Agnes Knipp of Southton, Somerset, acquitted following witchcraft charges
1675	Martha Rylens of Southton, Somerset, acquitted on five indictments for witchcraft; May Hill and Anne Huish married at Chobham, Surrey
1677	Declaration of Indulgence permits freedom of worship in specially licensed premises; publication of John Webster's *Displaying of Supposed Witchcraft*; Elizabeth Langley, wife of John Langley, faced trial on witchcraft charges in Wells (outcome unknown)
1680	Deaths of Robert Hunt and Joseph Glanvill; c.1680 Anna Rawlins acquitted at Wells, charged with bewitching Grace Atkins, spinster, 'by which she is much consumed, wasted, pined and lamed'; probable date of Lord North's trial of an unnamed man at Taunton for bewitching a thirteen-year-old girl (not guilty verdict)
1681	Publication of Glanvill's *Saducismus Triumphatus;* death of Richard Alleine
1684	Elenora/Eleanor, Susannah, and Marie Harris, and Anna Clarke/Cheeke acquitted at Taunton on charges of using witchcraft against Charles Atwell; publication of Richard Bovet's *Pandaemonium*
1685	Start of the reign of James II; Alice Molland hanged at Exeter, thought to be the last person executed in England for witchcraft; unnamed man acquitted on witchcraft charge at Taunton; Monmouth Rebellion culminates in the battle of Sedgemoor
1686	Beckington struck by typhus epidemic; Honora Phippen acquitted at Wells on charges of using witchcraft against Martha Welling and Katherine Goodson
1687	Elizabeth Langley found not guilty at Wells of bewitching Anna Payne
1688	The Glorious Revolution

CHRONOLOGY AND LOCATIONS

1689   Deposition of James II, start of the reign of William III; publication of the third edition of *Saducismus Triumphatus*; publication of *Great News from the West of England*; arrest of Margery Coombes, Elizabeth Carrier and Ann More of Beckington; death in gaol of Margery Coombes

1690   Trial at Taunton and release of Elizabeth Carrier and Ann More (April)

1691   Publication of Richard Baxter's *The Certainty of the Worlds of Spirits*; death of Richard Baxter

1692   Start of Salem witch trials

1693   End of Salem witch trials

1694   Swimming of three 'witches' at Rode, Somerset

1700   Death of May Hill

1705   Publication of John Beaumont's *An Historical Physiological and Theological Treatise of Spirits, Apparitions, Witchcrafts, and Other Magical Practises*

1710   Death of Lord Chief Justice Holt

1718   Publication of Francis Hutchinson's *An Historical Essay Concerning Witchcraft*

1719   Death of John Humfrey

1730   Witch-swimming episode at Frome

1736   Repeal of Jacobean witchcraft legislation

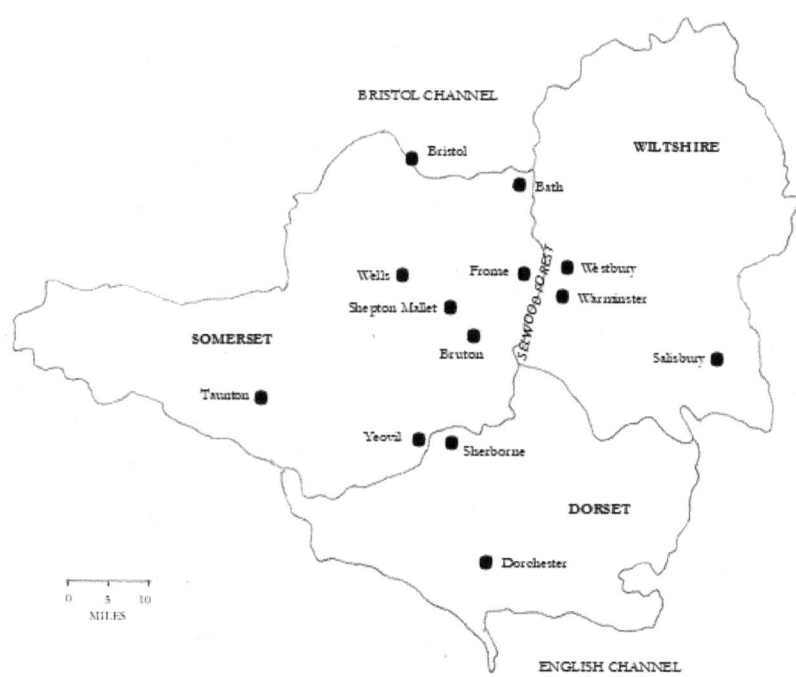

Map 1 The West of England.

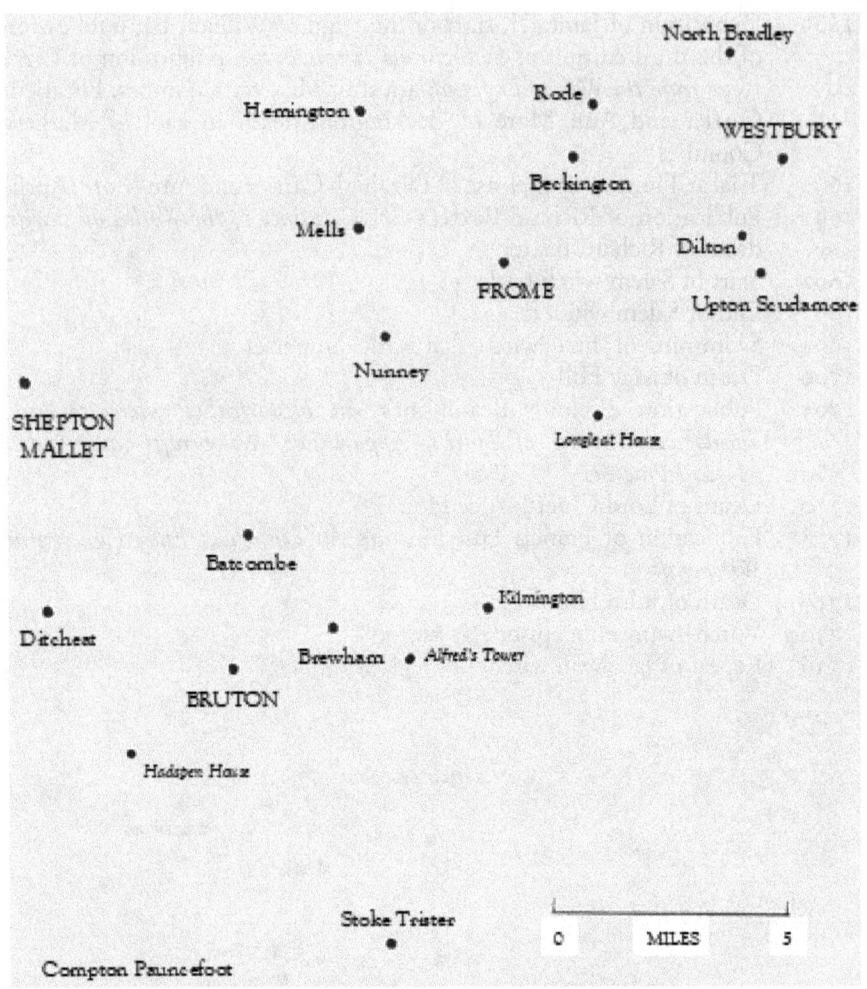

Map 2 *The Selwood Forest region of Somerset and Wiltshire.*

Batcombe, Somerset: 1613–1641 living held by Richard Bernard, author of *A Guide to Grand-Jury Men [...] in cases of witchcraft* (1627).
Beckington, Somerset: 1689–1690 scene of the bewitchment of two eighteen-year-olds, William Spicer and Mary Hill, and the subsequent arrest of three women, Elizabeth Carrier, Margery Coombes and Ann More.
Bruton, Somerset: location of the 1689 sessions at which the Beckington witchcraft case was examined.
Brewham, Somerset: setting for witchcraft coven and sabbat activity heard in the examinations of Christian Green and Margaret Agar in 1665.

CHRONOLOGY AND LOCATIONS

Compton Pauncefoot, Somerset: home of Robert Hunt, JP.

Dilton, Wiltshire: childhood home of May Hill, rector of Beckington at the time of the Beckington witchcraft episode of 1689.

Ditcheat, Somerset: location of a disturbing manifestation of the Devil in an account published in 1584; residence of a physician and cunning man named Compton involved in the 1665 Stoke Trister case.

Frome, Somerset: living held by Richard Baxter's colleague John Humfrey and then, 1662–1672, by Joseph Glanvill, author of *Saducismus Triumphatus*; location in 1730 of a fatal witch-swimming episode.

Hadspen House, Somerset: home of William Player – probably the 'Squire Player' who visited Beckington in 1689 to investigate the bewitchment of Mary Hill.

Hemington, Somerset: 1678–1736 living held by Stephen Hill, brother of May Hill, rector of Beckington.

Kilmington, Wiltshire: location of the alleged bewitchment of a 'young maid' in 1665.

Mells, Somerset: 1591–1619 living held by William Hill, author of *The First Principles of a Christian*.

Nunney, Somerset: possible home of Julian Cox, executed as a witch at Taunton in 1663.

Rode, Somerset: three women, Anne Haberfield and her daughters Elizabeth Kneall and Margaret Waddom swum here as witches in 1694.

Shepton Mallet, Somerset: 1657 scene of the bewitching of Richard Jones that led to the execution of Jane Brooks.

Stoke Trister, Somerset: setting for witchcraft coven and sabbat activity heard in the examinations of Elizabeth Style and Alice Duke in 1665.

Westbury, Wiltshire: 1582–1595 living held by Adam Hill, esteemed theologian and author.

BIBLIOGRAPHY

Sixteenth-, seventeenth- and eighteenth-century sources

Ady, Thomas, *A Candle in the Dark*. 1655.
Anon., *The Examination of John Walsh*. 1566.
Anon., *A true and most Dreadfull discourse of a woman possessed with the Devill*. 1584.
Anon., *Daimonomageia: A Small Treatise of Sickness and Diseases from Witchcraft*. 1665.
Anon., *Persecution Appearing with Its Open Face, in William Armour*. 1667.
Anon., *The Hartford-shire Wonder, or Strange News from Ware*. 1669.
Anon., *The Character of a Town-Gallant exposing the extravagant fopperies of some vain self-conceited pretenders to gentility and good breeding*. 1675.
Anon., *A Tryall of Witches at the Assizes held at Bury St Edmonds for the County of Suffolk; on the Tenth day of March, 1664*. 1680.
Anon., *A True Account of a Strange and Wonderful Relation of one John Tonken of Pensans in Cornwall*. 1686.
Anon., *Great News from the West of England*. 1689.
Anon., *A Full and True Account of the Apprehending and Taking of Mrs Sarah Moordike, Who is accused for a Witch*. 1702.
Alleine, Richard, *Cheirothesia tou presbyteriou, or, A Letter to a friend*. 1661.
—. *The Godly Man's Portion and Sanctuary Opened in Two Sermons Preached August 17 1662*. 1662.
—. *Vindiciae Pietatis, or, A Vindication of Godliness*. 1664.
—. *The World Conquered, or, A Believers Victory over the World*. 1668.
—. *Godly-Fear*. 1674.
—. *A Rebuke for Backsliders and a Spur for Loyterers*. 1694.
Aubrey, John, *The Natural History of Wiltshire*. 1691.
Bampfield, Francis, *A Name, an After-one*. 1681.
Baxter, Richard, *The Certainty of the Worlds of Spirits*. 1691.
Bayly, Lewis, *The Practice of Piety, directing a Christian how to walk that he may please God* (1611)
Beaumont, John, *An Historical Physiological and Theological Treatise of Spirits, Apparitions, Witchcrafts, and Other Magical Practises*. 1705.
Bekker, Balthazar, *The World Bewitched*. 1691-1694.
Bernard, Richard, and Richard Alleine, *David's musick, or, Psalms of that royall prophet, once the sweete singer of that Israel*. 1616.

Bernard, Richard, *A Guide to Grand-Jury Men Divided Into Two Bookes: In The First, Is The Authors Best Advice To Them what to doe, before they bring in a billa vera in cases of witchcraft, etc.* 1627.

Besse, Joseph, *A Collection of the Sufferings of the People Called Quakers*, Vol. I. 1753.

Blagrave, Joseph, *Astrological Practice of Physick.* 1671.

Blome, Richard, *The Fanatick History.* 1705.

Bovet, Richard, *Pandaemonium, or, The Devil's Cloyster being a further Blow to modern Sadduceism, proving the Existence of Witches and Spirits.* 1684.

Calamy, Edmund, *An Account of the Ministers, lecturers, masters and Fellows of Colleges and Schoolmasters, who were Ejected or Silenced after the Restoration in 1660.* Second edn, 1713.

—. *The Nonconformists' Memorial*, ed. Samuel Palmer. 1725.

—. *Of Credulity and Incredulity in Things natural, civil and divine.* 1668.

—. *A Treatise Proving Sprits, Witches and Supernatural Operations.* 1672.

Collinson, John, *The History and Antiquities of the County of Somerset.* 1791.

Cotta, John, *The Tryall of Witch-Craft, shewing the true and right Methode of the Discovery with a Confutation of Erroneous Wayes.* 1616.

—. *A True Discovery of the Empericke with the Fugitive Physition and Quacksalver.* 1617.

Cooke, George Alexander, *Topographical and Statistical Description of the County of Somerset.* c.1800.

Crook, John, *A True Information to the Nation, from the People Called Quakers.* 1664.

Dalton, Michael, *The Countrey Justice, containing the practice of the Justices of the peace out of their sessions.* 1618.

Defoe, Daniel, *A Tour Thro' the Whole Island of Great Britain.* 1724–37.

—. (under the name 'Andrew Moreton'), *Secrets of the Invisible World Disclos'd.* 1738.

Drage, W., *Daimonomageia: A Small Treatise of Sickness and Diseases from Witchcraft.* 1665.

England, John, *A Funeral Sermon for John Derbie, Esq.* 1713.

Fell, Margaret, *A Journal or Historical Account of the Life, Travels, Sufferings, Christian Experiences and Labour of Love in the Work of the Ministry of That Ancient, Eminent and Faithful Servant of Jesus Christ, George Fox.* 1694.

Filmer, Robert, *An Advertisement to Jury-men of England Touching Witches.* 1653.

Fontanus, Nicholas, *The Womans Doctour.* 1652.

Gaule, John, *Select Cases of Conscience touching Witches and Witchcrafts.* 1646.

Glanvill, Joseph, *Some Philosophical Considerations Touching Witches and Witchcraft.* 1666.

—. *A Blow at Modern Sadducism in some philosophical Considerations about Witchcraft.* 1668.

—. *Saducismus Triumphatus, or, full and plain Evidence concerning Witches and Apparitions.* 1681.
Goodcole, Henry, *The Wonderfull Discoverie of Elizabeth Sawyer a Witch, late of Edmonton, her Conviction and Condemnation and Death.* 1621.
Hart, John, *The Firebrand Taken out of the Fire.* 1654.
Higginson, Francis, *A Brief Relation of the Irreligion of the Northern Quakers, Wherein Their Horrid Principles and Practices, Doctrines and Manners, as Far as Their Mystery of Iniquity Hath Yet Discovered Itself, Are Plainly Exposed to the View of Every Intelligent Reader.* 1653.
Hill, Adam, *The Defence of the Article: Christ descended into Hell.* 1592.
Hill, William, *The First Principles of a Christian, or, Questions and Answers upon the Creed, the Ten Commandments, and the Lord's Prayer.* 1605.
Hobbes, Thomas, *The Elements of Law, Natural and Politic.* 1650.
—. *Leviathan.* 1651.
Humfrey, John, *An Account of the French Prophets and their Inspirations.* 1708.
—. *A Farther Account of Our Late Prophets.* 1708.
Hutchinson, Francis, *An Historical Essay Concerning Witchcraft.* 1718.
Jorden, Edward, *A Briefe Discourse of a Disease Called the Suffocation of the Mother.* 1603.
M. J., *The Hartford-shire Wonder or Strange News from Ware.* 1669.
Milton, John, *Paradise Lost.* 1667.
Moore, Mary, *Wonderfull News from the North, or, a true Relation of the sad and grievous torments Inflicted upon the Bodies of three Children of Mr George Muschamp, late of the County of Northumberland, by Witch-craft.* 1650.
More, Henry, *An Antidote against Atheisme, or, an Appeal to the natural Faculties of Minds of Man, whether there be not a God.* 1653.
North, Roger, *The Life of the Honourable Francis North, Baron of Guilford, Lord keeper of the great Seal, under King Charles II and King James II.* 1742.
Ozell, John (trans. from the French), *M. Misson's Memoirs and Observations in his Travels over England.* 1719.
Palmer, Samuel, *A Brief History of the Nonconformists.* 1774.
Perkins, William, *A Discourse of the Damned Art of Witchcraft.* 1608.
Prynne, William, *The county of Somerset divided into several classes, for the present settling of the Presbyterial government.* 1648.
Roberts, Alexander, *A Treatise of Witchcraft: wherein sundry Propositions are laid downe, plainely discovering the Wickednesse of that damnable Art.* 1616.
Salmun, William, *Aristotle's Master-piece Completed.* 1702.
Scot, Reginald, *The Discoverie of Witchcraft.* 1584.
Smith, Thomas [?], *A Gagg for the Quakers.* 1659.
Turner, William, *A Compleat History of the Most Remarkable Providences.* 1697.
Walker, John, *Sufferings of the Clergy.* 1714.
Webster, John, *The Displaying of supposed Witchcraft.* 1677.
Wesley, John, *The Journal of John Wesley.* 1735-90.

Whitehead, George, *A brief account of some of the late and present sufferings of the people called Quakers for meeting together to worship God in spirit and truth, being prosecuted by the statute of the 22th Car. 2. Cap. 1., entituled, An act to prevent & suppress seditious conventicles...* 1680.

Whitfield, Thomas, *A Treatise tending to Shew thet the Just and Holy God may Have a Hand in the Unjust Actions of Sinfull Men.* 1652.

Whiting, John, *Persecution Expos'd.* 1715.

W.P., *The History of Witches and Wizards Giving a True Account of all their Tryals in England, Scotland, Sweedland, France and New England; with their Confession and Condemnation.* 1720.

Nineteenth-, twentieth- and twenty-first-century sources

Adams, William Henry Davenport, *Witch, Warlock and Magician: Historical Sketches of Magic and Witchcraft in England* (New York: J.W. Boughton, 1889).

Anon., *History and Description of the Public Charities in the Town of Frome* (Frome, 1833).

Anon., *The National Gazetteer of Great Britain and Ireland* (London: Virtue, 1868).

Armitage, George, *The Publications of the Harleian Society for Marriage Licences Issued by the Vicar-General of the Archbishop of Canterbury* (London: Harleian Society, 1892).

Ashton, John, *The Devil in Britain and America* (Adelphi: Ward and Downey, 1896).

Barnes, Thomas G., *Somerset Assize Orders, 1629–1640* (Frome: Somerset Record Society, 1959).

Barry, Jonathan, Marianne Hester and Gareth Roberts (eds), *Witchcraft in Early Modern Europe* (Cambridge: Cambridge University Press, 1996).

Barry, Jonathan, 'Public infidelity and private belief? The discourse of spirits in Enlightenment Bristol' in Owen Davies and Willem de Blécourt (eds), *Beyond the Witch Trials: Witchcraft and Magic in Enlightenment Europe* (Manchester: Manchester University Press, 2004), 117–43.

Barry, Jonathan, and Owen Davies, *Witchcraft Historiography* (Basingstoke: Palgrave Macmillan, 2007).

Barry, Jonathan, *Witchcraft and Demonology in South-West England, 1640–1789* (London: Palgrave Macmillan, 2012).

Parry-Jones, B., Parry-Jones, W.L., 'Pica: Symptom or eating disorder? A historical assessment', *The British Journal of Psychiatry*, Volume 160, March 1992, 341.

Barstow, Anne Llewellyn, *Witchcraze: A New History of the European Witch Hunts* (San Francisco: Pandora, 1995).

Bates Harbin, E.H. (ed.), *Quarter Sessions Records for the County of Somerset:*

James I 1607–1625 (London: Somerset Records Society, 1907).

Bates Harbin, E.H. (ed.), *Quarter Sessions Records for the County of Somerset: Charles II 1625–1639* (London: Somerset Records Society, 1908).

Bates Harbin, E.H. (ed.), *Quarter Sessions Records for the County of Somerset, Volume 3: Commonwealth, 1646–1660* (London: Somerset Records Society, 1912).

Bath, Jo, and John Newton, 'Sensible Proof of Spirits: Ghost Belief during the Later Seventeenth Century', *Folklore*, 117:1 (2006), 1–14.

Bath, Jo (ed.), *Witchcraft and the Act of 1604* (Leiden: Brill, 2008).

Behringer, Wolfgang, *Witches and Witch-Hunts: A Global History* (Cambridge: Polity Press, 2004).

Bennington, B.D. (ed.), *The History of Parliament: The House of Commons 1660–1690* (London: Boydell and Brewer, 1983).

Berman, David, *A History of Atheism in Britain from Hobbes to Russell* (London: Routledge, 1988).

Bettey, J.H., *Wessex from AD 1000* (London: Longman, 1986).

Bever, Edward, 'Witchcraft Fears and Psychosocial Factors in Disease', *The Journal of Interdisciplinary History*, Vol. 30, No. 4 (2000), 573–90.

Bever, Edward, *The Realities of Witchcraft and Popular Magic in Early Modern Europe: Culture, Cognition, and Everyday Life* (Basingstoke: Palgrave Macmillan, 2008).

Bhatti, S., Malik, M., Rafaqat, A., Ishaque, U., Ayyaz, M., 'Acuphagia as a Cause of Gastric Bezoar Causing Gastric Outlet Obstruction', *Journal of the College of Physicians and Surgeons*, Pakistan 2014, Vol. 24 (Special Supplement 3): 190-192

Borman, Tracy, *Witches: James I and the English Witch-hunts* (London: Vintage Books, 2014).

Bostridge, Ian, 'Witchcraft Revealed' in Barry, Jonathan, Marianne Hester and Gareth Roberts (eds), *Witchcraft in Early Modern Europe* (Cambridge: Cambridge University Press, 1996).

—. *Witchcraft and Its Transformations, c.1650-c.1750* (Oxford: Oxford University Press, 1997).

Briggs, Robin, *Witches and Neighbours: The Social and Cultural Context of Witchcraft* (Oxford: Blackwell, 2002).

Clark, Stuart, *Thinking with Demons: The Idea of Witchcraft in Early Modern Europe* (Oxford: Oxford University Press, 1997).

Cleverdon, F.W., *The History of Mells* (Frome: Frome Society for Local Study, 2014).

Cockburn, J.S. (ed.), *Western Circuit Assize orders 1629–1648: A Calendar* (London: Royal Historical Society, 1976).

Cockburn, J.S., *Somerset Assize Orders 1640–1659* (Taunton: Somerset Records Society).

Cohn, Norman, *Europe's Inner Demons* (London: Pimlico, 1975, 1993).
Couzens, Phyllis, *Bruton in Selwood* (Sherborne: Abbey Press, 1968).
Creighton, Charles, *A History of Epidemics in Britain*, Vol. II (Cambridge: Cambridge University Press, 1894).
Crowley, D.A. (ed.), *A History of the County of Wiltshire: Vol. 8, Warminster, Westbury and Whorwellsdown Hundreds* (London: Victoria County History, 1965).
Cunningham, B.H. (ed.), *Records of the County of Wiltshire, being extracts from the Quarter Sessions Great Rolls of the Seventeenth Century* (Devizes: George Simpson, 1932).
Davies, Julie, *Science in an Enchanted World: Philosophy and Witchcraft in the Work of Joseph Glanvill* (London: Routledge, 2018).
Davies, Owen, *A People Bewitched: Witchcraft and Magic in Nineteenth-Century Somerset* (Bruton: 1999).
—. *Witchcraft, Magic and Culture 1736–1951* (Manchester: Manchester University Press, 1999).
—. *Popular Magic: Cunning-folk in English History* (London: Hambledon Continuum, 2003).
—. 'The Nightmare Experience, Sleep Paralysis, and Witchcraft Accusations', *Folklore* 114 (2003): 181-203.
Davies, Owen, and Willem de Blécourt (eds), *Beyond the Witch Trials: Witchcraft and Magic in Enlightenment Europe* (Manchester: Manchester University Press, 2004).
Deth, Ron van, *From Fasting Saints to Anorexic Girls: The History of Self-starvation* (London: Athlone Press, 1994).
Dunning, R.W. (ed.), *A History of the County of Somerset: Vol. III, Kingsbury (east), Pitney, Somerton and Tintinhull Hundreds* (London: Victoria County History, 1974).
Dunning, R.W. (ed.), *A History of the County of Somerset: Vol. VII, Bruton, Horethorne, and Norton Ferris Hundreds (Wincanton and Neighbouring Parishes)* (London: Victoria County History, 1999).
Dunning, R.W. (ed.), *A History of the County of Somerset: Vol. VIII, The Poldens and the Levels* (London: Victoria County History, 2004).
Durston, Gregory, *Witchcraft and Witch Trials* (Chichester: Barry Rose Law Publishers Ltd, 2000).
Dwelly, E., *Dwelly's National Records, Vol. I: Hearth Tax for Somerset 1664-5* (Fleet: E. Dwelley, 1916).
Elmer, Peter, 'Saints or Sorcerers: Quakerism, demonology and the decline of witchcraft in seventeenth-century England' in Barry, Jonathan, Marianne Hester and Gareth Roberts (eds), *Witchcraft in Early Modern Europe* (Cambridge: Cambridge University Press, 1996).
—. *Witchcraft, Witch-Hunting, and Politics in Early Modern England* (Oxford: Oxford University Press, 2016).

Eve, Paul F., *A Collection of Remarkable Cases in Surgery* (Philadelphia: J.B. Lippincott and Co., 1857).
Ewen, C. L'Estrange, *Witch Hunting and Witch Trials* (New York: The Dial Press, 1929).
—. *Witchcraft and Demonianism* (London: Heath Cranton, 1933).
Favazza, Armando, *Bodies Under Siege: Self-mutilation, Non-suicidal Self-injury, and Body Modification in Culture and Psychiatry* (Baltimore: Johns Hopkins University Press, 2011).
Fincham, Kenneth, 'The Restoration of Altars in the 1630s', *The Historical Journal*, 44, 4 (2001), 919–40.
Finucane, Ronald C., 'Historical introduction: the example of Early Modern and Nineteenth-Century England' in Houran, James, and Rense Lange (eds), *Hauntings and Poltergeists: Multidisciplinary Perspectives* (Jefferson: McFarland, 2001), 9–17.
Fix, Andrew, 'Angels, Devils, and Evil Spirits in Seventeenth-Century Thought: Balthasar Bekker and the Collegiants', *Journal of the History of Ideas*, 50:4 (1989), 527–47.
Foster, Joseph, *Alumni Oxonienses 1500–1714* (Oxford: University of Oxford, 1891).
Froide, Amy, 'Hidden Women: Rediscovering the single women of early modern England' in *Local Population Studies*, Number 68 (Spring 2002), 26–41.
Gaskill, Malcolm, *Crime and Mentalities in Early Modern England* (Cambridge: Cambridge University Press, 2000)
—. *Witchfinders: A Seventeenth-Century Tragedy* (London: John Murray, 2005).
—. 'Witchcraft, Politics, and Memory in Seventeenth-Century England', *The Historical Journal*, 50, 2 (2007), 289–308.
—. 'Witchcraft and Evidence in Early Modern England', *Past and Present*, 198 (2008), 33–70.
—. 'The Pursuit of Reality: Recent Research into the History of Witchcraft', *The Historical Journal*, 51, 4 (2008), 1069–88.
—. *Witchcraft: A Very Short Introduction* (Oxford: Oxford University Press, 2010).
Geiss, Gilbert, and Ivan Bunn, *A Trial of Witches: A Seventeenth Century Witchcraft Prosecution* (London: Routledge, 1997).
Gibson, Marion, *Reading Witchcraft* (London: Routledge, 1999).
Gillberg, Christopher, Soderstrom, Henrik, 'Learning Disability', *Lancet*, Vol 362, September 2003, 811-21.
Gittings, Clare, *Death, Burial and the Individual in Early Modern England* (London: Croom Helm, 1984).
Gordon, Alexander, (ed.), *Freedom After Ejection: A Review (1690–1692) of Presbyterian and Congregational Nonconformity in England and Wales* (Manchester: Manchester University Press, 1919).

Greenslet, Ferris, *Joseph Glanvill: A Study in English Thought and Letters of the Seventeenth Century* (Columbia: Macmillan, 1900).
Groves, Beatrice, 'Hal as self-styled redeemer: The harrowing of hell and *Henry IV Part I*' in Peter Holland (ed.), *Shakespeare Survey*, 57 (2004), 236–48.
Hamm, Thomas D., *Quaker Writings: An Anthology, 1650–1920* (London: Penguin, 2010).
Hartmann, Andrea S., Anne E. Becker, Claire Hampton, Rachel Bryant-Waugh, 'Pica and Rumination Disorder in DSM-5', *Pychiatric Annals*, 42:11 (2012), 426–30.
Hecht, Jennifer, *Stay: A History of Suicide and the Philosophies Against It* (Yale: Yale University Press, 2013).
Hindle, S., Shepard A., and Walter, J. (eds), *Remaking English Society: Societal Relations and Social Change in Early Modern England* (Boydell, 2013).
Houran, James, and Rense Lange, (eds), *Hauntings and Poltergeists: Multidisciplinary Perspectives* (Jefferson: McFarland, 2001).
Howard, Michael, *West Country Witches* (California: Three Hands Press, 2010).
Hunt, Henry, *A Peep into a Prison; or, the Inside of Ilchester Bastile* (London: Thomas Dolby, 1821).
Hunter, Michael, *Science and Society in Restoration England* (Cambridge: Cambridge University Press, 1981).
—. 'New light on the 'Drummer of Tedworth': conflicting narratives of witchcraft in Restoration England', *Historical Research* 78: 201 (2005), 311–53.
—. 'The Royal Society and the Decline of Magic', *Notes and Records of the Royal Society of London*, 65:2 (2011), 103–19.
—. 'The Decline of Magic: Challenge and Response in early Enlightenment England', *The Historical Journal*, 55:2 (2012), 399-425.
—. *The Decline of Magic: Britain in the Enlightenment* (New Haven: Yale University Press, 2020).
Hunter, Michael, and Simon Schaffer (eds), *Robert Hooke: New Studies* (Woodbridge: Boydell Press, 1989).
Hutton, Ronald (ed.), *Physical Evidence for Ritual Acts, Sorcery and Witchcraft in Christian Britain: A Feeling for Magic* (Basingstoke: Palgrave Macmillan, 2015).
Jobe, Thomas Harmon, 'The Devil in Restoration Science: Glanville-Webster Witchcraft Debate', *Isis*, 72: 3 (1981), 342–56.
Jones, David L., *The Ipswich Witch: Mary Lackland and the Suffolk Witch Hunts* (Stroud: The History Press, 2015).
Katz, David S., *Sabbath and Sectarianism in Seventeenth Century England* (Leiden: Brill, 1988).
Keeble, N.H. (ed.), *The Autobiography of Richard Baxter* (London: J.M. Dent and Sons, 1931, 1974).
Kermode, Frank, and Anita Kermode, *The Oxford Book of Letters* (Oxford:

Oxford University Press, 1995).
Kittredge, George L., *Notes on Witchcraft* (Massachusetts: The Davis Press, 1907).
—. *Witchcraft in Old and New England* (Massachusetts: The Davis Press, 1929).
King, Helen, *The Disease of Virgins: Green Sickness, Chlorosis and the Problems of Puberty* (London: Routledge, 2004).
Laurence, Anne, *Women in England 1500–1760: A Social History* (London: Phoenix Press, 1994).
Levack, Brian, *The Witch-Hunt in Early Modern Europe* (London: Pearson, 2006).
—. *Witch-hunting in Scotland: Law, Politics and Religion* (London: Routledge, 2007).
—. *The Devil Within: Possession and Exorcism in the Christian West* (London: Yale University Press, 2013).
—. *The Oxford Handbook of Witchcraft in Early Modern Europe and Colonial America* (Oxford: Oxford University Press, 2013).
Macfarlane, Alan, *Witchcraft in Tudor and Stuart England* (London: Routledge, 1970, 1999).
McGarvie, Michael, *The Bounds of Selwood* (Frome: Frome Society for Local Study, 1978).
—. *The Book of Frome* (Oxford: Barracuda Books, 1980).
—. *Marston House* (Frome: Foster Yeoman Ltd., 1985).
—. *St George's Church, Beckington* (Beckington: Beckington Parochial Council, 1990).
McKenzie, D.F., and Bell, Maureen, *A Chronology and Calendar of Documents Relating to the London Book Trade 1641–1700*, Vol. I 1641–1670 (Oxford: Oxford University Press, 2005).
McKenzie, D.F., and Maureen Bell, *A Chronology and Calendar of Documents Relating to the London Book Trade 1641–1700*, Vol. III 1686–1700 (Oxford: Oxford University Press, 2005).
McNaughten, Ben, Bourke, Thomas, Thompson, Andrew, 'Fifteen-minute consultation: the child with pica' Arch Dis Child Educ Pract Ed 2017; 102:226–229.
Marshall, Peter, *Mother Leakey and the Bishop: A Ghost Story* (Oxford: Oxford University Press, 2007).
Merrifield, Ralph, 'Witch Bottles and Magical Jugs', *Folklore*, 66: 1 (March, 1955), 195-207.
—. *The Archaeology of Magic and Ritual* (London: Batsford, 1987).
Molesworth, W., *The English Works of Thomas Hobbes, Vol. 3* (London: John Bohn, 1839-45), 9.
Morland, W.W., and Francis Minot, *The Boston Medical and Surgical Journal*, Vol. 61 (Boston: David Clapp, 1860).
Murray, Margaret, *The Witch-Cult in Western Europe: A Study in Anthropology*

(Oxford: Clarendon Press, 1921).
—. 'Witchcraft' in *Encyclopedia Britannica,* vol. 23 (multiple editions between 1929 and 1968).
Newton, John, and Thomas G. Barnes (eds), *Somerset Assize Orders 1629–1640* (Somerset: Somerset Record Society, 1959).
Notestein, Wallace, *A History of Witchcraft in England from 1558 to 1718* (Washington DC: American Historical Association, 1911).
Nuttall, Geoffrey K., and N.H. Keeble (eds), *Calendar of Correspondence of Richard Baxter*, Vol. 1, 1638–1660 (Oxford: Clarendon Press, 1991).
Nuttall, Geoffrey K., and N.H. Keeble (eds), *Calendar of Correspondence of Richard Baxter*, Vol. 2, 1660–1696 (Oxford: Clarendon Press, 1991).
Oldridge, Darren, *The Devil in Tudor and Stuart England* (Stroud: The History Press, 2010).
—. 'Light from Darkness: The Problem of Evil in Early Modern England', *The Seventeenth Century*, 27:4 (2012), 389–409.
Palmer, Kingsley, *The Folklore of Somerset* (London: Batsford, 1976).
Pearson, Jacqueline, "'Then she asked it, what were its Sisters names?': Reading between the lines in seventeenth-century pamphlets of the supernatural', *The Seventeenth Century*, 28:1 (2013), 63–78.
Petherbridge, Deanna, *Witches and Wicked Bodies* (Edinburgh: National Galleries of Scotland, 2013).
Pickering, Andrew, *The Witches of Selwood Forest: Witchcraft and Demonism in the West of England, c. 1625-1700* (Newcastle-upon-Tyne: Cambridge Scholars, 2017).
—. 'Great News from the West of England: witchcraft and strange vomiting in a Somerset village', *Magic, Witchcraft and Ritual* (University of Pennsylvania), Volume 13, Issue 1, Spring 2018.
—. 'Witchcraft and evidence in a seventeenth-century Somerset parish', *The Local Historian: Journal of the British Association for Local History*, Volume 48, Number 1, January 2018.
—. 'The Devil's Cloyster: putting Selwood Forest on England's seventeenth-century witchcraft map' in Nate, Richard, and Wiedemann, Julia (eds), *Remembering Places: Perspectives from Scholarship and the Arts* (Katholische Universität Eichstätt-Ingolstadt: Königshausen & Neumann, 2019).
Pickering, David, *Dictionary of Witchcraft* (London: Cassell, 1997).
Playfair, Guy, *This House is Haunted* (Guildford: White Crow Books, 2011).
Plomer, Henry Robert, *A Dictionary of the Printers and Booksellers who were at Work in England, Scotland and Ireland* (Oxford: Oxford University Press, 1922).
Price, Harry, *Poltergeist Over England: Three Centuries of Mischievous Ghosts* (London: Country Life Ltd, 1945).
Prior, Moody E., 'Joseph Glanvill, Witchcraft, and Seventeenth-Century Science', *Modern Philology*, 30:2 (1932), 167–93.

Pugh, R.B., and Crittall, Elizabeth, *A History of Wiltshire*, Vol. III (Oxford: Oxford University Press, 1956).

Raithby, John (ed.), *Statutes of the Realm*, Vol. 5: 1628–80 (London: The Record Commission, 1819).

Redgrove, Stanley, and I.M.L. Redgrove, *Joseph Glanvill and Psychical Research in the Seventeenth Century* (London: William Rider & Son, 1921).

Rhys, Ernest (ed.), Daniel Defoe, *A Tour Through England and Wales*, Vol. I (London: J.M. Dent, 1928).

Rideal, Rebecca, *1666: Plague, War, Hellfire* (London: John Murray, 2016).

Roper, Lyndal, *Witch Craze* (New Haven and London: Yale University Press, 2004).

Rose, E.A., Porcerelli, J.H., Neale, A.V., 'Pica: Common but commonly missed', *Journal of the American Board of Family Medicine, 13*(5), 2000, 353-358.

Rosenthal, Bernard, *Salem Story: Reading the Witch Trials of 1692* (Cambridge: Cambridge University Press, 1993).

Schiff, Stacy, *The Witches: Salem, 1692, a History* (London: Weidenfeld and Nicolson, 2015).

Scott, Walter, *Letters on Demonology and Witchcraft* (London: John Murray, 1830).

Sena, John F., 'Melancholic Madness and the Puritans', *The Harvard Theological Review*, 66:3 (1973), 293–309.

Sharpe, James, *The Bewitching of Anne Gunter: A Horrible and True Story of Football, Witchcraft, Murder and the King of England* (London: Profile Books, 2000).

—. *Instruments of Darkness: Witchcraft in Early Modern England* (Philadelphia: University of Pennsylvania Press, 2007).

Simpson, Jacqueline, and Stephen Round, *A Dictionary of English Folklore* (Oxford: Oxford University Press, 2000).

Skelton, Neil, *Church of the Blessed Virgin Mary, Old Dilton, Wiltshire* (London: The Churches Conservation Trust, 2006).

Stark, Ryan J., *Rhetoric, Science, and Magic in Seventeenth-Century England* (Washington DC: The Catholic University of America Press, 2009).

Stephen, Leslie, and Sidney Lee (eds), *Dictionary of National Biography* (London: Smith, Elder and Co., 1885–1900).

Stieg, Margaret, *Laud's Laboratory: The Diocese of Bath and Wells in the Early Seventeenth Century* (London and Toronto: Associated University Presses, 1982).

Sugg, R., *A Century of Supernatural Stories* (Createspace, 2015).

Summers, Montague, *Witch Covens and the Grand Masters* (*c.*1930; reprinted by Read Books, 2011).

Summers, Montague (ed.), *Pandaemonium by Richard Bovet, 1684* (Aldington: Hand and Flower Press, 1951).

Thomas, Keith, *Religion and the Decline of Magic* (London: Penguin, 1971).
Timperley, Charles Henry, *A Dictionary of Printers and Printings* (London: H. Johnson, 1839).
Tongue, Ruth, 'Some Notes on Modern Somerset Witch-Lore', *Folklore*, 74:1 (1963), 321–5.
—. *Somerset Folklore* (Glasgow: The University Press, 1965).
Toulson, Shirley, *Somerset* (London: Pimlico, 1995).
Treadwell, Michael, 'London Printers and Printing Houses in 1705' in *Publishing History*, 7 (1980).
Underdown, David, *Revel, Riot, and Rebellion: Popular Politics and Culture in England, 1603–1660* (Oxford: Oxford University Press, 1985).
—. 'A Reply to John Morrill', *Journal of British Studies*, 26:4 (1987), 468–79.
Uszkalo, Kirsten C., *Bewitched and Bedeviled: A Cognitive Approach to Embodiment in Early English Possession* (New York: Palgrave Macmillan, 2015).
Vandereycken, Walter, and Ron van Deth, *From Fasting Saints to Anorexic Girls: The History of Self-Starvation* (London: Athlone Press, 1994).
Walker, J. (ed.), *A Selection of Curious Articles from the Gentleman's Magazine* (London: Longman, Hurst, Rees, and Orme, 1809).
Walker, Simon, *The Witches of Hertfordshire* (Stroud: Tempus, 2004).
Walters, Cuming, *Bygone Somerset* (London: William Andrews & Co., 1897).
Weaver, Frederic William, *Somerset Incumbents* (Bristol: C.T. Jefferies and Sons, 1889).
Williams, Don E., David McAdam, David, 'Assessment, behavioural treatment, and prevention of pica: Clinical guidelines and recommendations for practitioners', *Research in Developmental Disabilities,* Volume 33, Issue 6, November-December 2012, 2050-2057.
Williams, Howard, *The Superstitions of Witchcraft* (London: Spottiswoode and Co., 1865).
Whitlock, Ralph, *Wiltshire Folklore and Legends* (London: Robert Hale, 1992).
Wightman, Samuel B., *The Anydate Calendar* (Redditch, 1938).
Wood, Juliette, 'The reality of the witch cults reasserted: Fertility and Satanism' in Barry, Jonathan, and Owen Davies (eds), *Witchcraft Historiography* (Basingstoke: Palgrave Macmillan, 2007), 69–90.
Wright, Thomas, *Narratives of Sorcery and Magic* (New York: Redfield, 1852; first published London: 1851).

Internet resources

Ancestry.co.uk: http://www.ancestry.co.uk/

Clergy of the Church of England Database: http://theclergydatabase.org.uk/

FreeREG: http://www.freereg.org.uk/

The National Archives: http://nationalarchives.gov.uk/

Oxford Dictionary of National Biography online edition entries
http://www.oxforddnb.com/

Burns, William E., 'Glanvill, Joseph'.
Coote, C.H., Curry, Patrick, 'Blagrave, Joseph'.
Cromartie, Alan, 'Hale, Sir Mathew'.
Wright, Stephen, 'Alleine, Richard'.
Greaves, Richard L., 'Bernard, Richard'.
Greig, Martin, 'Hill, Samuel'.
Halliday, Paul D., 'Holt, Sir John'.
Keeble, N.H., 'Baxter, Richard'.
Keene, Nicholas, 'Huish, Alexander'.
Malcolm, Noel, 'Hobbes, Thomas'.
Summerson, Henry, 'Hill, Adam'.
Vernon, E.C., 'Humfrey, John'.

Plymouth University electronic library
https://www.plymouth.ac.uk/
Somerset Heritage Centre
http://www1.somerset.gov.uk/archives/
Strode College electronic library
http://www.strode-college.ac.uk/
The Surman Index Online
http://www.qmulreligionandliterature.co.uk/research/surman-index-online/
Wiltshire BMD
http://www.wiltshirebmd.org.uk/
Wiltshire Family History Society
http://www.wiltshirefhs.co.uk/
Wiltshire and Swindon History Centre
http://www.wshc.eu/
Wiltshire Online Parish Clerks
http://wiltshire-opc.org.uk/

Wills retrieved from the digitised collections at The National Archives
http://www.nationalarchives.gov.uk/

PROB 11/122/277 Margery Greenhill, Widow of Westbury, Wiltshire,

BIBLIOGRAPHY

09/10/1613
PROB 11/135/286 William Hill, Clerk and Doctor of Divinity of Mells, Somerset, 10/03/1620/1
PROB 11/171/411 Elizabeth Hill, Widow of Upton Scudamore, Wiltshire, 30/06/1636
PROB 11/268/612 Thomas Smith, Fuller of Frome Selwood, Somerset, 27/11/1657
PROB 11/327/333 Alexander Huish, Rector of Hornblotten [and Beckington], 16/06/1668
PROB 11/336/194 Deborah Huish of Beckington, Somerset, 03/06/1671
PROB 11/364/612 Joseph Glanvill, Clerk, Rector of Bath, Somerset, 31/12/1680
PROB 11/370/155 Andrew Hill of Dilton, Wiltshire, 02/06/1682
PROB 11/429/288 Giles Hill, Yeoman of Upton Scudamore, Wiltshire, 02/12/1695
PROB 11/459/353 May Hill, Clerk of Beckington, Somerset, 17/02/1701
PROB 11/501/2 May Hill of Shorstreete, Wiltshire, 24/01/1708/9
PROB 11/511/391 Stephen Hill, Yeoman of Westbury, Wiltshire, 25/11/1709
PROB 11/533/130 Anne Hill, Widow of Beckington, Somerset, 16/05/1713
PROB 11/544/264 John Humphrey, Clerk of Saint Giles in the Fields, Middlesex, 12/02/1715/6
PROB 11/686/32 Stephen Hill, Clerk of Hemington, Somerset, 04/11/173

INDEX

Acuphagia, 158-65, 168
Ady, Thomas, author of *Candle in the Dark*, 124, 139
Albin, Henry, ejected minister, 139
Alcester, meeting of Cambridge Platonists at Ragley Hall (1665), 33
Alleine, Richard, rector of Ditcheat, 2, 31
Alleine, Richard, rector of Batcombe, 2, 9-12, 15, 17, 31, 40, 97, 104-5, 115-6, 199
Aster, John, ejected minster, 102, 105, 203
Aubrey, John, author of *Brief Lives* (1669-1696), 23-4, 41, 235
Bampfield, Francis, vicar of Sherborne, 105-7, 203-7
Batcombe, living of Richard Bernard, 1-3, 15, 51, 57, 104, 116
Batt, John, ejected minister, 104-5
Baxter, Richard, author of *Worlds of Spirits* (1691), 16-7, 25, 27, 107, 110, 125-6, 128, 144, 149, 162, 164-6, 169, 175, 178, 182, 184, 194-203, 208-10, 223, 232, 235, 237
Beaumont, John, author of *Spirits, Apparitions, Witchcrafts* (1705), 41-2, 232
Beckington, typhus epidemic (1686), 117-9, 130-2
Beckington, witchcraft case (1689-90), 123-189
Bekker, Balthasar, author of *The World Bewitched*, 126
Bennett, Edward, ejected minister, 103-5
Bennett, Philip, Somerset Clerk of the Peace, 103-4
Bernard, Richard, rector of Batcombe, 2-12, 25, 40, 51, 57, 61, 77, 80, 103-5, 111, 116, 124, 132, 136, 148, 153-4, 163
Bilson, boy of, 4, 153, 165
Blagrave, Joseph, author of *Astrological practice of Physick*, 139, 161, 163
Blome, Richard, author of *Fanatick History* (1660), 205, 207
Bolster, John, nonconformist preacher, 104
Bovet, Richard, author of *Pandaemonium* (1684), 109-13, 125, 136-7, 199, 220, 232
Boyle, Robert, author of *The Sceptical Chymist* (1661), 33, 35
Bradford-on-Avon, Chalfield House, 102
Brewham, witchcraft case (1665), 81-92
Bridgwater Gaol, 4
Bruton, witchcraft hearings (1689/90), 176-7, 183
Bury St Edmunds, 1665 witchcraft case, 60, 151
Butleigh, encounters with spirits, 42
Butler, Henry, ejected minister, 103, 106
Cary, John, J.P., 54, 56-7, 111
Casaubon, Meric, author of *Credulity and Incredulity* (1668), 3, 41
Castle Cary, witchcraft hearings (1657), 54
Compton, the cunning man of Ditcheat, 29-31, 71
Compton Pauncefoot, home of the Hunt family, 31, 39, 63, 87
Congregationalists, 17, 209
Conventicle Act (1664), ejected ministers and, 104-8
Cotta, John, author of *Tryall of Witch-Craft*, 4, 136, 138, 144, 150, 161
Crowley, Alastair, occultist, 91
Culpeper, Nicholas, herbalist, 4
Dalton, Matthew, author of *Country*

INDEX

Justice (1618), 3
Defoe, Daniel, views on spirits, 99, 219, 237
Devil's mark, 8-9, 69, 76, 82-3, 92, 176
Ditcheat, demonic-possession case (1584), 11-12
Dorchester Gaol, 105, 107, 204
Exclusion Bill, 1679, 109
Exeter, assizes, 168
Five Mile Act, 1665, 10, 105, 107
Fox, George, Quaker leader, 212
Frome, witch-swimming episode at Woodlands (1731), 228-9
Glanvill, Joseph, vicar of Frome Selwood, 9-12, 14-43, 51-2, 58-9, 62, 67, 74, 79-80, 83, 92, 108-12, 124-5, 136, 139, 174, 196, 198-9, 208-10, 216, 231-2, 235-7
'Great Ejection', 1662, of conformist ministers, 10, 16, 24, 103-7, 194, 203
Great Plague, 1665, 97-9, 115, 117, 131
Green sickness, 161-2
Hancock, Edward, nonconformist preacher, 107
Higginson, Francis, author of *Irreligion of the Northern Quakers* (1653), 210-3
Hill, Adam, vicar of Westbury, 25-6
Hill, May, rector of Beckington, 24-7, 30-1, 98, 100-1, 108-10, 115, 118, 123, 125-6, 128, 130, 132, 136, 145, 159-60, 162, 164, 169-70, 174-5, 182, 184, 195-203, 223, 232, 235-7
Hill, William, rector of Mells, 26
Hobbes, Thomas, author of *Leviathon* (1651), 5, 124, 232-5
Holt, John, Lord Chief Justice, 126-7, 145, 154, 168, 182, 184, 191-2, 219-21, 237
Hopkins, Matthew, 'Witchfinder General', 3, 39-40, 172
Horner, George, J.P., 107, 173
Huish, Alexander, rector of Beckington, 18, 26, 39, 100-2, 200, 203
Humfrey, John, vicar of Frome, 15-8, 106, 184, 196-203, 232, 237
Hunt John, J.P., 174
Hunt, Robert, Justice of the Peace, 9-10, 23, 29-31, 36, 38-40, 54, 56-7, 62-4, 68-9, 71-4, 77, 79-84, 86-9, 103, 107-8, 111, 135-6, 174, 208-9, 216, 232, 235
Hutchinson, Francis, author of *Historical Essay Concerning Witchcraft*, 42-3, 51, 126, 192, 220, 228
Ilchester Gaol, 81, 103, 173, 176-7, 183, 191, 204, 208, 214
Kilmington, witchcraft case (1666), 64
Laud, William, archbishop of Canterbury, 101
Magdalen Hall, Oxford University, 24, 27, 100, 203
Mapperton, witchcraft case (1663), 63-4
Marnhull, witch sabat, 75, 87
Mather, Cotton, author of *Wonders of the Invisible World*, 209
Mechanical philosophy, witchcraft and, 32-8
Milbourne, Thomas, London printer, 199-200, 237
Milton, John, author of *Paradise Lost*, 200
Mompesson, John, of Tidworth, 19-21, 31
Monmouth Rebellion (1685), 110, 113-5
More, Henry, editor of *Saducismus Triumphatus* (1681), 18, 33, 35-6, 38, 41-2, 50, 59, 62, 110-1, 198, 232, 235
Motcombe, witch sabat, 75
Murray, Margaret, author of *Witch-Cult in Western Europe*, 76, 91-2
North, Francis, Lord Chief Justice, 192
North Moreton, witchcraft case, 1604, 148, 165
Nunney, witchcraft tradition, 62-3
Paracelsus, alchemist-physician, 162
Parker, William, ejected minister, 104, 106
Pendle, witchcraft cases, 3, 73, 112, 135
Pepys, Samuel, diarist, 34
Perkins, William, demonologist, 7-8, 43, 112
Philips, Humphrey, ejected minister of Sherborne, 203-5
Pica, eating disorder, 158-65, 168

Pitminster, fairy fair, 112
Player, John, owner of Hadspen House, 145, 159, 169, 173-4, 232
Quakers, witchcraft allegations, 205-16
Rode, witch-swimming episode (1694), 223-8
Royal Society, 10, 19, 22-3, 33-7, 41-2, 111, 136, 235
Sacheverell, John, ejected minister, 107
Salem, witchcraft cases, 3, 42, 45, 51, 176, 209
Scot, Reginald, author of *Discoverie of Witchcraft*, 3, 9, 11, 123, 137
Seavington, witchcraft case, 137, 166
Shepton Mallet, witchcraft case (1658), 50-58
Sherborne, persecution of nonconformists (1663), 105-6, 203-7, 209
Sherborne, witchcraft allegations (1659), 205-8
South Petherton, apparitions, 30, 110, 112-13
Stearne, John, witch-finder, 3
Stoke Trister, witchcraft case (1665), 67-81, 87-92
Ston Easton, encounters with spirits, 41-2
'Strange vomiting', bewitchment and, 135-40, 149-70, 182-3
Summers, Montague, author of *History of Witchcraft*, 18, 90-1, 113
Sympathetic magic, 140
Taunton, witchcraft trials (1663; c.1680), 58-63, 192-3
Thynne family, of Longleat, 10, 18, 33
Tidworth, 'Tedworth Drummer' poltergeist case (1662-3), 19-24, 27-9
Toleration Act, 1689, 195
Turner, William, author of *Most Remarkable Providences*, 126
Uniformity Act, 1662, 10, 16, 24, 194, 203
Wagstaffe, John, author of *Question of Witchcraft*, 41
Warminster, meetings of nonconformists, 45, 103
Webster, John, author of *Displaying of Supposed Witchcraft* (1676), 41, 90, 136, 162, 234
Wells, witchcraft case, 4
'Werther syndrome', 160
West Coker, encounter with a demon, 112
Wincanton, witchcraft case (1665), see Stoke Trister
Winchester, gaol, 163
Witch-bottles, 139-40
Witch-scratching, 21, 51, 64
Witch-swimmings, 171-3, 223-31
Witches' familiars, 8, 37, 85, 108, 111, 123, 132-3
Witham Friary, meetings of nonconformists, 103, 106, 108
Woollen Act, burial in, 1678, 130-2
Wren, Christopher, 'Tedworth drummer' and, 24

About the Author

DR ANDREW PICKERING was, for many years, the Programme Manager for a University of Plymouth BA (Hons) degree in History, Heritage and Archaeology delivered at Strode College in Street, Somerset. His own undergraduate and postgraduate studies were undertaken at the universities of Birmingham, Keele, Bath and Leicester. He lives with his wife, Lisa, on Bruton's High Street, a few doors down from the former courtroom where the case of the Beckington 'witches' was heard 330 years ago. His wife's family on her mother's side includes numerous Greens from Brewham, the same surname as several people involved in the 1665 case examined by Robert Hunt of Compton Pauncefoot and made famous by Joseph Glanvill of Frome. He is a Fellow of the Royal Historical Society.

www.ingramcontent.com/pod-product-compliance
Lightning Source LLC
Chambersburg PA
CBHW050518170426
43201CB00013B/2000